BTEC First

media

Paul Baylis, Philip Holmes and Guy Starkey

www.harcourt.co.uk
✓ Free online support
✓ Useful weblinks
✓ 24 hour online ordering

01865 888118

Heinemann

From Harcourt

Heinemann Educational Publishers
Halley Court, Jordan Hill, Oxford OX2 8EJ
Part of Harcourt Education

Heinemann is the registered trademark of
Harcourt Education Limited

Text © Guy Starkey, Philip Holmes and Paul Baylis 2007

First published 2007

10 09 08 07
10 9 8 7 6 5 4 3 2 1

British Library Cataloguing in Publication Data is available from the British Library on request.

10-digit ISBN: 0 435464 70 1
13-digit ISBN: 978 0 435464 70 7

Edited by Melanie Birdsall
Typeset by Saxon Graphics Ltd, Derby
Original illustrations © Harcourt Education Limited, 2006
Illustrated by Saxon Graphics Ltd and Tek-Art
Cover design by Marcus Bell
Printed in China by South China Printing Co. Ltd.
Cover photo © Thinkstock/Alamy

Picture research by Zooid Pictures Limited

Websites
Please note that the examples of websites suggested in this book were up to date at the time of writing. It is essential for tutors to preview each site before using it to ensure that the URL is still accurate and the content is appropriate. We suggest that tutors bookmark useful sites and consider enabling students to access them through the school or college intranet.

Tel: 01865 888058 www.heinemann.co.uk

Contents

Acknowledgements

The authors and publisher would like to thank the individuals and organisations who granted permission to reproduce photographs, screenshots and text.

Pictures
Page 1 (opener), Nathaniel S. Butler / NBAE / Getty Images
Page 5 (Figure 1.2), John Powell / Rex Features
Page 6, Future Publishing
Page 7 (Figure 1.3), Joe Tree / Alamy
Page 10 (Figure 1.5), Jeff Christensen / Reuters / Corbis UK Ltd.
Page 1.6 (Figure 1.6), Michael Juno / Alamy
Page 14 (Figure 1.7), Columbia / Everett / Rex Features
Page 15, ITV
Page 23 (Figure 1.10), Ken McKay / Rex Features
Page 25 (Figure 1.12), Adobe
Page 27 (Figure 1.14), Ragnar Schmuck / Zefa / Corbis UK Ltd.
Page 31, reproduced by kind permission of Ofcom
Page 32, British Board of Film Classification
Page 33 (Figure 1.17), Martin Cleaver / Associated Press / Empics
Page 39 (Figure 1.21), *left and right:* MCPS-PRS Alliance; *centre:* Phonographic Performance Limited
Page 52, Katy McDonald
Page 61 (opener), Image Source / Rex Features
Page 63 (Figure 2.1), Getty Images
Page 78 (Figure 2.16), *left:* Activision Inc.; *right:* Ronald Grant Archive
Page 80 (Figure 2.18), Greg Wood / AFP / Getty Images
Page 80 (Figure 2.19), Ronald Grant Archive
Page 89 (Figure 2.25), Rex Features
Page 95 (opener), Fabio Cardoso / Zefa / Corbis UK Ltd.
Page 101 (Figure 3.4), Rex Features
Page 103 (Figure 3.5), Ronald Grant Archive
Page 105 (Figure 3.6), Fabio Cardoso / Zefa / Corbis UK Ltd.
Page 119 (Figure 3.10), William Sumits / Time Life Pictures / Getty Images
Page 123 (Figure 3.11), Pawel Libera / Corbis UK Ltd.
Page 127 (Figures 3.13 and 3.14), Claro Cortes Iv / Reuters / Corbis UK Ltd.
Page 128 (Figure 3.15), Getty Images / 43176
Page 130 (Figure 3.17), Getty Images / 43176
Page 131 (Figure 3.18), Keystone / Getty Images
Page 137 (opener), Mauricio-Jose Schwarz / Alamy
Page 162 (Figure 4.17), Sony UK Limited
Page 162 (Figure 4.18),vario images GmbH & Co. KG / Alamy
Page 165 (Figure 4.19), Philip Holmes
Page 187 (opener), picturesbyrob / Alamy
Page 191, Rob Harris
Page 195 (Figure 5.2), Empics
Page 199 (Figure 5.5), Empics
Page 203 (Figure 5.8), S2Blue
Page 209 (Figure 5.11), Arnos Design / Harcourt Education

Page 213 (Figure 5.12), Roger Ressmeyer / Corbis UK Ltd.
Page 214 (Figure 5.13), Peter Jordan / Alamy
Page 218 (Figure 5.15), Dagmar Schwelle / Alamy
Page 222 (Figure 5.16), Guy Starkey
Page 233 (opener), TNT Magazine / Alamy
Page 234 (Figure 6.1), Guy Starkey
Page 235, Yatin Vatland
Page 236 (Figure 6.2), Zooid Pictures
Page 237 (Figure 6.3), John Garett / Corbis UK Ltd.
Page 239 (Figure 6.4), source unknown
Page 240 (Figure 6.5), Hulton-Deutsch Collection / Corbis UK Ltd.
Page 242 (Figure 6.8), Rolf Adlercreutz / Alamy
Page 244 (Figure 6.9), Zooid Pictures
Page 251 (Figure 6.12), Adobe
Page 256 (Figure 6.14), Rex Features
Page 256 (Figure 6.15), Zooid Pictures
Page 259 (Figure 6.17), Photofusion Picture Library / Alamy
Page 261 (Figure 6.18), Adobe
Page 269 (opener), Allan Ivy / Alamy
Page 271 (Figure 7.1), Ronald Grant Archive
Page 272 (Figure 7.2), DreamWorks
Page 319 (opener), Darius Ramazani / Zefa / Corbis UK Ltd.
Page 321 (Figure 11.1), Zooid Pictures
Page 323 (Figure 11.3), *The Guardian*
Page 325 (Figure 11.4), Square Enix / Games Press Ltd.
Page 326, Martin Rockley
Page 327 (Figure 11.5), Empics
Page 355 (opener), Lise Gagne / iStockphoto

Text
Page 4 (Figure 1.1), ABC
Page 66 (Figures 2.3 and 2.4), NMA
Page 82 (Figure 2.21), ABC
Page 198 (Figure 5.4), Guy Starkey, *Radio in Context*, Palgrave Macmillan
Page 201 (Figure 5.6), bbc.co.uk
Page 202 (Figure 5.7), this advert was produced for NIACE, the National Institute of Adult Continuing Education, as part of its Write Where You Are campaign, funded by the Department for Education and Skills and the European Social Fund in 2005
Page 204 (Figure 5.9), Zebra Music
Page 283 (Figure 7.6), ASA
Page 283 (Figure 7.7), CAP
Page 322 (Figure 11.2), BBC & James Payne
Page 326 (Figure 11.6), Channel 4 News
Page 329 (Figure 11.7), David Walliams / Matt Lucas
Page 331 (Figure 11.8), *The Guardian*
Page 332 (Figure 11.9), *Sun*
Page 346 (Figure 11.15), BBC & James Payne
Page 346 (Figure 11.16), Michael Butt

Introduction

Welcome to the First Certificate and First Diploma in Media. This is a relatively new qualification and there have been changes to it in September 2006. These changes mean that the qualification reflects some of the very latest developments in media production practices and technology in the dynamic media industry.

Understanding how the media industry works, the ways in which media producers make their products and the job roles in this industry are becoming ever more important. The First Certificate and Diploma are not just for people who want to work in the media industry when they finish their education. Many of the techniques and skills needed for this qualification are transferable – i.e. they can be used in a wide variety of other situations. The planning, research and organisational skills you will be developing through your work will be very useful in almost any career or profession. Being able to present information in a lively and engaging way, such as using a video, audio, interactive or printed product, can be a real boost to a person's career.

You may want to move on from this qualification to GCE or National Award, Certificate or Diploma in Media. The skills you develop in your First Certificate or Diploma will be an excellent starting point.

Media plays an important part in everyone's lives. In your work for this qualification, you will be looking at what media producers make and how their output is influenced by what people want. You will be able to investigate just what the media industry is in all its many forms and where you might fit into this industry. You will be able to make media products, show them to an audience and reflect on what you have made.

How to use this book

You will see that this book is divided, like the qualification, into units. These units are the core units for the First Certificate and the Diploma and some of the specialist units. The specialist units provide the underpinning skills you will need in Video Production, Audio Production, Print Production and Writing for the Media, as well as how to use these skills in Advertising Production and the Media Production Project for the Diploma.

Your teacher will advise you on the best approach to developing skills depending on the facilities and other resources available in your school or college.

You should consider how the work you undertake on one unit could be linked to your work in other units. For example, imagine you have decided to produce a promotional video advertisement for Unit 7 Advertising Production. In order to do this you will have to make a video product. So why not also work on Unit 4 Video Production? You could use the skills you develop in Unit 4 to make the best video product you can for Unit 7. You could also use the video work you do in Unit 7 as extra evidence of your skills in video production for your assessment in Unit 4.

You should see this qualification as being an opportunity to seamlessly produce a range of media products while developing an understanding of the media industry, research techniques and media audiences.

At the start of each unit you will see a list of 'Learning outcomes'. These state exactly what you should 'know, understand or be able to do' as a result of completing the unit. Your teacher will provide suitable assignments to enable you to complete work in the required units and to achieve a Pass, Merit or Distinction. You must bear in mind that in order to achieve a Pass grade you must complete all the assessment criteria at Pass level. In order to achieve a Merit grade you must achieve all the Pass criteria and all the Merit criteria. In order to achieve a Distinction grade you must achieve all the Pass criteria, all the Merit criteria and all the Distinction criteria. Your teacher will provide you guidance on how you might improve your work in order to achieve an appropriate final unit grade.

We have tried hard to make this book appealing and engaging, so you will want to learn more. Getting a high grade depends on you doing your best to follow the guidance in the book. You should look carefully at the assessment criteria for the unit, study the information provided in the unit, use the 'Assessment tasks' and follow the guidance in the 'Assessment evidence' boxes. You will see that there are ticks against sections of the assessment evidence boxes. These ticks indicate how you might provide evidence of Pass (✓), Merit (✓✓) and Distinction (✓✓✓) for these assessment tasks.

We hope that you find this book helpful and we wish you good luck for your First Certificate/First Diploma in Media.

Paul Baylis
Philip Holmes
Guy Starkey

Understanding the language of the grading grids

In the specification for this qualification, you will see that each of the units has a grading grid, which provides advice for you and your teacher on the evidence that you need to produce to gain a Pass, Merit or Distinction grade. You will see that the same words appear regularly in the grids so you need to be aware of what these words mean.

Describe – this requires you to provide a correct but unelaborated response to the task. For example, you may be asked to describe the conventions of factual media productions. In this example, you will provide evidence that you understand what a factual production is by describing in simple terms two or three examples.

Identify – this requires you to note down relevant issues or points. For example, you might identify that in the UK there are BBC and commercial television channels. You will identify that the BBC is a public service broadcaster and that commercial television is driven by the sale of advertising space.

Discuss – you must discuss using appropriate illustrative examples. This means that you will produce material in some detail and you will make comments on it. For example, you might provide examples of the range of BBC programmes or media sectors that they cover. You will also provide examples of the range of programmes or sectors covered by commercial television and the companies involved.

Critically discuss – this means that any observations you make or arguments you engage in should be fully explained, justified and supported. You should be able to provide some sort of evaluation or comparison to support your critical discussion. For example, you might choose to compare the range of television news programmes produced for local consumption with the nationally produced news or BBC24. All your observations and examples should be supported by reasoned argument.

You must remember that 'critical' does not mean that you have to criticise.

Correct terminology – this means that you use the right words in the correct context. You will be able to use the terminology currently used in the media industry. For example, when discussing the BBC you will be able to produce sentences such as 'The BBC is a public corporation operating as a public service broadcaster.' Likewise, when talking about your production work you will be able to use terms that are relevant to your chosen media sector.

Fluent language – this means that you will use language that is appropriate to the audience, your meaning will be clear and you will maintain engagement with your audience.

Explain – this requires you to justify or support your comments in some way. For example, you might make a claim that the BBC news has a generally unbiased view of world affairs, while the news on a commercial TV channel seems to be influenced by the political views of its owner. You would need to back this up with evidence of your research into news programmes and with specific examples of news coverage that supports your claim.

Competently – this means that you will be demonstrating your ability in a certain area, but you may not be using your skills with complete confidence or imagination. For example, you may be a member of a video production team and you handle the camera, put up the tripod, erect the lights and take all the equipment back after the shoot – if you carry out all these tasks well, this would be regarded as working competently. However, in order to gain a higher grade you would have to do more – for example, take responsibility for the shoot, make creative decisions, allocate roles to the team and appear to be confident in your role.

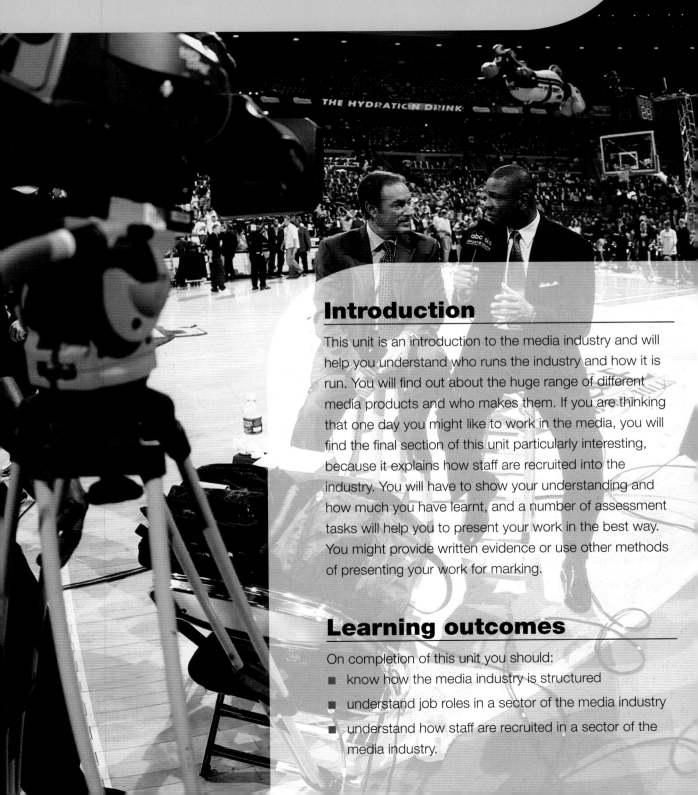

1 Introduction to Media Industries

Introduction

This unit is an introduction to the media industry and will help you understand who runs the industry and how it is run. You will find out about the huge range of different media products and who makes them. If you are thinking that one day you might like to work in the media, you will find the final section of this unit particularly interesting, because it explains how staff are recruited into the industry. You will have to show your understanding and how much you have learnt, and a number of assessment tasks will help you to present your work in the best way. You might provide written evidence or use other methods of presenting your work for marking.

Learning outcomes

On completion of this unit you should:

- know how the media industry is structured
- understand job roles in a sector of the media industry
- understand how staff are recruited in a sector of the media industry.

1.1 How the media industry is structured

The media industry is made up of different areas known as 'sectors'. These are: radio, television, film, print and interactive media.

You need to describe and discuss how the media industry as a whole is structured. In this section we will look at the different sectors in the media and how media organisations differ, depending on their size and shape and who owns them. Three assessment tasks will help you present your work in the correct way.

Industry sectors

The media industry continues to grow as new developments in technology bring new ways for audiences to receive media products. Some of the oldest media, such as print, film and radio, are still growing, and the public's appetite for their products is just as strong as ever. Each part of the media industry is called a 'sector'. You need to know and be able to show your understanding of how the whole of the media industry is structured. Then you will go on to study job roles and recruitment in just one sector for sections 1.2 and 1.3.

The growth of the Internet is challenging the traditional ways of distributing media products to audiences. For example, broadband provides fast download times as well as video and audio on demand. In the media the term 'convergence' has come to mean the breaking down of barriers between the original forms of distribution. Text, images and sound are all now available through alternative 'platforms' and the boundaries between different sectors are becoming increasingly blurred. For example, many people listen to the radio through their televisions, or read newspapers online.

The **media industry** has developed due to scientific discoveries, audience demand and investment by business people. At first, humans could only communicate with each other in person or by sending messages via couriers or by using signals – with smoke, beacons or flashing lights. The development of *mass media* has enabled individuals to send messages to larger audiences, made up of people they are unlikely to ever meet. **Audience** demand for media products changes as the choices available to them develop. At the beginning of the twentieth century, music halls were very popular for their comedy, dance and song routines. As the cinema developed, music halls began to close down.

Some sectors of the media industry are dominated by a few very large organisations. In others there is a wide range of large and small organisations, some in competition with each other and some working together. Some **media companies** are suppliers and others are customers – for example, a feature film company (customer) may hire a

What does it mean?

Media industry – *the industry in which the main activity is focused on communication through mass media – like other business industries, its purpose is to make money*

Media company – *an organisation which is mainly concerned with communication through one or more of the mass media*

Audience – *a group of people targeted by the media industry because they share broadly similar characteristics and interests*

specialist animation company (supplier) to provide certain scenes, or the opening and closing sequences of a production.

As the media industry has grown, and the range of products has increased, audiences have become more able to choose between alternatives. The development of the Internet, multimedia and satellite transmission has even enabled audiences to access content from all over the world.

We are all becoming more choosy about what we consume from the media. The days when people could always discuss the previous night's television at school or at work are long gone, because now the choice of television channels is so great that people are more likely to have watched different programmes.

Did you know?

Here are some key dates of when different forms of mass media began.

- *1450 – Johannes Gutenberg developed the first ever printing press, but it was two hundred years before the first daily English-language newspaper began.*

- *1895 – Two brothers, Auguste and Louis Lumière, patented a projector they called the* Cinématographe *and then opened the world's first cinema in Paris.*

- *1906 – Experimental radio broadcasting began, using the new 'wireless' technology first used to send personal messages from point to point.*

- *1936 – The BBC began the world's first regular television service, but it closed down when World War II broke out.*

- *1990s – Multimedia, combining text, images, video and audio, developed worldwide in a range of disk-based formats and the Internet.*

- *2004 – The term 'podcasting' was given to audio broadcasting through Internet downloads.*

Now let's look at each sector of the media industry in turn, beginning with the oldest.

Press

The press publish newspapers, magazines and comics. Despite the increase in online information, there is still a huge market for print products and the print industry will continue to be an important sector of the media for a long time to come. For example, magazine sales in the UK have been rising by 6.6 per cent a year, with more new titles being added all the time.

The table in Figure 1.1 shows how the national daily newspaper market is dominated by a small number of titles. They are owned by an even smaller number of media organisations. The biggest of them is News International, which also owns a large part of Sky Television.

The more serious newspapers used to be called 'broadsheet' because their size was much larger than the 'tabloids'. Because of declining sales, the publishers of the broadsheets decided to change the format in order to revive their sales. In September 2003 *The Independent* was the first broadsheet to change to a smaller size which could be more easily read on public transport – where people often sit in cramped conditions. *The Times* quickly followed, publishing large and small versions simultaneously for a while, before dropping the original broadsheet format altogether.

Because they wanted to maintain a different identity from the tabloids, the publishers of these newspapers invented the term 'compact', even though they were now the same size as the 'tabloids' such as the *Sun,* the *Daily Mirror*, the *Daily Star*, the *Daily Mail* and the *Daily Express*. Redesigning a newspaper often greatly increases sales. When the *Guardian* adopted its new 'Berliner' style in 2005, flagging sales were immediately revived – after hearing reports of the changes, old readers returned and new readers bought the newspaper for the first time to see what it was like.

The Sun (News International Newspapers Ltd)	3,226,053
The Daily Mail (Associated Newspapers Ltd)	2,314,601
Daily Mirror (Trinity Mirror plc)	1,635,915
Daily Express (Express Newspapers Limited)	909,258
The Daily Telegraph (Telegraph Group Limited)	882,307
Daily Star (Express Newspapers Limited)	747,289
The Times (News International Newspapers Ltd)	658,023
The Guardian (Guardian Newspapers (UK) Ltd)	336,283
The Independent (Independent Newspapers (UK) Ltd)	222,826
Financial Times (Financial Times Ltd)	126,551
Total	**11,059,106**

■ **Figure 1.1** *United Kingdom average daily newspaper sales and ownership, 3–30 January 2005. Source: Audit Bureau of Circulation.*

Did you know?

Regional and local newspapers now tend to be owned by big publishing groups, but some of them are still independent, and may even be locally owned. Modern print technology allows production to become centralised, rather than close to regional audiences. You may be surprised to find that your local newspaper looks very similar to local newspapers with similar titles elsewhere in the country.

There are a number of big magazine publishers, such as EMAP, which publishes *Kerrang!*. Until recently EMAP's *Smash Hits* title was very popular with teenagers, but when sales declined they stopped production of the magazine, even though a television channel of the same name was doing very well. Magazines tend to be much more specialised than newspapers, and looking at the shelves in a large newsagent's (see Figure 1.2) will give you a good idea of the enormous range of magazines available for different audiences.

■ **Figure 1.2** *Some of the enormous range of magazines for different audiences on offer at a newsagent's.*

Case study

Future Publishing

Future Publishing began as a specialist magazine company in 1985, just as the home computer games market was taking off. Its first title was *Amstrad Action*, and editor Chris Anderson used a £10,000 bank loan to finance the launch. The first publisher to give away computer programmes on the cover, Future Publishing used the latest page layout software, and the company quickly grew. Today, it owns 120 consumer magazine titles worldwide, runs a number of popular websites, and organises events such as Metal Hammer's Golden Gods Awards.

Theory into practice

Visit the ABC's website to investigate the sales figures for:

- national Sunday newspapers
- regional and local newspapers in your area
- magazines.

Identify the best-selling titles and which media organisations own them. Your research will be useful when you describe how the press sector is structured.

Film

The biggest film production companies in the world are based in the United States, where Hollywood makes movies that are shown (distributed) all over the world. Few other countries produce such a large number of films and with such large budgets. Film production in the UK decreased in the 1960s as cinema audiences began to decline due to the increasing popularity of television. Some independent film producers have survived, and in 1982 Channel 4 television began investing in film production for the cinema. Many of these films are still shown on the Film Four channel. In India, home-grown Bollywood films draw big audiences, and at international film festivals such as at Cannes, some very interesting films from around the world are shown, even if they may not make it to your local multiplex.

Did you know?

Some of the biggest earners at cinema box offices worldwide have been:

Titanic (1997)	$1,835,300,000
Lord of the Rings: The Return of the King (2003)	$1,129,219,252
Harry Potter and the Philosopher's Stone (2001)	$968,600,000
Star Wars Episode I (1999)	$922,379,000
Lord of the Rings: The Two Towers (2002)	$921,600,000
Jurassic Park (1993)	$919,700,000
Shrek 2 (2004)	$880,871,036

Theory into practice

Visit the websites of the big multiplexes, the British Film Institute and some film producers in the UK and abroad, to find out what's going on in the movie world. Read *Sight & Sound* and *Empire* magazine, too. Where is the most money being invested in film production at the moment, and what kind of films are businesses prepared to invest in?

Distributors move the films around the world, taking care to prevent them being pirated and sold on DVD and video, while chains of cinemas operate in every big town and city in the country. Cineworld is one of the biggest cinema chains in the UK. In the past 20 years, the development of exciting cinema multiplexes, often in out-of-town retail parks, has greatly stimulated the market for cinema going – particularly among young people. Some small, independent cinemas still survive, especially in London, often showing 'art' films, classics and foreign-language films that are made on much smaller budgets than Hollywood movies.

Radio

Radio is now more than 100 years old – the first actual radio programme was transmitted by a Canadian in 1906. Some of the biggest changes in production methods have occurred since the early 1990s, with the introduction of digital production, so radio is by no means old-fashioned. In the 1920s it was radio that first brought popular mass entertainment into the home – whole families would gather around their one wireless set to tune in to programmes featuring well known music hall stars who had transferred their acts to this new national 'stage'.

■ **Figure 1.3** *A modern DAB radio.*

In the UK the radio sector is divided into the BBC and the commercial stations. There are five BBC national networks and three national commercial networks. Then there are BBC regional and local stations and more than 300 regional and local commercial stations. New Digital Audio Broadcasting (DAB) sets (Figure 1.3), the Internet and even satellite and Freeview television bring even more BBC and commercial stations within reach of most people. Most of the commercial stations are owned by big groups, such as GCap Media, EMAP and The Local Radio Company. Networking allows radio production to be centralised, so the big commercial groups make some programmes for all their stations and then computer software inside each station customises it with local adverts and station jingles to adapt the output to the local area.

Theory into practice

Visit the BBC radio website and also those of GCap Media, EMAP and your local stations. What differences are there between the BBC stations and the commercial stations? What audiences are the different stations targeting, and how do they make their programmes appeal to these audiences?

Television

When television first brought live pictures into the home, radio suffered a big decline in evening listening, and small single-screen cinemas in town centres also lost business – many closed down or were turned into bingo halls. Initially, television was restricted to a small number of analogue terrestrial channels, but satellite and cable companies, as well as the development of digital terrestrial television – Freeview in the United Kingdom – massively increased the amount of choice on offer.

Independent Television (ITV) began in 1955 as a network of regionally owned and operated companies. They shared the most popular programmes and produced many that were intended to be shown only in their own regions. Carlton and Granada began buying other ITV companies in the 1990s, and, by the time the two merged in 2004, the new ITV plc owned almost all of them. Since then ITV production has become increasingly centralised in the south east of England.

BBC2 began in 1968, when the BBC began colour transmissions. Channel 4 began in 1982. The Sky Channel was joined by three more channels when Sky TV began a major push to develop satellite television in 1988. So you can see that until the 1990s there really was not much choice for television viewers – not when compared to today's wide range of channels. However, many channels just recycle repeats.

■ **Figure 1.4** *Television viewers have more choice today than ever before.*

Did you know?

Some of the most popular television programmes are bought in from the United States – feature films made for the cinema are also popular. Television companies also sell their programming overseas whenever they can, because foreign channels will pay well for programming that their own audiences will want to see. Often they will sell an idea or a format – for example, the BBC's Fame Academy *is even more popular in France, where Endemol produces it for the main commercial channel, TF1.*

Setting up a new television channel is much easier if it uses a digital platform like Sky, Freeview or the Internet to reach its audience. Some channels make their own programmes, and some, such as Channel 4 and Five, act as publisher–broadcasters, commissioning programmes from independent producers or even other broadcasters and paying them to produce them.

Theory into practice

Visit the websites of the BBC and the other UK television companies. Pay particular attention to the kind of programming each one broadcasts. How much of it is original production made in-house, and how much has been bought in or repeated?

Music

The music industry is divided into publishers, recording companies, distributors and record labels. They all need composers and performers too, of course, or they wouldn't have anything to sell to the public. Music publishers publish and print sheet music – the notes and lyrics making up some of the more popular songs of today and from the past. Musicians buy the sheet music in order to perform the music. Recording companies do just what their name suggests – they own and operate or hire recording studios, where songs are recorded for the record labels.

The record labels try to spot new talent – singers and musicians – and find ways of marketing them that will make money for themselves and for the talent. Some of the biggest labels also own smaller labels that they have created themselves or that they have bought up. Distributors get the finished product into the shops in time for it to be on sale when the public wants to buy it. There would be little point in a record label investing in a new band, getting them publicity and then not managing to get copies of the product to the shops in time for it to be bought by the public. Today, an increasing amount of music is sold through Internet downloading.

■ **Figure 1.5** *The music industry and other media industries have a lot in common, and sometimes it is difficult to see where the boundary lies.*

Interactive media

Websites, video games and CD-ROMs have grown in importance over the past ten years. Most are produced by companies wishing to make a profit from selling them on to customers. All interactive media products begin with an initial idea, which has to be fully worked through as an initial proposal, indicating how that idea will look, read and sound to the customer. This may be in response to a request from a client, in the form of a brief, or it may be an original idea intended to make money from sales or subscriptions – or to promote another product or a cause. Usually the product will be carefully targeted at a particular audience or market.

Companies usually want a website to communicate with new and existing customers. Clubs, societies and pressure groups – who may want to change government policy on a particular issue – often simply want to publicise what they do or believe. The purpose of DVDs and CD-ROMs can be to entertain, persuade or to inform – and some do all three. Video and computer games are usually written in order to exploit the vast home entertainment market. Whether on disk or the web, often the purpose is to sell the games, and sites such as Amazon and Argos have cataloguing and purchasing functions that enable customers to view products, select from those most likely to appeal to them and buy them.

The BBC's website is one of the most visited in the world, and many large media organisations with a big output use interactive media. However, the low cost of web production means that almost anyone with the equipment and the skills required can create their own alternatives to mainstream print, audio and even television. Blogging and podcasting are two examples of how individuals can get involved – but only blogs and podcasts that get highlighted by television, radio, the press or the most popular websites will reach mass market audiences. There are simply so many of them.

Photo imaging

This sector includes high street photographers who take portraits for families, photograph weddings (Figure 1.6) and other festive occasions and ceremonies and produce portfolios for would-be fashion models. Other photographers work for the press, providing pictures on demand when there is a news event that needs covering or chasing after celebrities in the hope that the press will buy the pictures afterwards. A big exclusive photograph can earn a photographer large amounts of money, but the regular work, such as wedding photography, can provide a steady income, too.

■ **Figure 1.6** *Some of the smallest of media companies are photographers, working alone.*

Advertising and marketing

Most big companies, whatever their business, have marketing departments. Even small companies plan and produce marketing material, which may take the form of websites, flyers, catalogues, DVDs and so on. There are also some specialist advertising and marketing companies who will do marketing for other companies for a fee.

Did you know?

All photography used to be done on light-sensitive film that needed developing in a dark room with chemicals used to fix the image on the reels of film. The images would then be projected onto light-sensitive paper that would also need fixing so the images could be viewed out of the dark room. Now, digital photography produces instant pictures that can be manipulated using software, and sent electronically to newspaper and magazine editors, picture libraries and picture agencies, for sale and publication.

Theory into practice

Use a copy of BRAD, or visit BRAD's website, to see which advertising agencies are representing the biggest and best known companies. Visit some of the agencies' sites, to investigate further the kind of work they have been doing.

Advertising agencies are often expert in devising and producing advertising – for use in radio, television, cinema and the press. Some of the large agencies work for the biggest blue chip clients, dreaming up exciting and original advertising for big-name household brands. This kind of work can be very glamorous, involving photo shoots and location recordings for print, television and the cinema, using top-flight producers and directors, celebrity actors and famous models.

Assessment task 1

Describe the main features of each sector of the media industry. Be methodical, clearly separating each sector from the others. Explain what makes it different from the others and why.

Assessment evidence

✔ Describe each sector, saying which are the biggest organisations within the sector and why.

✔✔ Use examples to explain why some organisations in each sector are the biggest or most successful, and why others are not.

✔✔✔ Use correct terminology in your explanations, making sure they are detailed and supported by strong evidence of your conclusions.

Size and shape

The size of a media organisation affects the scale of its operation. The BBC is one of the biggest in the world, yet there are many tiny media organisations – perhaps in your own town or city. Because some media organisations are very complex, they are not all organised in the same way – they are often *shaped* differently.

Size

There are many ways in which size really matters in the media. Economies of scale are cost savings gained by a large organisation which can use its assets much more effectively than if it were smaller. For example, a large organisation or a group of companies can concentrate certain functions in one place, using specialists to 'service' each part of the network. Examples include:

- Personnel – recruiting new staff and handling all the various administrative tasks relating to employing people.

- Accounts – keeping track of finances, preparing financial reports, invoicing clients for money they owe and paying bills and staff for work done.

- Advertising sales – selling advertising space or airtime, particularly to national clients who may be some distance away from local radio stations, for example.

Geographical scope

Size may relate to geographical factors: i.e. a small media organisation may operate only locally, within a single area, while a larger organisation may operate over one or more regions, or even nationally. Some big organisations are international, operating in more than one country.

Most media organisations are much smaller than the BBC. Channel 4 broadcasts a single analogue terrestrial television channel and a small number of digital-only channels, such as Film Four, More4 and E4. Channel 4, as a 'publisher–broadcaster', makes very few programmes itself – instead it commissions other companies to make the programmes

 Case study

The BBC

The British Broadcasting Corporation operates several television channels for terrestrial or satellite distribution, over 50 different radio stations and the websites bbc.co.uk and bbcnews.com. There are regional opt-outs, with studios and newsrooms in many different locations around the United Kingdom, that provide alternative bulletins and news magazine programmes for viewers of BBC1. BBC Wales has a major television and radio production centre in Cardiff, while Bush House in London is the home of the BBC World Service. Together with other national, regional and local services that the corporation provides, this all adds up to make it one of the world's most complex media organisations. By 2012 the BBC plans to have moved hundreds of jobs from London to Manchester, in an attempt to make its output more relevant to audiences in the North.

it wants to broadcast. At first this policy encouraged the growth of many small television production companies, some of which have grown much bigger since then. Similarly, the introduction of the Welsh fourth channel, S4C, encouraged the growth of several companies based in Wales and specialising in programmes in Welsh. They have to compete for commissions with BBC Wales, which also makes programmes in Welsh for S4C.

Although there are big groups of commercial radio stations, some are independently operated. That means that they are owned by a number of individual shareholders or perhaps small numbers of shares in them are owned by private companies – but no other organisation has enough voting rights on the company board to have overall control. Community radio has been licensed in the United Kingdom since 2002. Small groups of enthusiasts have been allowed to set up and run not-for-profit stations aimed at specific communities that may feel underserved by commercial or BBC stations.

There are large groups of newspapers too – local and regional titles, as well as national newspapers, often belong to large conglomerates however local they may seem to their audiences. For example, the largest newspaper group, Trinity International Holdings, owns ten per cent of the local newspaper market, including the *Sunderland Echo* and the *Belfast Telegraph*.

It is the big Hollywood studios which dominate the film industry, because of the large amounts of money they are able to invest in film production. The United States provides a very large home market for Hollywood movies, and these very commercially successful movies are also popular in many other countries around the world (Figure 1.7). The Hollywood studios are able to make big profits from the most popular films – a worldwide box office success can reward investors with profits worth many times their original investment. But sometimes films that look promising on paper can flop instead, losing money on a grand scale.

■ **Figure 1.7** *Hollywood movies reach worldwide audiences.*

Did you know?

A number of small, independent film companies have successfully made feature films for screening in cinemas. One example is Aardman Animations, which first made its name by making animated short films. Later on the company's owner Nick Park was able to invest in producing longer Wallace and Gromit features.

Status

The status of a media organisation can depend on its size and its role. There are other factors, too – for example, the television channel Five is much smaller than the BBC's massive organisation, and smaller too than ITV. Because it is one of only five terrestrial television channels, though, it is much more important than, for example, UKTV, which operates several channels but not a single one of them is available through an ordinary analogue television set and aerial. When analogue switch-off occurs, Five's status will be greatly reduced, because it will become just one of many more multi-channel television choices.

Here are some other reasons for the differences in status between media organisations:

■ Small and medium-sized businesses may have only limited status because there are much bigger ones that operate over larger areas or have bigger audiences. For example, a local newspaper has a lower status than a national one.

■ Independent organisations may not have as much power and influence as those which form part of a group, because they find it harder to make themselves heard. For example, the managing director of a small local commercial radio station does not have as much influence as one who manages a whole group of stations.

■ Subsidiary organisations are owned by parent companies, which may not value their opinions and may buy or sell them – or even close them down – in order to maximise their own profits. For example, a special effects company owned by a Hollywood film studio may be closed or moved to another country in order to save money.

 Case study

ITV plc

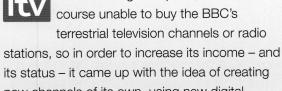 When looking to expand, ITV was of course unable to buy the BBC's terrestrial television channels or radio stations, so in order to increase its income – and its status – it came up with the idea of creating new channels of its own, using new digital technology.

ITV's first venture into digital terrestrial television was called ON Digital. Because viewers were slow to subscribe to the service, it was rebranded ITV Digital in the hope it would have greater appeal. It collapsed because the income from subscriptions never did cover the massive investment ITV made in buying up rights to broadcast Champions League football matches. The BBC, Sky and Crown Castle stepped in to take over the digital frequencies and use them to launch Freeview, which was unexpectedly an outstanding success, reaching four million homes in its first two years. So by 2006, and keen not to miss out, ITV had set up four new free-to-air channels, all funded by advertising and premium phone lines.

Each organisation involved in production or distribution wants to succeed financially. That may require diversification, which could mean developing new types of products or buying up smaller companies.

Assessment task 2

Describe two very different organisations from each sector of the media industry. Be methodical, clearly separating each sector from the others. Explain what makes them different from each other.

Assessment evidence

✓ Describe the size and shape of each organisation, pointing out differences in geographical scope and in status.

✓✓ Use examples to explain those differences in geographical scope and status.

✓✓✓ Use correct terminology in your explanations, making sure they are detailed and supported by strong evidence of your conclusions.

Structures and ownership

We have seen that the media industry is made up of many different organisations. They can differ in the way they are structured – or organised. They can also differ in the way they are owned – or who controls them.

Structure

There are a number of ways in which pooling content can enhance a large organisation's products. For example, national and international news can be gathered centrally and repackaged by each local company according to the interests of their own audiences.

Now some commercial radio groups operate news 'hubs', in which a regional newsroom compiles bulletins for a number of different radio stations in the region, even covering stories for them. A single newsreader reads different news bulletins for several stations, recording them one at a time for each of the different stations to broadcast simultaneously. Very few listeners to a local station will realise that the same newsreader can also be heard on neighbouring stations that could be only 30 or 40 miles away.

Did you know?

*The BBC is an example of a **cross-media** organisation that is able to exploit its content to great advantage. For example, reporters are able to produce news for radio, television and online use because the same information and recordings can be packaged and repackaged in different ways for different media, and different local, regional and national versions can be prepared within the same media.*

What does it mean?

Vertical integration – *different parts of an organisation come under others involved in the same process. For example, a Hollywood studio could produce films, own a distribution company that gets them to cinemas on time, and even own some of the cinemas which show the films.*

Horizontal integration – *different parts of an organisation don't supply or depend on each other, and may even operate in different media. For example, one of the BBC's local radio stations is a part of the same organisation as the BBC1 television channel, but they each lead a very separate existence, with the only similarities in content being in the national and international news they broadcast.*

Cross-media – *an organisation which operates in a number of different media, such as the BBC.*

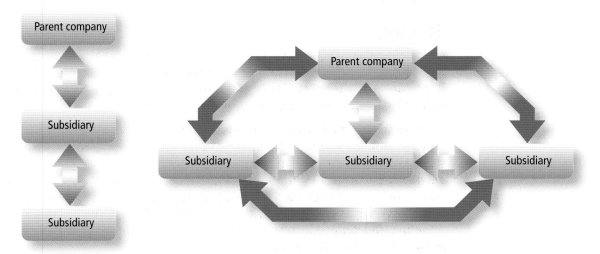

■ **Figure 1.8 *Vertical* and *horizontal integration*.** *The organisation represented on the left is vertically integrated, while the one on the right is both vertically and horizontally integrated, as some departments work together and for each other.*

Ownership

Most media organisations are **privately owned**, which means that individuals or other businesses have invested money either in setting them up from scratch or in buying them from someone else. Usually they do this in order to make a profit. Companies which make a loss either go bust and close down or they are bought up by someone else who wants to try to make them profitable.

In some parts of the industry there are **publicly owned** organisations. That means that the state owns them on behalf of its citizens. Only in broadcasting is state ownership of the media very significant – that is because in 1926 the government's Crawford Committee recommended that radio was too important to be left to private companies to run. There were very few frequencies available, which meant that not everyone who might have wanted to broadcast could do so. A small number of companies taking control of this new medium would have concentrated ownership in a few powerful hands and they might have used it to exert undue influence over the population.

So, in 1927 the British Broadcasting Company became the British Broadcasting Corporation, and it wasn't until 1955 that Independent Television (ITV) became the first official commercial competition that the BBC had ever had to face. Independent Local Radio (ILR) followed in 1973. Most people agree that having to compete for audiences since then has made the BBC more competitive and improved choice overall.

The press, the film sector and most music and interactive media companies have always been privately owned, because only broadcasting developed with a scarcity of basic resources.

Anyone with enough money to invest can set up a newspaper, start a recording company or label, make a film or set up a website. However, launching a daily or a weekly newspaper, for example, can cost many millions of pounds, without any guarantee of success. In 1987 a new weekly newspaper called the *News on Sunday* lost its owners £10 million and closed after just seven months. Fortunately, it costs only a tiny fraction of that amount to create and maintain your own website and you can call it whatever you like.

Did you know?

Not every media organisation is big and profitable. Even the biggest of them can lose money if their earnings are less than their outgoings. On the other hand, some small companies manage to make a profit on very small earnings, providing their costs are also small.

What does it mean?

Public ownership – *an organisation is owned for the public by the state*

Private ownership – *an organisation is owned, bought or sold by other companies and individuals. In many cases shares in the organisation are traded on the stock exchange. Foreign companies have invested heavily in buying media companies in the United Kingdom.*

Assessment task 3

Identify a privately owned media organisation from each sector of the media industry. Explain how its ownership is different from one publicly owned organisation, such as the BBC. Explain one example of vertical integration and one of horizontal intergration across different media.

Assessment evidence

✔ Describe the differences between private and public ownership *and* between vertical and horizontal integration. Horizontal integration should be cross-media.

✔✔ Use examples to explain these differences in ownership and structure.

✔✔✔ Use correct terminology in your explanations, making sure they are detailed and supported by strong evidence of your conclusions.

1.2 Job roles in the media industry

You need to identify, describe and discuss the job roles in *one* sector of the media industry. In this section we will look at the various jobs in the media, professional working practices and the terms and conditions of employment. Three more assessment tasks will help you present your work for this section.

Job roles

In the media industry, job roles differ widely, depending on the size and shape of an organisation, as well as which sector it is in. Broadly, they come under the following headings:

- **Technical** – setting up and operating equipment, making sure all stages of production are carried out to the quality level required.

- **Creative** – thinking of initial ideas, researching them in order to find out if they will work, getting additional information and writing complete scripts or articles.

- **Editorial** – choosing between available ideas, commissioning the most promising ones and rejecting others, doing pre-production work including research and planning.

- **Managerial** – leading teams of people in order to get the best out of them and to produce the best media products for their audiences.

- **Sales and marketing** – selling and promoting sales of media products so that they reach the biggest audiences possible.

- **Administration** – booking people, equipment and studios, organising catering and accommodation if needed on location.

- **Financial** – keeping records and accounts, making sure that people and suppliers are paid and collecting income earned from sales and advertising.

Did you know?

The media industry employs nearly 160,000 people across all of its different sectors in the United Kingdom. Even the simplest of television programmes provides work for many people.

Now let's investigate the sectors one by one, to see what jobs there are in each sector. Media organisations differ greatly even within the same sector, but they are generally organised according to the production processes involved in their operations. Understanding these processes will help you to make sense of the way they are organised. Your own interest in the media may lead to employment in such an organisation, and understanding how everything works could be essential to having a successful career. Even if you never work in the media, you will understand more about the products you consume as part of the media companies' audiences.

Press

There are four key stages to the production of newspapers and magazines. The first is **pre-production**, and this stage begins with the publication being commissioned. Of course, regular publications continue to be produced on a daily, weekly or monthly basis, depending on how frequently they appear. Every publication has to start somewhere, though, and the first edition of a magazine or a newspaper undergoes an initial period of research and development before its design and content are finally agreed.

The **production** stage involves generating words, images and graphics, putting these together into the desired layout and design, and then the actual printing and collation of the completed product. The original words used in a print product are called 'copy'. Images and graphical information can be as important as the copy in communicating the right message and ensuring that the correct target audience notices the product in the first place. For example, there are literally hundreds of magazines on display in most newsagents, and an image-rich front page that sells the magazine to potential readers is an important way of marketing a title. Digitised images can be resized and enhanced using software such as *Adobe Photoshop*.

Pre-press is the generic term for all of the design and layout work that takes place before the product can actually be printed. As with other areas of the media industries, the traditional labour-intensive methods of pre-press layout have been replaced by desktop publishing software packages. This has meant that the hand-crafted skills associated with cut-and-paste methods have been superseded by the design and software skills needed to operate DTP and design software such as *Adobe InDesign* and *QuarkXpress*.

Print finishing is the final stage in print production. It involves trimming and cutting the pages to the correct size, folding and collating them in the right order, and then using some form of staple or stitching to bind them together in a finished product.

■ **Figure 1.9** *The design team has to get the look of a new publication just right.*

Who does what?

Editors are the team leaders in print production, but they report to a **publisher** or, in the case of many newspapers, a **proprietor**. The proprietor is the owner of the company – some newspaper proprietors lead colourful lives that make them the subject of news stories themselves, while others are rarely heard of because they choose to live discreetly, away from the limelight. In the press sector of the media industry, there are a number of roles which are specific to each of the four key stages.

Planning the design, style and layout of a new publication is the job of specialised **designers**. They have to make sure the look and content of the finished product are right for the audience.

Journalists are employed by the newspaper and magazine industries and they often work under a lot of pressure and to very tight deadlines. They need to be creative and skilled wordsmiths with a good, broad knowledge base. Sometimes their work will require the assistance of specialist **researchers**, and the biggest newspapers employ **librarians** to manage their in-house libraries of information, past editions and cuttings.

In newspapers and magazines it is the **editors**, and **sub-editors** under them, who check and refine the copy produced and manipulate it if necessary to fit the space available. In reality, most newspaper editors simply don't have the time to be involved in the production of every page – they give a lot of this work to **section editors** who have responsibility for one section of the paper, such as the travel, motoring, gardening, business or entertainment pages.

A few of the larger companies still employ in-house **photographers**, but most now use freelance photographers with the skills required for particular projects, or they buy images from a photographic agency. It is the role of the pre-press **designers** and **art workers** to ensure that the words, images and graphics are combined in an effective manner.

Printers are needed to run the printing presses. Digital printing methods are replacing older, manual methods such as offset litho and gravure, and this means that fewer printers are needed. Once the pages of a magazine or newspaper have been printed, then the **print finishers** get to work – sorting, folding and packaging the product.

Television and film

Television and film production begins with an initial idea, which may be entirely new or based on something that has been produced before. In order for production to take place and the idea to be turned into a finished product, somebody has to finance it. In the case of film production, backers may need to be found. Sometimes, the backers are handsomely rewarded with big profits because the income from the film greatly exceeds the cost of producing it. There is an element of gambling to this process, though, because if a film flops, large amounts of money can be lost.

Television has a huge appetite for new material – otherwise its output would consist entirely of repeats. News journalism must be carried out on an almost continuous basis – especially where the product is a rolling news service, such as BBC News 24. Other types of programme often come after a producer has made a successful bid to a TV channel for a commission to develop an idea, perhaps into a whole series.

Agreeing the finances is one of the first stages of **pre-production** – this can only be done once a budget has been worked out, based on what it will actually cost to make the product. Other pre-production activities include developing scripts, carrying out a recce of locations to be used, casting for actors and presenters, and arranging any logistical requirements. These include arranging transport to different locations, booking studios, equipment and a crew to do the work and organising catering. Drama productions may require many hours of rehearsals, costume design and production and make-up.

Production – in studio or on location – can be time-consuming, as there is often little chance of being able to go back and re-record something if it isn't right on the day. Actors may not be available later, and locations may look different after a period of time. So everyone on the production team has to ensure that their work is carried out according to the script and the other production paperwork.

■ **Figure 1.10** *Television presenters have to be very skilled in getting everything right first time.*

Live television production, such as for news programming, has the added complication that mistakes can't be covered over by re-recording and editing at the post-production stage. Luckily, television audiences mostly understand that in live situations things can go wrong – and as long as it doesn't happen too often, they seem to tolerate, and even enjoy, such occasions.

With recorded TV programmes and feature films, there may be a lengthy **post-production** stage, in which different shots are edited together, mistakes are removed and scenes are placed in the correct order. Music can be added, and for big-budget films that are distributed internationally, additional language soundtracks are recorded. Special effects and subtitles can also be added at this stage. Films and television programmes then need marketing.

■ **Figure 1.11** *A good way to start work in television is as a runner (see page 24).*

Who does what?

Producers are the team leaders, and they report to **executive producers** or the owners of film studios, or in television to **network controllers** who commission the programmes they produce. In film production, although the **producers** are important because without them the production wouldn't take place, it is usually the **director** whose name becomes most closely associated with the production. This is because it is the director's job to turn the script into a finished film by interpreting the script and deciding how it should be shot and edited, as well as directing the actors – these are big creative decisions which determine whether or not the film will be a success.

Not surprisingly, the Walt Disneys, Martin Scorseses and Steven Spielbergs of the film world become very famous, because of the importance of their roles in creating box office successes. Their successes, though, would not be possible without large numbers of other people performing a number of roles in the pre-production, production and post-production stages.

Researchers perform some of the most important work, finding out historical facts to be included in a script or researching locations before recces can take place. **Script writers** turn initial ideas into the detailed set of words for presenters and actors to speak, as well as instructions for the people responsible for costume, props, make-up, camera, sound and lighting.

Script writers often become famous too, because when audiences like their stories they will want to see more of them. It is unusual for any of the other people involved in pre-production, production or post-production to become celebrities.

In news production, **journalists** usually work on their own news stories, but sometimes a number of them may work together on a big story – and they often use researchers to help find out facts or get footage from an archive to be able to show past events as background to something that has just happened.

A television studio needs several people to operate it, simply because of the large numbers of tasks that have to be performed simultaneously. Each camera needs a **camera operator**, who will follow instructions from the director in the gallery. A **lighting director**, a **vision mixer** and a **sound mixer** will each follow the requirements of the script and the instructions from the director, to ensure operations run smoothly. On the floor of the studio a **floor manager** will also receive instructions from the gallery, and make sure they are carried out – giving **actors** or **presenters** cues to begin, for example.

A **sound recordist** is an important member of a location team when shooting drama, and **boom operators** can be as necessary away from the studio as in it, if microphones have to be kept out of sight. **Runners** perform odd jobs, carrying messages and getting last minute items to where they are needed (Figure 1.11). On location, **reporters** take crews with them, to operate a camera and make sure the sound is broadcast or recorded correctly. Sometimes they need **interpreters** and even **minders**, too.

The various post-production jobs are done by **editors**, **special effects designers** and **musicians**. **Foley artists** create overlays of sound to produce particular effects and mixes.

Radio

Despite the recent changes in technology, pre-production in audio is still as important as it is for the moving image. Audiences often think radio is just about presenters chatting informally between songs. It all sounds so effortless, most people can't imagine the considerable preparation that goes into a 'sequence programme' like a breakfast show.

Most music stations operate a playlist, organised by a computer program, and the individual programme teams have to work with the songs they are scheduled to play. Presenter chat is often the result of careful research, looking for interesting stories in the press or seeking information on the Internet. Competitions need to be prepared in advance, perhaps because a number of songs have to be edited together, or questions and answers need working out for a quiz, for instance. There may also be guest interviews to arrange.

Most radio stations run newsrooms, or at least contribute to news gathering for the region they cover. A news bulletin is a compilation of several stories, some from the local area and some supplied by a national and international news service. Every news story requires careful research and the checking of facts, be it locally or far away, before it can be read on the radio.

Commercial stations funded by advertising must first sell the advertising time to clients, who then pay either the station itself or an agency to produce the adverts. Writing copy for radio commercials requires imagination, creativity and also attention to detail, because they must be both catchy and memorable, as well as accurate in the claims they make and the offers they describe. Once completed, the advertising campaign needs scheduling, so each advert is played at the right time. Then the client needs billing for the cost of airing their advertisement.

The national BBC networks make programmes that local radio stations could not afford to produce. Comedy programmes like the original *Little Britain*, science fiction series like *The Hitchhiker's Guide to the Galaxy* and orchestral concerts by the BBC's own orchestras require vast resources and big budgets to support them. Any programmes involving large numbers of people – for example, drama, light entertainment or panel discussions produced as outside broadcasts, such as Radio 4's *Any Questions* – require planning, varying amounts of scripting and, if on location, getting permission from the site owners. Transport, catering and security need to be planned for and arranged in advance.

Radio work demands great professionalism – especially when microphones are live – no matter how informal the programme may sound. Luckily, recorded programmes can be edited and re-mixed if necessary in post-production (Figure 1.12). Non-linear editing software is used to remove mistakes, to edit together material that was recorded at different times, and to add music and effects.

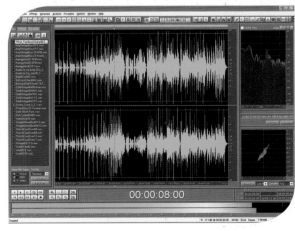

■ **Figure 1.12** *Editing out mistakes on a PC is an important skill in itself.*

Who does what?

Producers are the team leaders on each individual programme or project. They report to the **programme controller**. The title may differ slightly between organisations – some call them **programme directors** and many local BBC stations have **programme organisers**. BBC networks each have a **controller** instead, who commissions programme proposals from producers.

Then there are a number of roles in the pre-production, production and post-production stages. **Researchers** work to a brief from a **producer**, investigating a topic and arranging interviews to be recorded or broadcast live at a later date. Often it will be the producer who does this work if the programme team is small or they are working to a tight budget. Producers also book studios, hire actors and make any arrangements needed to make a production a success. At the news desk, it is the job of a **reporter** to research and write stories, preparing reports. The **editor** then selects stories for the next bulletin. A magazine programme might also use a reporter to prepare recorded items or even to report live from an event that will be of interest to the audience.

Script writers work on drama productions, researching facts as they need them. Music will be scheduled by the **head of music**, who decides what songs should go on the station playlist, and which should come off it, how often they should be played and at what time of day.

Producers usually want to be in the studio – or the control room – while a programme is in production. They can make sure things run smoothly and to time. **Presenters** link different

Hello. I want to be a big star!

■ **Figure 1.13** *Radio stations large and small employ people who work on and off air.*

items together and carry out live interviews with studio guests or 'down the line'. A complicated programme, like a drama or a magazine, might have a **technical operator** or an **engineer** operating the equipment (called a **studio manager** or a **broadcast assistant** in the BBC).

Sales executives sell airtime, while **copywriters** write the advertisements. Scheduling adverts is the job of the **traffic manager**. Commercials are made by **creative producers**, who take the script that has been agreed by the client and use **voiceover artists** to record them. Often in radio there will be a **station sound producer** in charge of recording jingles and station promotions, mixing items for competitions and producing other features for use in sequence programmes.

Music

Record companies are run by **executives** who manage the business and keep a close eye on finances. The Artists and Repertoire (A&R) department spots 'talent' and signs new bands and singers. **A&R people** do this work. They then manage the **talent** to get the best out of them in terms of music sales. In recording companies and studios it is the **producer** who manages the creative process, balancing the different sound sources – each instrument and each voice – and deciding on the final mix. **Sound engineers** assist with this, setting up microphones and making sure cables are connected properly.

Interactive media

Websites, video games or CD-ROMs all begin with an initial idea, which has to be fully worked through as an initial proposal, indicating how that idea will look, read and sound to the consumer. This may be in response to a request from a client, in the form of a brief, or it may be an original idea intended to make money from sales or subscriptions – or to promote another product or cause. Usually developed further in a treatment (a detailed description of the content of the proposed product), the product will be carefully targeted at a particular audience or market.

Content production may be simple or complex, depending on the nature of the product. It may include writing, shooting and editing video material, finding and editing audio or creating and manipulating entirely new images, as in the case of video games. Putting the various parts of an interactive media product together requires careful selection of the best and most appropriate material, in order to create a quality product that fits the brief. Interactive media products, and especially games, need to be extensively tested before release, to identify any problems with them and bugs in the software.

■ **Figure 1.14** *Many workers in interactive media work alone, even at home.*

Who does what?

People who work in interactive media production tend to be so multi-skilled that they can perform most functions themselves. Many of them work to a brief from a client, either as a freelancer or working within a section of a large company – for example, a Public Relations department. One of the biggest interactive media production centres is BBC Online, which provides web support for a vast range of the corporation's television and radio programming. Large numbers of **content producers**, **bulletin board editors** and **designers** work together in teams that report to the **producers** of individual programmes. Some specialise in turning audio and video produced for broadcast into web downloads.

The Public Relations department of a non-media organisation will have **copywriters** working on both print and online materials, perhaps including an in-house newspaper, marketing leaflets and press releases. This work may be overseen by an **editor**, or the copywriters may report to the **head of marketing**, a **director** of the company or someone else who occupies a senior, but apparently unrelated position.

The production process begins with an idea being explored by a **commissioning editor** or a **publisher**. An **editor** may control quality, organise **proofreaders**, and commission a **picture editor** to find appropriate illustrative material – which could of course include video or audio material created by specialist **producers**.

As multi-skilling is very common in multimedia production, it may be difficult to distinguish between production and post-production. A **web designer** may create the 'look' of a site or a page, and then hand it over to someone else to administer, while a **web master**'s role is ongoing, managing a site on a continuous basis.

DVD and CD-ROM production also depends heavily on design. The **producer** gathers and edits material, then physically positions it within the product. Packaging material, such as inlay cards and accompanying booklets and manuals will be the responsibility of **designers**, **proofreaders** and **copywriters**.

Photo imaging

Photography is a very personal activity, and **photographers** often process their own work – either in a darkroom or on computer. Alternatively, photographic film may be sent to a laboratory for processing by **technicians**. Picture libraries are organised by **picture librarians**. They handle enquiries from customers wishing to buy photographs and make sure payment is received and a fair share given to the photographer.

Assessment task 4

Choose one *sector of the media industry. Identify and discuss a range of the main job roles in that sector.*

Assessment evidence

✓ Describe the different job roles in detail, clearly showing how they differ from each other.

✓✓ Use examples to explain the reasons for the differences between job roles.

✓✓✓ Use correct terminology in your explanations, making sure they are detailed and supported by strong evidence of your conclusions.

Professional working practices

Media producers have to work within a wide range of different constraints. Some are legal, relating to the laws of the land. Some are ethical, relating to questions about how to treat people – as well as animals and the environment. A third category of constraints is the professional codes of practice – some of these are imposed by **regulatory bodies** and some originate from the industry's **self-regulatory bodies**, such as the British Board of Film Classification (BBFC) and the Press Complaints Commission (PCC), or membership organisations, such as the National Union of Journalists (NUJ).

There are different reasons for keeping within constraints imposed on the media industries. A media producer could be sent to prison or fined for breaking the law. Large amounts of money could be lost in damages

What does it mean?

Regulatory body – *an organisation set up by law to control an industry – its powers are given to it by law, and it has to abide by that law*

Self-regulatory body – *an organisation set up within the media industry to set standards for the industry – the intention is to keep the industry's reputation clean by being responsible and showing it is capable of running itself without outside intervention*

Remember

Employers and commissioning editors will be impressed by a good, working knowledge of the industry rules and regulations. They want to employ reliable people who can be trusted to work well with a minimum of supervision, so this awareness could open a number of doors for you later on.

paid to angry people who have been wrongly treated. When media employees make bad mistakes, their professional reputations suffer and they might lose their jobs if it looks like they could be careless enough to make similar mistakes in the future.

This shouldn't put you off working in the media, but it should make you want to know how to make sure you don't break the rules. It is very rare for someone working in the media to be taken to court, for example, so rest assured that if you learn what not to do and always use your common sense, you will stay on the right side of the law and the ethical and professional codes of practice.

Codes of practice

The media industry has a number of codes of practice governing how media producers should handle some of the most difficult issues. Most come from either regulatory or self-regulatory bodies.

■ **Figure 1.15** *On television the watershed is at 9 p.m.*

Case study

Ofcom

Ofcom
OFFICE OF COMMUNICATIONS

The most important code for radio and television is Ofcom's *Broadcasting Code*, because the public can complain to Ofcom about matters of taste and decency in any television or radio programme.

There are clear rules on the suitability of content for children, for example, and when children are to be included in programming or advertising. On television there is a watershed at 9 p.m. Before this time content of a violent or sexual nature should not be shown, and language should be moderate. After 9 p.m. the levels of violence and sexual content and the use of bad language are allowed to increase, particularly on certain channels which have a target audience that are considered to be relatively unshockable. All television channels are required to advise viewers before programmes if the content might be considered to be particularly shocking or disturbing, so viewers may switch off or to another channel.

In radio there is no watershed, just a recognition that later on in the evening children are less likely to be listening. In the past Radio 1 has broadcast material during the daytime that featured strong language and sexual references, and there have been many complaints about such content. Commercial radio stations have to attract advertising in order to survive, and if they want to maximise their audiences, they have to be very careful about the content that they air – parents of young children are more likely to switch off or to another station if their children are going to hear material that is unsuitable for them.

The BBC's *Editorial Guidelines* includes rules for its staff on all these issues. Producers and presenters working for the BBC are expected to follow them, including the sections on not causing offence.

The Ofcom code also covers advertising, and a separate document lists many types of goods and services that may not be advertised on television and radio. These include illegal services such as prostitution or drug pushing, and there are many other categories that are either banned or strictly controlled. Gambling is one, as is anything to do with faith healing, communication with spirits or fortune telling. Medicines and any products which claim to improve health are controlled too.

There are specific rules about using children in advertising and advertising that is aimed at children. Certain categories of advertising must be checked by experts. You can visit Ofcom's website in order to see the complete sets of rules for yourself.

Theory into practice

Visit the Ofcom website and the BBC website to see the *Broadcasting Code* and the *Editorial Guidelines* for yourself. Read through some of the more interesting sections of each to get a flavour of them.

Case study

British Board of Film Classification

In the cinema, it is the British Board of Film Classification which regulates film. This is a self-regulatory body, set up by the film industry itself. The BBFC works to a set of guidelines over content, which is based on age certification. Producers and directors know that, in order to get shown in most cinemas in this country, their films need a certificate – and one that is going to allow the target audience to see the film in large numbers.

There is little point in investing very heavily in a madcap teen comedy that will mostly appeal to people under sixteen if some of the content is so raunchy it ends up getting an 18 certificate. The target audience won't be able to get in to see the movie, and those who can will consider it too young for them, and stay away. Likewise, it is pointless keeping the content clean enough for a 12 certificate, if the story will be unappealing to teenagers because they will consider it too childish for their tastes.

The BBFC will view new films and advise film studios if cuts are required in order for them to get particular certificates. Advertisements and trailers intended for the cinema are also checked in the same way.

■ **Figure 1.16** *The number of people allowed to see a film can make or break it at the box office.*

Case study

Press Complaints Commission

Newspapers and magazines have their own self-regulatory bodies: the Press Complaints Commission (PCC) deals with complaints about news coverage and unfair treatment, while the Advertising Standards Agency (ASA) oversees printed advertising and billboards. The PCC has a number of editors on its board, and most of the industry has agreed to stick to its rules.

Unfair treatment complaints can come from anyone, from celebrities and footballers to politicians and even members of the royal family. Sometimes a member of the public who feels he or she has been unfairly treated makes a complaint – often this is someone in business who has been 'exposed' by a newspaper, but feels the coverage has been biased in some way, or that he or she has not been able to put the other side of the story. If the PCC judges that a publication has broken the code of practice, it can demand that an apology is printed. Publications usually comply with such rulings, but often the apology is much smaller and less noticeable than the original story – particularly if the story was a big one with several pages of coverage and bold headlines.

The PCC does not regulate standards of taste and decency in the press. Providing they do not contravene the Obscene Publications Act, or any other law, newspapers and magazines may set their own standards. For example, the serious newspapers will only feature nudity when it is essential to some feature item or news story, whereas some of the red-top tabloids print topless pictures to attract and entertain male readers. The amount of nudity featured in the *Daily Sport*, for example, shows that the newspaper thinks its readership likes soft-core pornography and is not particularly interested in hard news.

■ **Figure 1.17** *Newspapers have voluntarily agreed to stick to the PCC code.*

Professional codes of practice

Some professional bodies have their own professional codes. The National Union of Journalists (NUJ), for example, has a code of conduct which calls for its members to report issues and events honestly and truthfully without distortion or bias. It states that journalists should avoid 'falsification by distortion, selection or misrepresentation'. They should also avoid the 'expression of comment and conjecture as established fact'.

This code is in fact ignored by many newspaper journalists, whose editors and proprietors may expect them to support one political party or another. Broadcast journalists work within stricter regulatory constraints and so tend to take the NUJ code more seriously.

The interactive media are unregulated except for having to comply with the laws of the land like everyone else. There are no separate bodies with the job of regulating their output. However, many producers working in this sector will be working to client briefs, and the clients will have their own expectations and standards of taste and decency, depending on the intended purpose of the interactive products.

Workplace codes

As well as the written codes of practice, every professional in the workplace has to keep to a range of behavioural codes. These cover everything from how to dress at work to how to treat other people, including colleagues, managers, clients and the public. Standards of dress and behaviour differ from workplace to workplace. Some organisations expect their staff to dress formally, while others are much more relaxed and informal. The important thing when you are offered a job in the media is to find out as quickly as possible what the expected standards are and to follow them in your own dress and behaviour.

Legal restrictions

The law of the land is divided into criminal law and civil law. Criminal law is there to protect others, and to ensure that the country is as safe a place as possible for everyone to live and work in. If you break the criminal law you may be prosecuted.

Civil law relates mainly to the rights of individuals and the duties of people to others. For example, it allows one person or an organisation to sue another if the terms of a contract have been broken, or for breach of copyright if an idea is stolen.

Health and safety

It makes a lot of sense to start our consideration of legal restrictions with health and safety. This is because the safety of yourself and others should always come first. As well as considering our own safety, we each have legal responsibilities to consider everyone else's safety, too. Health and safety laws don't just apply to the media industries, but to every profession in every industry.

 Remember

Everyone in the workplace should be treated with dignity and respect, and they should treat others in the same way. Good timekeeping, completing work to deadlines and responding to correspondence promptly – including emails – are all part of professional conduct. Working to high professional standards will show that you expect to be treated professionally, too.

In fact, the Health and Safety at Work Act makes it a criminal offence for anybody not to take all reasonable care to ensure the safety of the people around them. Managers have to take particular care regarding the conditions in the workplace. They must take reasonable safety precautions on location work as well as within the office or studio. If someone dies at work or as a result of careless or wilful actions, a criminal court may find the person responsible guilty of manslaughter. That is an offence punishable by many years of imprisonment.

If there is a faulty piece of equipment, a sharp exposed edge or a liquid spill on a smooth floor, someone might get hurt on it (Figure 1.18). If you see a hazard at work, you should report it immediately or, if you have the skills, fix the problem yourself. In many circumstances, you will only be qualified to cordon off the affected area, so people are warned about the hazard and are able to avoid it.

Always report accidents and enter the details in the accident book in case there is any follow-up required, such as an investigation or a court case.

The best practice in order to avoid accidents is to carry out a risk assessment. The very nature of accidents means that often they are unpredictable. However, if you can provide evidence that you took all reasonable precautions, employers and staff alike can at least avoid prosecution.

■ **Figure 1.18** *Some accidents could easily be avoided, if only someone would take action first.*

A risk assessment involves identifying any likely hazards. For example, you could say that anyone working outdoors could be struck by lightning, but that this risk is probably only worth considering in very stormy weather. Sending a reporter or a film crew out on a very stormy day will involve a greater risk than on other days – you have to use your common sense when thinking about the risks involved in a particular activity.

Most employers have safety officers to carry out risk assessments and first aiders who can respond quickly in case of any accidents causing injury at work. Knowing some first aid can save a life, as you may be able to keep a seriously injured colleague alive until paramedics arrive.

Copyright

The media industry is an ideas industry, and producers earn their living from developing popular ideas that get audiences interested. Copyright protects these ideas from being copied by other people without permission.

Copyright protects performance, too, such as singing a song, doing a rap or acting in a production. Almost every literary, dramatic, artistic or musical work has had some investment made in it. That investment may

 Think it over

Copyright might seem to cause us problems, because it prevents us using other people's work without obtaining proper permission, but in fact it is there to protect us and our own ideas, too.

Supposing you come up with a brilliant idea for a new programme format, an exciting new magazine or an appealing story that would work well in print, on radio and on screen. You will expect to be able to earn a good share of the profits from exploiting that idea, if it proves popular with audiences. Imagine your annoyance if your idea earns you nothing, while other people make a fortune from what is rightfully yours.

 Think it over

If someone was selling illegal copies of Hollywood films in very large quantities, far fewer people would pay to see the film at the cinema or buy the official DVD. The income of the Hollywood studios would drop rapidly and they would have to stop making new movies. Copyright law is there to prevent this happening.

be time spent working on it, the use of specialised equipment to produce it, and even money spent on marketing and promotion. Copyright law helps to ensure a return on the investment made.

The Copyright, Designs and Patents Act 1988 is there to protect the owners of copyright work. Stealing someone else's copyright work can result in being sued under the civil law and that could lead to paying out large sums of money in damages. Many media products, such as films and TV programmes, cost a lot of money to produce, and the investors in those products have the right to benefit from them.

A television production company such as Endemol, which produces *Big Brother*, needs to protect its entertainment show formats from unofficial exploitation by other television companies. Under international copyright agreements, no other TV companies are allowed to copy the format, so Endemol can earn money by producing *Big Brother* in different countries.

If you look closely at most printed products you will see the copyright symbol © somewhere, plus the name of the copyright owner and the year. The copyright declaration is usually found on a page near the front of a book (it is on page ii in this book), at the bottom of the last page of a newspaper and near the list of editorial staff in a magazine. It is almost always to be seen briefly at the end of the final credits on a film or a television programme (Figure 1.19), and on inlay cards and sleeves of DVDs, videos and CDs.

It would be very difficult for radio stations to use a visual copyright mark, but that doesn't mean that radio programmes, news bulletins, competitions and so on are not copyright. Otherwise rogue stations could steal other stations' news bulletins, for example, without making any investment whatsoever in news gathering. Radio is a special case, and copyright law automatically covers radio broadcasts, without any statement having to be made.

The Internet is the most problematic media area in terms of copyright law. In theory all material on the web is someone's copyright, and you will often see statements to that effect on websites. However, there are a large number of sites which infringe other people's copyright.

Did you know?

Some television companies write the year of copyright in Roman numbers – one of the reasons for this, is that when programmes are repeated, it isn't so obvious to viewers how old the programme is.

Did you know?

One music download site began as a file-sharing service which enabled members to access copyright songs without the copyright owners' permission. The music industry took legal action to prevent this, and as a result, the website became a legal source of music downloads, offering songs for payment – with the permission of the copyright owners, who now receive royalties for their work.

Copyright does expire after a particular length of time – and how long depends on what it is. For example, Mozart's compositions are no longer under copyright because he died more than 70 years ago. You could therefore perform his music without having to gain any permissions or pay any royalties. The table in Figure 1.20 shows the different terms of copyright that apply in the United Kingdom at the time of writing this book.

© **Gigolo Sun Productions MMVI**

■ **Figure 1.19** *A copyright mark from 2006.*

Type of work	Length of copyright
Literary, dramatic, musical or artistic work	70 years after the death of the author
Sound recordings and broadcasts	50 years from creation
Typographical arrangements (for example, producing a new version of a book that is out of copyright)	25 years
Databases	70 or 15 years, depending on the complexity

■ **Figure 1.20** *Different types of work are covered by copyright for different lengths of time.*

Anybody who owns the copyright to a literary, dramatic, artistic or musical work that is in copyright may sell it or simply give it to someone else. So the copyright transfers to that person, for him or her to do with as he or she thinks fit.

You have to be very careful with copyright because there may be different rights in a work, owned by different people. The works of Mozart consist of the sheet music from which they are played. It is that sheet music – his compositions – which is free for you to use. If you wish to use a *recording* of any of Mozart's work that was made within the last 50 years, then the musicians will own the rights to their performance. If it was recorded more than 50 years ago but is now being re-released, then the recording company or record label still owns the rights to the performance.

In order to use copyright material, media producers are usually required to report seven essential pieces of information, as shown in Figure 1.22 on page 40.

The owner of the copyright in a work will often grant permission for it to be used. That permission may be free of charge, or it may be in return for a fee. Sometimes the permission is called a 'licence'. In the UK, most radio stations have copyright licensing agreements with three bodies set up to collect royalties on behalf of their members. Some television channels have them, too – for example, ITV does. These licensing arrangements are called 'blanket agreements'. Most commercially sold music is represented by the three organisations shown in Figure 1.21. The information sent to the licensing bodies is known as 'copyright returns'.

Performing Right Society

Represents composers, when you broadcast their work

Phonographic Performance Limited

Represents record companies and performers, when you broadcast their work

Mechanical Copyright Protection Society

Represents publishers and songwriters, when you make recordings of their work

■ **Figure 1.21** *The three copyright licensing bodies in the United Kingdom. Each one represents different groups of copyright owners.*

Did you know?

The best-selling author, Dan Brown, was unsuccessfully sued in 2006 by a team of authors who claimed he had stolen an idea of theirs for his book The Da Vinci Code. *The former English teacher's novels have earned him millions of pounds from book sales and royalties from the blockbuster film based on his book.*

Remember

Permission must be obtained for using any copyright material, not just music. The producer of a television programme cannot use a film clip or a clip from another TV show without permission. Likewise, using print material created by someone else usually requires permission. Even showing a company's logo on screen can be a breach of copyright, if the company that owns the logo has not agreed to this.

Artist	Title	Composer	Publisher (of the title)	Record label	Serial number	Duration used
Natasha Bedingfield	These words	N Bedingfield/ S Kipner/ A Frampton/ W Wilkins	EMI/Sonic Graffiti/EMI/ Ingenius	BMG	82876 637022	3′41″

■ **Figure 1.22** *The seven different pieces of information needed when noting the copyright details of a commercially released music track.*

The licensing bodies do not offer blanket agreements for using their members' music in radio or television commercials. Every song or instrumental track to be used in an advert has to be cleared separately, by contacting the rights owners and gaining their permission. If the rights owners sense that big business is behind the advert, they are likely to ask for a very large fee for the use of their work. If the rights owner does not want to have the music associated with the product, he or she is likely to refuse permission.

An alternative, if the budget is large enough, is to have some music specially recorded. It could sound *quite* like the original, or at least make the audience think of the original. But if it is too close a copy, the copyright owners of the original work may decide to sue – and the court may agree with them! Some companies produce library music especially for media producers to use in commercials, as 'beds' for radio presenters to talk over and in opening and closing sequences for television and radio programmes. There is usually a fee for their use.

Rights clearance for other uses of music can be very time consuming, and television and film producers often prefer to commission original music. For a feature film it is quite normal to have a musical director and performers working for months on writing and recording a musical score that fits the action.

Libel law

Libel law is one of the trickiest areas for media producers. It presents many pitfalls and it is wise to tread carefully if there is even a small risk of being sued for **libel**. Libel is a form of **defamation** and it occurs when someone publishes or broadcasts something about someone that is untrue and is damaging to his or her reputation.

Anyone working in the media industry should take advice from somebody more senior, or even specialist libel lawyers, if at all concerned about the possibility of libel. Someone once said that being involved in a libel case is a bit like playing poker, because neither side quite knows what evidence the other side is going to produce. Certainly, at the start of most libel cases, it is difficult to predict the verdict.

The law assumes that everyone has a natural right to a good reputation, whoever they are, unless they do something to deserve being thought badly of. Therefore, a court will presume that a statement that is

Did you know?

The sums awarded in successful libel cases can be enormous. Of course, exposing wrongdoing is one of the most important roles media producers can play – but the risk of losing their own jobs is high. If a libel case goes wrong for them, their employers might consider that they are not careful or responsible enough to be trusted with controversial stories again.

What does it mean?

Defamation – *unfairly damaging somebody's reputation*

Libel – *defamation that is broadcast, published, distributed to a large number of people on a leaflet or posted on the Internet*

Slander – *defamation on a small scale, for example through word of mouth. Because slanderous remarks can be repeated from one person to another, they can still be very damaging. Slander can occur in any area of human activity, including the workplace, school, college, clubs and societies – not just the media.*

published or broadcast, and which could damage someone's reputation is libellous *unless* the media producer can convince the court that the statement made was true.

That is why it is important for investigative reporters working on stories intended to reveal wrongdoing to keep evidence of the facts they report. That evidence may one day have to be very convincing to a jury in a libel case – and so 'half-knowing' something or having a 'gut feeling' about something is simply not strong enough to justify the publication or broadcast of damaging statements.

Unless media producers are very thick-skinned, being sued for libel can be a very worrying experience. Not knowing how a libel case will turn out, and the risk of losing, can become unbearable over the lengthy period such cases often take. The average length of a libel case is two years, from the issuing of the original notification – in the form of a writ – to the verdict and the awarding of any damages.

Before you take fright and decide that you never want to work in the media, you should consider that libel cases are very rare. Think of how many news stories and feature items are published and broadcast in a typical day, without there being any problems over libel at all. That is because almost all media producers know the law, and they have taken the time either to avoid something that might result in a libel action or to collect enough evidence and seek suitable advice and guidance.

Did you know?

Libel and *slander* are both types of **defamation**. *People often confuse the two, but generally in media production it is libel which concerns us most. Your own production work should take into account the different constraints placed upon it by libel law.*

Theory into practice

Here are some examples of claims that might damage a person's reputation:

- Saying an actor was drunk on stage and couldn't remember his lines – what casting director would give that actor another part?
- Alleging that a shop assistant stole money from the till – who would trust that person with money in the future?
- Claiming that a politician has lied in order to get votes, and cannot be trusted – why would people vote for such a politician in the future?
- Alleging that a driving instructor doesn't understand the Highway Code – who would pay for lessons with that instructor?
- Saying that a footballer has slept with another footballer's wife or girlfriend before an away match – could the other player trust him ever again, and could such difficulties affect their performance on the pitch?
- Claiming a man is violent towards his wife or children or that he sexually abuses them – he may have to go into hiding for his own safety.

Court reporting

Matters that go before a court of law can be very difficult for the media. Statements made in court may not be true, and repeating them without making clear that they are merely allegations could turn out to be libellous. Another problem is that reporting should not damage the proper working of the court system. If it is read, heard or seen by the members of a jury, it could affect the outcome of a trial.

Reporting criminal cases from the courts is a very specialised role within the media industry. The book *McNae's Essential Law for Journalists* (published by Oxford University Press) contains very detailed information of all the different restrictions that apply in different circumstances. Reporters refer to that book frequently, making sure they are using an up-to-date edition, so that they know about any recent changes in the rules.

Being found in contempt of court carries severe penalties, including fines and imprisonment, so media producers and presenters need to know the basic guidance that will keep them on the right side of the law. Broadcasting opinions about a criminal case while it is in progress is against the *sub judice* laws.

Did you know?

In December 2003, two presenters on a radio station in Shropshire broke the sub judice *laws – while the trial was in progress, they discussed on air the high-profile trial of Ian Huntley for the murder of two schoolgirls. They expressed the opinion that Ian Huntley's evidence was unbelievable and said that he should just give up 'and admit that he did it'. They even asked their listeners to phone and text in with their own opinions.*

If members of the jury had heard the presenters' comments, it could have influenced their verdict. It doesn't matter under the law that the local radio station in Shropshire was a long way from the court – the programmes of many local radio stations are now available outside their normal broadcast areas via the Internet.

Special rules apply to minors – children and young people under 16 years of age – involved in court or who are talked about in court. Generally, minors cannot be identified in the media – unless the court case is about antisocial behaviour and results in an ASBO being put on the young person. In these exceptional cases, identifying the minor concerned is considered to be part of the punishment, and a deterrent to stop them causing further trouble – precisely because people *can* identify them. Adult victims in rape proceedings are protected from being identified, too.

Data protection

Every person or organisation has to work within the Data Protection Act. This law restricts the use of personal data, in order to protect people from inaccurate or misleading information being compiled about them without their knowledge, and then being shared by different organisations. It is not hard to imagine how, without any controls on data collection and use, this kind of information sharing could lead to some very unfair decisions being made about people – preventing them access to credit, for example.

Most organisations or individuals wishing to collect personal information have to be licensed for this purpose. Anyone whose information is held has the right to be able to access it and check that it

What does it mean?

Sub judice – a Latin term which literally means 'under justice'. It is used to refer to a judicial process that is taking place. In order that justice takes its natural course, special restrictions apply to all reporting of a criminal court case.

Remember

All media products must follow the rules regarding what can what cannot be reported once a criminal case has started. The rules apply to the Internet, too, when content has been created or is hosted in this country.

■ **Figure 1.23** *Storing personal information is covered by the Data Protection Act.*

is correct. Anyone collecting information about people – and particularly if they are using computer-based equipment to process it – must abide by this law. Storing and editing interview material on computer comes under the law. Most employers will already have the correct licences that allow them to collect and store personal data, as well as the correct procedures for dealing with enquiries about such data – your college or school almost certainly will.

Race

One of the most important legal restrictions on media producers concerns race. Because of the Public Order Acts of 1936 and 1976, it is an offence to cause incitement to racial hatred, and so anyone who sets out to cause divisions between the different ethnic groups in the country can be prosecuted. Where racial violence has broken out in the world, it has often been very bloody and caused further deep divisions between people.

Media producers who are reporting on certain events might unwittingly fall foul of this aspect of the law. If, for example, a reporter is covering a demonstration or a public speech given by a racist and includes some of the inflammatory words used by the speaker in his or her report, the reporter could be prosecuted. When running a debate on a phone-in or having a guest interviewee on a programme, producers and presenters have to be very careful that racially inflammatory words do not get broadcast, because they could themselves be prosecuted.

Remember

It is actually very rare for people to be prosecuted for incitement to racial hatred. It is even rarer for it to be media producers who are in the firing line. This may be because of widespread knowledge and understanding about the law, and what it allows people to do and what it prevents them from doing. Most people in Britain seem to be aware of the dangers of racism and willingly uphold this law.

Assessment task 5

From the one *sector of the media industry that you have chosen, identify and discuss a range of professional working practices that apply to the jobs you listed in Assessment task 4.*

Assessment evidence

✔ Describe the different professional working practices in detail.

✔✔ Use examples to explain these professional working practices and why they are important.

✔✔✔ Use correct terminology in your explanations, making sure they are detailed and supported by strong evidence of your conclusions.

Contracts, conditions and pay

The larger the organisation, the more specialised the people who work there tend to be. Each part of the production process is performed by specialised people who are expert in their own area. In smaller organisations, staff tend to work across more different job roles. This is often because there is not enough work in one specialised field to keep one person fully occupied. Each person may become expert in a number of roles, as a small organisation often cannot afford to employ people who are not busy all the time.

Contracts for staff and freelancers

The media industry makes great use of freelancers – individuals who work for organisations when they require their services, but who do not have a permanent job with the company.

■ **Figure 1.24** *Time is money in the media industry, and staff, freelancers and actors cost money whatever they are doing.*

Some very specialised roles are carried out by freelancers who are brought in to perform a particular task for a one-off fee. For example, most actors and actresses get work in broadcasting for short periods at a time – it would be uneconomic to employ them to sit around waiting for a suitable part in a drama or commercial to come along.

So, in the media industry paid work is done by staff or freelancers. Even unpaid volunteers may have to sign a contract, agreeing to keep to certain rules or codes of conduct. In a media organisation, paid staff may be either:

- full-time – meaning they work for the organisation all week

or

- part-time – meaning they work for the organisation for just part of the week.

Their relationship with the company is formally established by a contract of employment, which they have to sign when they first accept the job. The contract will contain details of the employee's obligations to the organisation and the organisation's obligations to them. These obligations will most likely include pay, holiday entitlement, hours to be worked and where the work is to be done, and any pension contributions to be deducted from the pay. Current good practice for contracts includes referring to the job specification that was sent to all applicants for the job when it was first advertised – as well as listing the duties of the post, it will indicate who the employee's line manager is.

The contract may include other information, such as rules about not smoking at work and perhaps about complying with rules on equal opportunities and regulators' codes of practice. There will be a period of notice which the employee must give the employer if they want to leave the organisation – for example, to take up a better or more highly paid job elsewhere.

There are considerable advantages to having a full-time contract, rather than a temporary one. The most obvious is that you can then decide when *you* want to leave the organisation, rather than your time in the job simply running out at a predetermined date when you might not have found a new job to go to. A full-time contract will often allow you to join a company pension scheme and some employers give employees longer holidays once they have worked for them for a certain length of time. Working on temporary contracts, even if these are renewed over several years, can often mean that you miss out on benefits such as these.

Remember

Staff contracts may be either **permanent** or **temporary**.

A temporary contract is for employment that is for a fixed term only – perhaps to cover someone else's absence, while that person is on maternity or paternity leave, for example. The employee cannot expect to be employed after the end of the contract, unless he or she is offered a new contract – this could be for the same job or for a different one.

Remember

It is worth reading a contract of employment very carefully before signing it, and raising any queries with the **human resources department** of the organisation – or even seeking specialist advice from a solicitor, your local Citizens' Advice Bureau or a **trade union**.

Freelance contracts relate only to the performance of specific tasks, and a typical freelancer might be working on different contracts for more than one organisation at the same time. Freelance work offers no job security or benefits beyond what is specified in the current contract, so, again, it is important to check the contract before signing.

Some people working in the media like the flexibility of working on temporary or freelance contracts because they can move around different organisations and choose when they work. Sometimes, because the work is less secure than a full-time staff post, organisations have to offer higher rates of pay in order to attract the right people to do the work. In broadcasting, for example, presenters may be hired for only a single series of programmes, but be paid very generously – especially if they are already famous names.

Not everyone who works freelance manages to find work all the time. There may be some long periods of unemployment. However, busy freelancers and **stringers** are able to pick and choose between different jobs, turning down work that doesn't pay so well and discriminating between interesting and less interesting work, or people they do and do not want to work with.

Moving around the industry certainly means meeting and working with a greater variety of people, and one way to further your career is to build up a long list of contacts – people you have worked with in the past, who might be helpful when you are looking for more work. This is called 'networking' because over time you develop a network of supportive contacts.

Another disadvantage of working freelance is that you have to keep accounts (Figure 1.25) and file tax returns with details of your income and business expenses. Many freelancers pay accountants to do this for them, and this cost to their business can be offset against tax they owe, as can other costs they incur in their work.

Everyone who works has to pay National Insurance. This is a scheme run by the state, which helps to finance sick pay when you are ill (although this does not apply to self-employed people), medical treatment when you need it and a very basic old age pension when you reach retirement age. It is wise to contribute to an additional pension scheme as soon as you can.

Michael Foan, *Broadcaster and Writer*

Income and expenditure account for the year ended 30th April 2006

	£
INCOME FOR WORK DONE:	22068

Deduct: EXPENSES

Motor running costs	2011
Telephone (business use)	291
Work clothes for professional appearances	301
Stationery, postage & sundries	274
CDs & DVDs purchased for professional use	451
Reference books, etc.	101
Computer expenses	30
Use of room as office	230
Accountancy fees	180
	3869

NET SURPLUS OF INCOME OVER EXPENDITURE:	18199

■ **Figure 1.25** *The accounts of a freelance writer and broadcaster.*

Work patterns

Because the media industries mostly work round the clock, on a 24/7 basis, many staff and freelancers work to different patterns from the nine-to-five day found in many office jobs and other industries. Programmes have to be broadcast live at all times of the day and night, news does not stop out-of-hours, and often filming a blockbuster movie has to take place at the weekend when disruption to traffic will be reduced. Readers now expect newspapers on bank holidays – and certainly at weekends. So, while many people working in the media, particularly those in administration, management and financial jobs, do keep regular hours, many do not.

What does it mean?

Stringers – *freelance journalists who usually work for news organisations, often covering interesting court cases for newspapers or radio stations who cannot spare staff to sit in court for a whole day. They provide coverage of other types of news story, too – sometimes providing a tip off to a news editor.*

Remember

Typical work patterns include:

- **Shift work** – doing the equivalent of a working day, but at night. The 24-hour day can be broken up into three equal eight-hour shifts.

- **Office hours** – a roughly nine-to-five pattern, normally starting and finishing a little earlier or later.

- **Irregular hours** – changing almost daily, some days more hours are worked and then other working days are a little shorter to make up for the leisure time lost.

- **Antisocial hours** – work done early in the morning, late at night, on bank holidays and at weekends. Often this kind of working is shared around a team on a rota basis, and some workers are lucky enough to be paid bonuses for working at antisocial times.

Pay

Once established in their careers, most people working in the media industry want to be properly paid for their contribution to an organisation's success. We would not want to be exploited for long periods of working for nothing, just to gain 'work experience', so it is reasonable to expect that someone who is qualified and experienced enough to do a particular job regularly is worth paying properly. Payments can be made in a number of ways:

- Salaried staff – people on permanent or fixed-term contracts receive an annual salary, usually paid monthly into their bank accounts.

- Hourly payments – these are usually made to freelance or temporary staff and are paid according to the number of hours worked for the organisation. Some weeks they may work more hours than others and are paid accordingly.

- On completion – a payment for a job completed. Usually paid to freelancers who accept a commission or fee to perform a particular task, such as compose a soundtrack, write a script or work on a photo shoot.

Assessment task 6

From the one sector of the media industry that you have chosen, identify and discuss the different types of employment contracts that apply to the jobs you listed in Assessment task 4. Explain how these are paid.

Assessment evidence

✔ Describe the different types of employment contracts in detail.

✔✔ Use examples to explain these types of employment contracts and how they differ.

✔✔✔ Use correct terminology in your explanations, making sure they are detailed and supported by strong evidence of your conclusions.

1.3   How staff are recruited

You need to describe and discuss how staff are recruited in *one* sector of the media industry. In this section we will look at the skills and qualifications needed to work in the media and how media organisations recruit staff. Three more assessment tasks will help you present your work in the correct way.

Skills and qualifications

Education and training

These two words are very closely related, but people tend to have different expectations of what will result from each of them. Education is the term favoured by schools, colleges and universities, because it suggests development of the individual person in lots of ways that relate to work and life, such as literacy, numeracy and how to relate to others. Training, on the other hand, is a term that often appeals more to employers, because it suggests learning specific skills that are focused on one task or a small number of tasks involved in performing a particular job role. In fact, most of us would probably get most out of life from a balance between the two – being better educated will enable us to think more clearly, to find solutions to problems, to get information and to know what to do with it once we have found it, while being trained in job-specific skills will enable us to succeed at work and to develop a career.

Very few people begin working in the media industry in senior positions. Most begin in low-paid, low-status jobs and work their way up their own personal 'career ladder'. This is fine for young people who do not yet have mortgages and families to provide for.

Climbing up the career ladder does not happen automatically, though, and it is important to develop the skills to identify career opportunities and submit successful applications in order to benefit from them. Networking helps, but so do being well qualified, learning new skills and getting to grips with changes in technology and working practices as soon as possible.

Depending on where in the production processes you begin, there are a variety of different pathways in each area of the media industry. Sometimes a freelancer working from home will be tempted to join the staff of a company. Equally staff may decide to go freelance – this tends to happen a lot when companies run into financial difficulty and have to make a number of employees redundant. Redundancy can be very distressing at the time, but sometimes a forced change of career path can open up new avenues and ends up being seen as an opportunity. Often there is financial compensation for redundancy, which is sometimes enough to purchase equipment and make the first few months as a freelancer easier financially.

Case study

Katy McDonald

Katy McDonald is a radio journalist. She studied for a Media Production degree at the University of Sunderland, and stayed on for a further year to complete a postgraduate course – an MA in journalism.

As a student, she did some work experience at Sky Television, and then talked her way into Metro Radio in Newcastle, where she began by also working for free. After a short while she was being paid to do the technical operation on the Saturday afternoon sports programme and a five nights per week phone-in on Metro's sister station, Magic 1152.

As soon as she got her qualifications in journalism – including the National Council for the Training of Journalists (NCTJ) certificate – Katy got a full-time

job on the newsdesk, where she quickly became morning news editor, compiling and presenting bulletins on Metro and Magic.

Generally, the best way to further a career in the media industry is through education and training – being as skilled and qualified as you can be, with certificates to prove it. Learning should not stop once you have settled into a job, but should be part of a life-long process that will help you to adjust to changes as they come along.

Education and training can take a number of different forms:

- Full-time education – in school, college and university. This leads to recognised qualifications, such as BTEC First and BTEC National awards, GCE, HND, degree and postgraduate certificates, diplomas and masters degrees. Normally there is time left in the week to do some part-time work, and if this is in the media industry, it can provide valuable experience and contacts that could lead to a full-time job once the course is finished.

- Part-time education – also in school, college and university. Many of the qualifications above can be studied part-time, leaving more time free in the week for paid work, if you can get it. Of course, it will take longer to get the qualifications – perhaps several years more – because you are spending less time studying each week. People who graduate from universities often study for postgraduate qualifications on a part-time basis, often later in life, when their children have grown up, for example.

- On-the-job training – many employers recognise the need to train employees, perhaps beginners who need to develop essential skills in a new workplace or with unfamiliar equipment. Training on the job tends to focus narrowly on those essential skills, because, to an employer, your time is money. Some employers have formal training schemes, perhaps with the job title of trainee – but the pay tends to be low to reflect the cost to the employer of taking on someone who needs training. Modern apprenticeships fit into this category, although they tend to be few and far between.

- Continuing professional development – a formal scheme run by an employer which focuses on individual employees, identifying training and development needs, then seeking to address them. Employees normally negotiate with their manager what development should be offered each year, working to targets and goals which both employer and employee feel will benefit them.

- Self-training – often, if an employer doesn't offer much in the way of continuing professional development, an individual might take on the responsibility to gain extra skills and understanding in order to progress professionally. This can involve taking part-time courses out of working hours, or finding teach-yourself materials in books, on disks or on the Internet.

- National Vocational Qualifications (NVQs) – once someone has developed skills at a certain level, they can be certified through this scheme. NVQs are not taught qualifications, but measurements of a person's skill level at the time of the test. They are a way of getting recognition for skills you have developed, without necessarily having been taught them on a course.

Level

The level of a qualification is determined by its placing in the National Qualifications Framework (NQF), shown in Figure 1.26.

Level 8	D (doctoral) Doctorates
Level 7	M (masters) Masters degrees, postgraduate certificates and diplomas
Level 6	H (honours) Bachelor degrees, graduate certificates and diplomas
Level 5	Diplomas of higher education and further education, foundation degrees and higher national diplomas
Level 4	C (certificate) Certificates of higher education
Level 3	A levels
Level 2	First diploma, GCSEs Grades A*–C
Level 1	First certificate, GCSEs Grades D–G

■ **Figure 1.26** *The National Qualifications Framework.*

You will notice that the BTEC First Certificate and Diploma are NQF levels 1 and 2. It may look like you have a long way to go, but you may want to aim to get qualifications higher up the framework, such as a degree, and maybe after that a postgraduate certificate, diploma or masters degree.

Sources of information

There are lots of ways of finding out about the various skills and qualifications that would be useful for a career in the media. Skillset is the national training organisation for the audio–visual industries, and on their website, www.skillset.org, they offer lots of information for beginners and established professionals alike. Other training organisations include the National Council for the Training of Journalists (NCTJ) and the Broadcast Journalism Training Council (BJTC), which also have websites. Skillset has devised a whole suite of National Occupational Standards relating to most areas of the media.

Trade unions, such as the National Union of Journalists (NUJ) and the Broadcasting, Entertainment, Cinematograph and Theatre Union (BECTU), also provide careers advice on their websites – and of course, they would like you to join them as members once you have a job in the media.

Your school or college will certainly be able to help you access a careers advice service – although you should remember that they may not have much specialist knowledge of the media industry. Do not be discouraged by people who say that media students are unlikely to get jobs in the media – these views have been proven to be wrong by the Skillset surveys, which show that large numbers of people in the media do have qualifications in media subjects.

Finally, anyone wanting to enter the media industry would be well advised to read the trade publications regularly. These include *Broadcast*, *Media Week*, *The Radio Magazine*, *Campaign* and the *UK Press Gazette*.

Did you know?

A 2001 survey of workers in broadcasting, multimedia and film found that:

- *60% had joined the workforce since 1994*
- *50% were working on a freelance basis*
- *30% were graduates in media subjects*
- *30% had a postgraduate qualification*

Source: Skillset and the DCMS AV Industries Training Group

Theory into practice

Build up a research file of cuttings of interesting-looking jobs in one or more sectors of the media industry. Identify the skills and experience employers are looking for, and find reasons why certain ones keep cropping up. Ask yourself how you could get the skills and experience the employers are looking for. Are there further courses you could go on to in order to make yourself more employable?

Assessment task 7

From the one sector of the media industry that you have chosen, identify and discuss the different skills and qualifications needed for the jobs you listed in Assessment task 4.

Assessment evidence

✔ Describe the different skills and qualifications in detail.

✔✔ Use examples to explain these skills and qualifications and how and why they differ.

✔✔✔ Use correct terminology in your explanations, making sure they are detailed and supported by strong evidence of your conclusions.

Transferable skills

Skills which are useful in many different industries are called transferable skills. They include basic numeracy, literacy and IT skills, as well as self-confidence, the ability to make presentations, effective communication skills and the ability to work well with other people. They also include professional behaviour in the workplace, which we looked at on page 34.

Personal attributes

The survey quoted in the Did you know? box on page 54 also asked employers in the industry what they wanted from new recruits.

Employers said that they wanted new recruits to:

✔ distinguish themselves from 'the pack'

✔ be multi-skilled where relevant (for example, in newsrooms), but specialisation remains important in several areas

✔ maintain a willingness to learn, work hard and be flexible over working practices

✔ be enthusiastic and not to arrive thinking they know it all

✔ be disciplined

✔ balance common sense with creativity.

Reasonable employers will understand that you cannot know everything yet about how to do the job, but they will also expect you to understand the contexts within which you will work and know how you fit into the bigger picture of the organisation and the wider industry around you.

It seems like employers want a lot from their workers – but you have a right to be treated fairly in return. That means not being exploited, having equal opportunities whatever your gender, your ethnic and social background and whether or not you have any disability. Fairness at work also means others have the right to expect the same from you.

Even very experienced graduates with media degrees may find adapting to the world of work challenging. For a start, they are expected to turn up punctually every day, and to stay behind late if something needs finishing off for a deadline. It can be a big shock, too, to have only four weeks of holiday a year plus bank holidays and maybe days off in lieu.

Key skills

In the 1990s the government developed five key skills areas. You can provide evidence for these by doing this qualification.

For this qualification, you will be working to demonstrate key skills at NQF level 2, but as people progress onto more advanced courses of study, they aim to demonstrate key skills at the appropriate higher level. For example, going on to do a National Diploma or a GCE Advanced in Media would lead to covering key skills at level 3.

Remember

The five key skill areas are:

✔ application of number

✔ communication

✔ information and communication technology

✔ improving own learning and performance

✔ working with others.

Assessment task 8

From the one sector of the media industry that you have chosen, identify and discuss the transferable skills needed for the jobs you listed in Assessment task 4.

Assessment evidence

✔ Describe the transferable skills in detail.

✔✔ Use examples to explain these transferable skills and how and why they are important.

✔✔✔ Use correct terminology in your explanations, making sure they are detailed and supported by strong evidence of your conclusions.

Methods of recruitment

The media industry can be difficult to break into for beginners, but once inside it often seems to get much easier, as you gain experience, skills, understanding and, of course, contacts. Media organisations recruit new staff in a number of ways. The most obvious way is advertisements placed in the national and trade press, as well as on the Internet. The most popular place to find press advertisements for jobs in the media is the *Media Guardian*, every Monday.

Because advertising in the *Media Guardian* is so expensive, some organisations try to save money by targeting their adverts in publications that people with the skills they are looking for are likely to read, such as *The Radio Magazine*, which costs much less and is read widely in the radio sector. For print journalists, the *UK Press Gazette* is often the best place to look for work. Some websites are becoming just as useful and just as popular.

Did you know?

Other ways in which media organisations recruit staff include:

- *Word of mouth – an employer asks people to ask around, to see if someone suitable can be found through indirect personal contact.*

- *Personal contact – an employer knows someone, perhaps someone who has done work experience in the company, who might be suitable, and makes a direct approach, either offering the job straightaway or inviting that person to apply formally for it.*

- *Internal promotion – someone already inside the organisation is suitable for promotion to a more senior, and better-paid, position. These job opportunities may not even be known about by people on the outside, because they are only publicised internally.*

Figure 1.27 *The jobs pages of the* Media Guardian *are often the first pages media workers turn to.*

In most media jobs, maintaining a portfolio of your best work means you will be able to demonstrate your suitability for promotion or an opportunity in another organisation without delay. This might mean keeping cuttings of stories written for printed publications, keeping recordings of moving image or audio work or keeping examples of multimedia that you have worked on. Unless a specific job advertisement asks for more, audio and video demos should be short – three to four minutes maximum, because the people who will be deciding which applicants to put on a shortlist and invite for interview will probably be very busy, and will not be able to set aside much time for trawling through lots of material.

Only include *copies* of your *very best work* in your demo or a portfolio – the moment employers come across anything of a poor standard, they will almost certainly move on to the next application. Presentation is crucial. The covering letter and any application form must be very well presented and without spelling errors. Disks and tapes must be neatly and clearly labelled with your name and contact details, in case they become separated from the rest of the material, and work on paper or card needs special protection to prevent it becoming spoilt.

As this course is at an introductory level, your best career option may well be to go on to further study first.

CURRICULUM VITAE

Name:	Michael Foan
Age:	24
Qualifications and dates:	B.A. (Hons.) in Media Production (Television & Radio) 2/1, University of Sunderland, 2004 Advanced GCE in Media (A) 2001 Advanced GCE in English (A) 2001 Advanced Subsidiary GCE in History (C) 2000 GCSE English (A) 1999 GCSE Maths (C) 1999 GCSE History (A) 1999 GCSE French (C) 1999 GCSE Geography (B) 1999
Employment history:	Presenter, Oldtown FM, June 2004-present, evening show Station Assistant, Oldtown FM, September 2001-June 2004, working on Saturday sports & music show Work experience at Oldtown FM, 2 weeks in August 2001 Shelf filler, Bestco supermarket, Oldtown, January 1999-August 2001

...terests: Music, sport and writing. I have written four magazine articles for the music press, as well as my first novel (currently available for publication).

...er experience: Duke of Edinburgh's Award (Silver) Oldtown orienteering club member since 1999

■ **Figure 1.28** *Your CV won't be as impressive as this one yet, but you will be able to add to it as you gain experience.*

Assessment task 9

From the one sector of the media industry that you have chosen, identify and discuss the ways in which they recruit people for the jobs you listed in Assessment task 4.

Assessment evidence

✓ Describe the different methods of recruitment in detail.

✓✓ Use examples to explain those methods of recruitment and how and why they differ.

✓✓✓ Use correct terminology in your explanations, making sure they are detailed and supported by strong evidence of your conclusions.

2 Research for Media Production

Introduction

Research is a very important process that underpins all media production. The films and television programmes that we watch, the radio programmes that we listen to, the newspapers and magazines that we read and the websites and computer games that we interact with have all been carefully planned and researched to try to make them as successful as possible.

Media products are often very expensive to produce, and there is a lot of pressure on the people who plan and produce them to get them right. Because of these pressures, media companies put a lot of time and effort into researching a product to make sure that it will attract the right audience and that this audience will react to it in the right way. They also plan the production process thoroughly to ensure that it can be completed in the required time and within the allocated budget.

In this unit you will learn about the different research methods and techniques that are used for media production. You will then be able to use this knowledge to carry out your own research for the practical work that you will be undertaking in your other units.

Advertising is an important source of income for many media products and a lot of research is carried out on sales and audience preferences to help media companies decide what media products they want to make and where they can best place these products in the market or schedules.

Learning outcomes

On completion of this unit you should:

- understand research methods and techniques
- be able to identify and gather research material
- be able to collate and store research material
- be able to present results of research.

2.1   Research methods and techniques

Research can be carried out for many different reasons. A media production company that is producing a magazine, for example, will need to research and gather material for the content of the stories, articles and features that they are going to include. They will also need to research what the target audience would like to read in the magazine, what the publisher requires and what the companies that they hope will advertise in it expect. They also need to research what income they can expect to receive from these advertisers as well as from sales of the magazine.

They can then begin to research the costs of producing the magazine so that they can work out if their ideas are viable.

A lot of the research used by media producers is carried out for them by specialist organisations who become experts in their particular area.

For example, the **National Readership Survey (NRS)** is a non-profit-making organisation that provides information to the industry on who reads what publication.

It provides a breakdown of the readership of each major newspaper and magazine according to a range of different factors, including gender, age

Think it over

Think about the sort of things that you would have to budget for if you were producing a magazine for the national market. What sort of people would you need to employ? What technology would you need? What about marketing and distribution?

■ **Figure 2.1** *A magazine being printed.*

and social class. This information is very valuable to companies and agencies that are planning to launch a new product, or that buy and sell advertising in the print medium, as the data allows them to target the right audience more effectively.

The NRS collects data covering more than 250 newspapers, newspaper supplements and consumer magazines – the data is then made available to its subscribers via its website.

The **Audit Bureau of Circulation (ABC)** also provides circulation information to the newspaper and magazine industry and includes directories, leaflets and websites in its range of products researched.

Theory into practice

Go to the websites of the NRS and ABC to find out more information about these two organisations.

Choose one magazine and one newspaper and, using the information from either of the websites, find out as much information about each publication as you can. You will also find more information about your chosen newspaper on the Newspaper Marketing Agency (NMA) website.

Write up your findings in the form of a report.

Try to find out the names of other organisations that specialise in media research. Here are two more names to get you started:

*   **Broadcasters' Audience Research Board (BARB)**
*   **Radio Joint Audience Research Limited (RAJAR)**

How many more can you find?

Remember

The four main methods of research that you need to understand are:

■ primary
■ secondary
■ quantitative
■ qualitative

Whatever the different reasons are for research, many of the methods and techniques used are the same, and once you have learnt the basics you will be able to apply your knowledge and skills to a range of different situations.

Primary and secondary research

One of the basic distinctions to be made is between **primary** and **secondary research**.

Primary research is original research that is carried out for a specific purpose in order to obtain original data. The techniques used include conducting a survey in the street, interviewing people over the phone and running a focus group.

Did you know?

Most major film studios show newly completed films to a small sample of the target audience to check if they like them. If they don't, then they will often change parts of a film before it is released.

One example of this is the science fiction film Blade Runner, *which was made in 1982 by Ridley Scott. The preview screenings suggested that the audience did not understand parts of the story and did not like the way the film ended. The studio that had paid Scott to make the film added additional voiceovers to explain certain scenes, removed the now famous 'unicorn scene' and added a happy ending.*

Ridley Scott later released a 'Director's Cut' version with the additional voiceover removed, the unicorn scene restored and the original ending. It is now this version that is seen by many as the better one.

Theory into practice

Try to find out the details of other films that have been changed because of the feedback received from preview screenings.

An example of primary research is when a film company shows a preview of their new film to a group of people (often called a **focus group**) and asks them what they think of it.

Secondary research involves the use of data and information that have already been published or are already available within an organisation. Secondary research techniques include reading books and magazines, searching on the Internet (Figure 2.2) and taking notes from research studies that already exist.

An example of secondary research is when a media organisation uses data and information that has already been gathered and analysed by another company to add to and maybe even to replace their own primary research.

Media research organisations such as the National Readership Survey (NRS) and the Audit Bureau of Circulation (ABC) undertake primary research of their own and then sell the findings and results of this research to other media companies. This data will be used by the companies as secondary research to add to any primary research that they are carrying out themselves.

■ **Figure 2.2** *A researcher at work – using a range of secondary sources.*

Quantitative and qualitative research

The other two main methods of research that you need to understand are **quantitative** and **qualitative**.

Quantitative research produces data and information that you can measure and count. The data can usually be shown as a set of numbers and is often presented in the form of tables, charts and diagrams (Figures 2.3 and 2.4).

Quantitative research can involve both primary and secondary techniques, and the information produced can include such things as ratings, circulation and viewing figures, as well as the counting and measuring of items or space in a particular media product.

The other main method, qualitative research, produces information about people's opinions, views and preferences about something. Again,

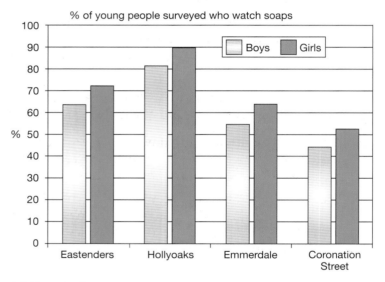

■ **Figure 2.3** *Example of a bar chart showing quantitative data.*

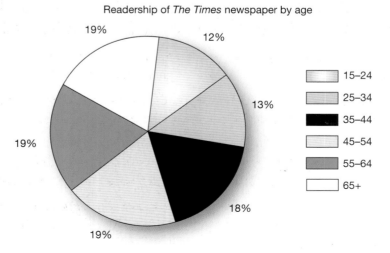

■ **Figure 2.4** *Example of a pie chart showing quantitative data* (source: NMA website).

| Rob | I really like the picture of the woman on the front of the magazine. It reminded me of an ex-girlfriend. I liked the way that she dressed, but I do not think that I would buy the magazine. I might read it if a friend of mine had already bought it. |
| Jane | I though the woman on the front of the magazine looked ugly. Her make-up looked old fashioned and her hair was not very trendy. I do not think that I would buy the magazine as I don't think it would appeal to me and it is also over priced. |

■ **Figure 2.5** *Examples of qualitative information from a survey about a new magazine.*

both primary and secondary research techniques can produce qualitative data. Qualitative research is often very important within the media industry as it is used to find out what individuals and groups think and feel about a particular media product.

Depending on the nature of the research and the types of questions asked, it is not always possible to analyse the results of qualitative research statistically, particularly if the responses are personal and subjective (Figure 2.5).

A film company asking a focus group what they think about a new film is likely to produce both quantitative and qualitative data. For example:

■ The group might fill out a short questionnaire before the film starts, showing that 55 per cent of the women and 38 per cent of the men visited the cinema in the last month. This is quantitative data.

■ After the film has finished the company will ask each individual what they thought about the film. What were their feelings about the main character? What did they understand about the storyline? What did they think of the ending? These questions will provide qualitative data.

What does it mean?

Primary research – *original research to obtain original data, using techniques such as interviews, questionnaires and focus groups*

Secondary research – *research using existing data and information that has already been gathered by other people or organisations – often available in books, magazines or on the Internet*

Quantitative research – *research based on measurable facts and information that can be counted, producing numerical and statistical data*

Qualitative research – *research based on opinions, attitudes and preferences rather than hard facts*

Assessment task 1

Think carefully about the four key methods of research outlined above and, in your own words, describe each one. You then need to describe the different techniques that can be used for each method and give examples of different situations in which each of the methods and techniques would be used.

In your report you should try to use appropriate language and make sure you check your spelling and grammar.

Assessment evidence

✔ Describe the main methods and techniques used in research. This is an important piece of evidence that underpins the whole unit.

✔✔ You will be able to try to achieve a merit or distinction grade when you begin to apply and use these techniques in your own research later in the unit.

2.2 Identifying and gathering research material

In this section you will be using the research methods and techniques that you learnt about in section 2.1 to carry out some research of your own. You can carry out a series of small stand-alone research projects, or you might want to link your research to the production work that you are planning in some of your other units.

Before you can begin to successfully apply the main methods and techniques to your own research, you need to understand in more detail what the advantages and disadvantages of the different techniques are and what you need to do to make your research a success.

Questionnaires

One of the main techniques used in primary research is asking people questions, and it is highly likely that you will use some form of questioning technique in the research that you carry out yourself.

The use of a questionnaire is perhaps the most popular form of primary research, but you will need to think carefully about the way that it is presented. You also need to work out the best way to write the questions so that the questionnaire makes sense.

Questionnaire design

If you are going to send your questionnaire to people for them to fill in, it is important that the questionnaire itself looks attractive and professional and does not put people off. Put an appropriate title at the top of the page and include a brief introduction so that people are clear who you are, what the purpose of the survey is and what the results will be used for. You should also include clear instructions on how the survey should be completed. This is particularly important if people are going to complete the questionnaire by themselves, as you will not be there to explain anything to them that they do not understand.

Don't forget to include details of where people should return the questionnaire to once they have finished it.

How many hours do you spend watching TV every day?

■ **Figure 2.6** *A student doing primary research using a questionnaire in the street.*

 Remember

Time spent planning and checking your questionnaire will be time well spent, and should improve the effectiveness of your research project

The questions
There are two main types of question that you can use in a questionnaire or interview. One type is known as a **closed** question and the other is an **open** question.

As a general rule you should start your questionnaire with some straightforward closed questions that are easy to answer.

What does it mean?

Open questions – *these allow the person answering to give his or her own views and opinions on a particular subject and often start with such words as:*

- *What*
- *Why*
- *When*
- *How*
- *Who*

Closed questions – *these are more limited in terms of the potential answers that can be given and are often answered with yes, no or don't know, or an answer picked from a range of given options*

Q1: How old are you?

15 or younger ☐   16–18 ☐   19–21 ☐   22+ ☐

Q2: What is your gender?

Male ☐   Female ☐

Q3: Which of the following television services do you have in your home? (You can tick more than one box.)

Terrestrial ☐   Satellite ☐   Cable ☐   Freeview ☐

Q4: Do you have broadband at home?

Yes ☐   No ☐   Don't know ☐

■ **Figure 2.7** *Examples of closed questions used in a questionnaire.*

Asking people their age, gender and occupation, for example, should get them into the process of completing the questionnaire, and will also provide you with some basic information about the people that you have interviewed which you can use later when analysing your results. It will also allow you to check that you have covered the right sample of people, and allow you to include some more people in the survey if you have not.

When using closed questions, it is often easier to include the potential answers within the questionnaire itself, with a tick box for people to select the answer. If you use this method it is important that you include all of the potential answers, and you need to decide whether to include an 'Other' or 'Don't know' option.

Closed questions, where there is a limited number of potential answers that are listed in the questionnaire, are good to use in this form of survey – they are relatively easy for the respondents to answer and will provide you with quantitative data which you can easily analyse and represent in the form of graphs, charts and diagrams.

However, more open style questions, where you might be asking people to write down a personal response to something, often provide you with qualitative information that gives a more meaningful insight.

Both open and closed questions are sometimes used together in a **paired** question, as shown in the example in Figure 2.9.

As a general rule, your questionnaire should contain a mix of both open and closed questions, and require both simple tick box responses as well as more in-depth, written responses.

Q5: Why did you choose to take a media qualification?

Q6: What three words or phrases best describe your feelings about digital radio?

1. _____
2. _____
3. _____

■ **Figure 2.8** *Examples of open questions used in a questionnaire.*

Q7a: **Do you play computer games?**

Yes ☐   No ☐

Q7b: **If you answered yes to 7a, please explain in the space below what you like about playing computer games.**

```


```

■ **Figure 2.9** *An example of a paired question, containing both open and closed elements.*

Theory into practice

Design a simple questionnaire that uses both open and closed questions.

Use the questionnaire to survey a chosen group of people.

Analyse the results and write up the findings in a short report.

Using a scale

For some questions you might want to know how much people agree or disagree with a particular statement, or how strong their feelings are on a particular topic. To do this you can use a rating system or a response scale of some kind. The three most popular scales used in research are: **Likert scale**, **rank order scale** and **semantic differential scale**. Examples of these three types of scale are shown in Figures 2.10 to 2.12.

What does it mean?

Likert scale – *the people completing the questionnaire are asked how strongly they agree or disagree with a series of statements*

Rank order scale – *people are asked to indicate their order of preference from a list of given answers, usually by putting a number next to each answer*

Semantic differential scale – *uses a sliding scale between two opposing words and asks people to indicate where on the scale their opinion comes*

Q8: What do you think of the game? Tick one box for each statement.

	Strongly agree	Agree	Neither agree nor disagree	Disagree	Stongly disagree
a) The game is easy to play					
b) The design of the game is attractive					
c) The game is good value for money					
d) I would buy this game					

■ **Figure 2.10** *Example of a Likert scale in a questionnaire asking what people think about a new computer game.*

Q9: How do you prefer to buy your music? Rank the followng formats in order of preference, with 1 being your most preferred and 5 being your least preferred format.

Internet download   1   Vinyl   3

CD single   4   DVD   5

CD album   2

■ **Figure 2.11** *Example of a rank order scale used to find out what format young people prefer to buy music in.*

Q10: Place a cross on the scales below to show what you feel about the product being advertised.

Looks Attractive ....x.................. **Looks Unattractive**

Healthy ....x......... **Unhealthy**

Good value ....x............................ **Poor value**

■ **Figure 2.12** *Example of a semantic differential scale.*

Theory into practice

Look back at the questionnaire that you have designed. Try to redesign one or more of the questions to include at least one of the scales you have learnt about, or introduce a couple of new questions that use one of the scales.

Test how this new style of question works by using it with some of your sample audience.

Write up your findings of how well the new questions worked.

Think it over

When filling out the questionnaire, what factors would encourage you to answer truthfully, and what would put you off?

The way in which you approach people and explain to them what you want them to do is also very important to a successful survey. You are really asking people to do you a favour by spending some time answering your questions, so you need to do all you can to encourage them to say yes in the first place and to then complete all of the questions.

Some companies will offer people a reward for filling out a survey for them, such as an entry into a prize draw, a discount off one of their products or a small gift of some kind.

You also need the people who complete your questionnaire to put some thought into the answers that they are giving you. Try to make sure that your questions will encourage people to answer honestly and not put down silly answers or answers that are not true.

The overall look and design of a questionnaire is also important. The questionnaire should look neat and tidy and as professional as possible. Nobody will be impressed by a few scribbled notes on a scruffy piece of paper. You might also want to group specific questions together into different sections, perhaps with a separate heading for each section. This can make the questionnaire look more attractive and appealing and may also give people a sense of achievement when they have completed a section, so the questionnaire does not seem so long.

Keep the language of your questions as simple as possible and avoid asking questions that are difficult to understand. Questions that are too vague or too complex are unlikely to provide you with useful answers, if they are answered at all. You should also try to avoid asking leading questions that suggest a particular answer to the respondent, or the use of strong or emotive language that, again, might push people into giving a particular type of answer.

■ **Figure 2.13** *Making your questionnaire enjoyable to fill in will ensure that more people take part in your survey.*

Think it over

Can you see any problems with the following questions?

Q11: Why do you think game shows are good?

Q12: What do you think about the media?

Q13: Do you prefer vector-based or pixel-based image generation and manipulation software programs and what are your thoughts about the use of CGI in CD-ROMs?

 Remember

When designing a questionnaire you need to think very carefully about the form and structure of the questions that you are asking. You need to make sure that people will be able to understand and answer the questions that you are asking, and that the answers will provide you with the information that you require.

Conducting surveys

Of course not all surveys are presented to people face to face. Some surveys are carried out over the telephone, some are posted out and many nowadays are sent out via email or completed online on the Internet. Some questionnaires are included in a magazine or newspaper.

Asking people questions either face to face or over the telephone is very time-consuming, particularly if you are covering a large sample of people, but it does allow you to be very selective about who you include in the survey and how many people you include. It also allows you to explain any questions that might need further clarification. If you use either of these two methods you will need to think carefully about how you are going to record people's responses. Using a tally chart or data recorder might be more efficient than filling out an individual questionnaire sheet for each respondent, though you will need to think about how you will record individual answers to more open questions.

If you post or email the questionnaire, or include it within a publication, people can complete the questionnaire in their own time and in their own home – this might mean that some people are happier to give you confidential information, though of course you have little control over how many people actually complete the questionnaire or return it to you!

 Think it over

What do you think the advantages and disadvantages are of the different ways of presenting your questionnaire?

Q	Answers	Responses	Total
Q1	15 or younger	|||	3
	16–18	||| |||	8
	19–21	|||		6
	22+	|||	3
Q2	Male	||| ||||	9
	Female	||| |||		11

■ **Figure 2.14** *Example of a simple tally chart for recording answers to closed questions.*

Pre-testing

Pre-testing your questionnaire on a small sample of your audience before you start conducting your full survey is a very good idea, as it will allow you to identify any potential problems with specific questions or the design and layout of the questionnaire, in good time for you to make any changes.

Focus groups

Focus groups are pre-selected panels of people who are chosen to represent a particular target audience. They are often used by marketing and advertising agencies to test the likely response of the target audience towards the product that is being advertised and to the advert itself.

As we saw earlier, film studios use focus groups in preview screenings of major films, to try to ensure that the audience reaction is the one that they are looking for and that the film will be well received. Companies that are launching a new computer game, magazine, radio show or television programme may also show a preview of the product to a focus group to test it out and get feedback before they launch the full product.

Remember

If you are going to use a focus group as part of your research you will need to think carefully about who you invite to be in the group, where you will hold it, how you are going to manage the discussion and what you will use to record what is said.

■ **Figure 2.15** *A focus group of young people being shown an advert for a new computer game.*

Secondary research

There is a lot of information and research data already available in books, journals and on the Internet, and you will need to carry out some form of secondary research to add to and support your own primary research. When doing secondary research it is important that you clearly understand what the original purpose of the research was, who commissioned it and when it was conducted. Not every piece of research that you may come across is necessarily reliable or valid.

Remember

Simply collecting pages and pages of information from the Internet does not in itself count as secondary research. Any information that you print off from the Internet, or photocopy from books and journals, needs to be read and understood, perhaps annotated by highlighting key points and writing brief notes in the margin, and then used to inform or supplement your own primary research.

Types of information

When doing secondary research you might need to identify different types of information. For example, you might find lots of written information in the form of reports, articles, newspaper stories and transcripts of interviews. You might also find visual information in the form of photographs, drawings and cartoons, or audio–visual information from films and television programmes. If you are looking at other research projects, then much of the information might be presented in charts, tables and diagrams.

Whatever types of information you discover, you should not simply copy other people's work that you find. Some research work will have **copyright** rules attached to it. This means that it is against the law to copy or use the work in any way without first asking the permission of the owners of the copyright. The copyright owner might be the author of the work or the company that paid for the work to be carried out.

Theory into practice

Do some secondary research of your own to find out more information about copyright. You could start by looking back at pages 36–40 in Unit 1.

Remember

It is important that you clearly reference any work that you use and make sure that you do not break any copyright rules that may apply.

What does it mean?

Copyright – *any work that is protected by copyright cannot normally be used without the permission of the owner. Copyright can be bought and sold, and copyright owners can choose to licence others to use their work while keeping copyright ownership over the rights themselves.*

Targeting the right audience

When planning any form of primary research it is important that you target the right audience for your sample. Dividing the audience into different categories makes it easier for researchers to make sure that they sample the correct range of people. It reflects the way in which media producers identify and target groups of people with the same needs and wants. This is covered in more detail in Unit 3, but we will have a quick look at the four main categories that are used to divide up a target audience: age, gender, culture and social class.

■ **Figure 2.16** *All films and many computer games have age certificates.*

1. Age

The age of the target audience is an important factor for many media producers, and one of the reasons for this is that some kinds of product can only be shown or bought by certain age groups. The British Board of Film Classification (BBFC) puts an age category on all films, videos and DVDs that are shown and offered for sale or rental in the UK, and also classifies many of the video and computer games that are available (Figure 2.16).

Advertisers are also interested in what media products different age groups are reading and watching, as they can then decide whether or not to place advertisements within certain products. For example, the table in Figure 2.17 shows that the *Daily Star* has a higher number of young readers than the *Daily Telegraph*. This difference will affect the kinds of products that are advertised within the two newspapers.

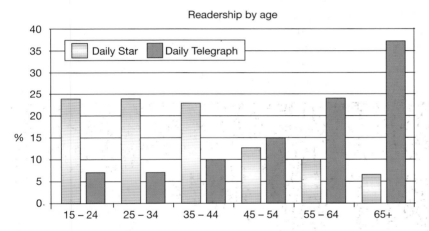

■ **Figure 2.17** *Chart showing the age breakdown of the readers of two national newspapers.*

Theory into practice

Choose one magazine that you think is read by mainly young readers and one that you think is read by older readers.

Do an analysis of the types of products that are advertised in the two magazines.

Write up your findings in the form of a short report, or present your results to the rest of the class.

2. Gender

Gender is also an important category to think about as many media products may be targeted at either men or women. This is perhaps most clearly seen within the magazine market, which has specific magazines targeted at males and others targeted at females (Figure 2.18).

Think it over

Try to think of the different ways in which some magazines target men and some target women. Can you think of any that target both?

■ **Figure 2.18** *Some magazines target men, while others target women.*

■ **Figure 2.19** Bride and Prejudice, *a recent Bollywood-style film that was made in the UK.*

3. Culture

People's needs and wants as consumers will also vary according to their culture, language and background, and a number of media products are available to meet this need. The media industry is now very much a global one and newspapers, magazines, radio and television programmes from all over the world are readily available to people living in Britain. There is also a growing production base in the UK for media products that target different cultures and ethnic groups (Figure 2.19).

4. Social class

Any potential audience can also be linked to a rough idea about their social class. Social class is often determined by a person's income, which can be an important factor for advertisers who need to target the relevant income group as accurately as possible. There is no point in advertising a top-of-the-range sports car to people who are unemployed or have a low disposable income.

Social grade	Social status	Chief income earner's occupation	Examples
A	Upper middle class	Higher managerial, administrative or professional	• experienced doctor • bishop • police superintendent • board director of a medium to large company
B	Middle class	Intermediate managerial, administrative or professional	• recently qualified doctor • vicar • solicitor • farmer with 2–9 employees • chief clerk in a bank
C1	Lower middle class	Supervisory or clerical and junior managerial, administrative or professional	• student doctor • supervisor of 25 or more employees • inexperienced journalist • monk or nun
C2	Skilled working class	Skilled manual workers	• police constable • bus driver • roadside rescue mechanic • bricklayer • plumber
D	Working class	Semi- and unskilled manual workers	• supermarket shelf stacker • traffic warden • fisherman • apprentice
E	Those at the lowest level of subsistence	State pensioners, casual or lowest grade workers	• state pensioners with no secondary pension • seasonal fruit pickers

■ **Figure 2.20** *Table showing Standard Occupational Classification.*

Most companies involved with media research and production use a scale that puts people into different categories according to the sort of job they do and the amount of income that they are likely to have available to spend. The scale is only a very rough one and does make some very general assumptions about what people earn. The scale is called Standard Occupational Classification and was developed in the 1950s. It puts people into one of six groups: A, B, C1, C2, D or E as shown in Figure 2.20, depending on the profession of the main earner in the household. Group A is considered more 'upmarket' than B, B than C1, and so on. Figure 2.21 shows how different newspapers fit their readership into the different groups.

Some people are very surprised when they see which group this method puts them in. The different categories relate quite closely to family income – the better paid jobs tend to be in category A – but don't reflect the most important people in terms of who we need in emergency situations, for instance, when there is a leak or our house is on fire!

Title	% of total readership by socio-economic scale					
	AB	ABC1	ABC1C2	C1	C2	DE
Daily Telegraph	58	87	95	29	9	4
Guardian	60	90	94	30	4	5
Daily Mail	29	64	85	35	21	15
The Sun	11	33	64	23	31	36
Daily Mirror	12	38	68	27	29	32
Daily Star	9	29	62	19	34	38

■ **Figure 2.21** *Table showing the socio-economic profile of a selection of national newspapers (November 2005).*

Assessment task 2

Plan, design and carry out a research activity that includes both primary and secondary research methods, and allows you to gather both qualitative and quantitative information.

The research activity that you design can be a stand-alone task, but it is perhaps better and more relevant if you link it to one of the practical projects that you are carrying out for one of the other units.

If, for example, you are planning to produce a video for Unit 4 then you may want to carry out the following research tasks:

■ *Conduct a survey of a sample of your target audience, or ask a focus group what they think of your ideas.*

■ *Interview some people to find out information for your video, or to find out if they will be suitable to appear in your video.*

■ *Do a recce of the potential locations that you might use and research the equipment that is available to you.*

■ *Search in books, magazines and on the Internet for relevant information that you could include as content in your video. If you are planning to produce a video on global warming, for example, you will need to read up about the relevant issues and debates around the subject and get some up-to-date facts and figures that you can use.*

Don't forget to keep examples of your work as you go through each of the different stages, and to keep a diary or commentary that explains what you are doing.

Assessment evidence

✔ Identify sources of information and use relevant methods to gather material from these sources.

✔✔ Ensure that the methods and techniques used have been consciously chosen and that there is a sense of purpose behind the activity. There will also be evidence of some level of discrimination and order to the material gathered.

✔✔✔ Demonstrate a systematic approach to your work. This means that you should have set clear objectives at the start of the research and then developed a strategy to obtain the best information that you can.

2.3 Collating and storing research material

The amount of information that is gathered when undertaking a research study can often be very large, particularly if the research is linked to a production that is very complex involving lots of different aspects. One of the key skills that you will need to learn when undertaking your own research is the ability to sift through the information that you have gathered, and to select and use the material that is of value to your needs. Far too many students simply put all of the primary and secondary research that they have produced and found into a folder and expect to receive a good mark for it.

Collating information

Collating your research material involves sifting through the material to identify what is useful and what needs to be disregarded, and then sorting it into categories – this will allow you to easily find what you need at a later date.

■ **Figure 2.22** *Sifting through your research material is an important task.*

Because you will have designed and carried out your primary research yourself, it is likely that most of the results obtained will be useful to you and so you will want to keep them. There may, however, be situations where your research results are no longer relevant. You may, for example, have carried out a survey with a particular target audience and then changed the target audience following feedback from your client, so that the results of this original survey are no longer valid. Similarly, you might have conducted an interview with somebody on the problems of underage drinking, and then decided not to include this article in your magazine.

It is much more likely that you will decide to disregard some of your secondary material, as this is material that you have found. You will need to check and sort through to see what, if anything, is relevant to your particular project. Carefully sifting and sorting your secondary research material is very important, as teachers and moderators have seen far too many research folders that are filled with pages and pages downloaded from the Internet that often have little or no relevance to the project being carried out and are simply there to pad out the research folder.

If you have already completed Assessment task 2 above, then you will now have lots of primary and secondary research material that will need to be collated and stored.

Remember

If you are aiming for more than just a pass in this unit, then you must make sure that you carefully sort through your research material and only include relevant, well-annotated pieces of secondary research.

Storing information

Once you have sorted out the information that you require, and disgarded the information that you do not, you now need to ensure that all of the information is carefully logged, organised and stored to ensure it is secure, whilst also allowing you easy access to it.

If you haven't already got one, create a research folder in which you can store all of your relevant research material. This research folder needs to have a clear index system so that you can easily find a relevant piece of information. Any secondary material that is stored should also be highlighted and annotated in some way so it is clear what you have selected from it and what you have used it for. It is also a good idea to include some form of written commentary in your folder that explains to the tutor and moderator what is in there, how it was obtained, why it has been included and how you have used it or are going to use it.

You may of course also store some or all of your information electronically. Copies of your questionnaire and any questions that you used in an interview or for your focus group are best stored on a computer and backed up on a disk or other storage device. You may find it best to store your hard data in a spreadsheet or database as well as the paper versions that you may have produced whilst carrying out the research.

Assessment task 3

Collate your primary and secondary research data by sifting through it and sorting out what you want to keep and what you want to discard. Write a commentary of what you are doing to include in your research file together with the material that you have kept.

Once you have decided what material you are going to keep, put it into order and index it so that you know what is in the folder and where any named piece of evidence is. The easiest way of doing this is to give every sheet a page number and divide the folder into different sections. Having a section for primary research and one for secondary research is a good starting point.

Look through your research information and decide what sections will be best for your folder.

Assessment evidence

✔ Collate and store the research material that you have gathered in some sort of order and so that a specific item can be accessed.

✔✔ Demonstrate that you have sifted the material to ensure that the selected material is relevant to the research undertaken. You should store this material in such a way that it can be easily accessed and specific information easily located.

✔✔✔ Demonstrate a systematic approach to your work. This means that you will have evaluated and sifted all of the information gathered, and stored all the relevant material in such a way that any specified piece of information is immediately traceable.

2.4 Presenting the results of research

The results of your research can be presented in the form of a written report, as an oral presentation to the rest of the class or in a suitable audio–visual format. If you choose to present your findings in the form of a presentation you must make sure that this is recorded so that your mark can be checked by the moderator towards the end of the course. However you decide to present your findings, you will need to think carefully about the structure and content of what you produce as well as the language that you use.

Oral presentation skills

One of the ways in which you may choose to present your findings is in the form of an oral presentation to the rest of the class. Conducting an effective presentation is not an easy task, and you will need to identify what presentation and communication skills you already have and which ones you need to develop further.

There are three key aspects for you to consider when planning an oral presentation. These are your **spoken words**, your **non-verbal communication** (or **NVC** as it is known) and any **visual aids** that you choose to use.

Non-verbal communication

The saying that first impressions count certainly applies when giving a presentation – the way in which you present yourself to your audience, the way that you dress, your posture, position, hand and arm movements and facial expressions are all important aspects to consider.

Think it over

Think about your communication skills. Are you confident when speaking to other people? What can you do to improve the way in which you get your ideas across?

What does it mean?

Non-verbal communication (NVC) – *all of the body language that occurs during interpersonal communication, including the clothes that you wear, your posture, facial expression and hand and arm movements*

Spoken language – *this includes not only what you say but also the way that you say it – known as* **paralanguage**

Paralanguage – *the way that you speak, including pitch, tone, pace and volume, as well as all of the fillers and hesitations that we use in everyday language (e.g. 'er', 'well', 'OK', 'um')*

Visual aids – *props, objects and examples that you include in your presentation, also slides, images and posters that can help to structure what you say*

Paying careful attention to these features of your non-verbal communication can make your presentation look more professional and be more effective. It can also make you feel more confident.

When presenting your ideas, you need to dress to impress. What you say and do will look and sound more authoritative if you present yourself in a professional

■ **Figure 2.23** *Your body language and gestures can be more important than what you actually say.*

manner. You need to think carefully about who will be in your audience and what their expectations will be, as well as the context and location of the presentation, when deciding what to wear and how to present yourself. It is also important that you feel comfortable in what you are wearing and that you practise in your presentation clothes before you do the actual presentation.

The way in which you hold and position your body can also communicate a lot of information to your audience, and your aim is to demonstrate that you are a confident, professional person who is in control and knows what they are doing.

Your audience will not appreciate looking at the back of your head while you talk to the screen behind you, and you won't come across well if you are slumped in a chair or have your arms folded across your body in a defensive manner.

You will probably be nervous when you are presenting to your audience, and tell-tale signs of these nerves can 'leak out' and distract from what you are trying to communicate. An audience can end up focusing on the presenter who paces up

■ **Figure 2.24** *Looking at a presenter talking to the screen is boring for the audience.*

Theory into practice

Look at the ways in which TV presenters and people who are good at talking in front of an audience present themselves. Look at the way in which they use their hands and arms, the way that they move and position their body and the clothes that they wear. How do all of these things make them look? Is there anybody you can think of who is not very good at this sort of thing?

Figure 2.25 *Mr Bean would probably not be very good at doing an oral presentation!*

and down and waves their hands and arms around too much, rather that listening and trying to understand what they are proposing.

Your facial expressions are often the hardest part of your non-verbal communication to control, and can be another area where your nervousness can leak out. Smiling is good. It makes you feel better and puts your audience at ease.

Think it over

The face is the most communicative area of your body and it can communicate hundreds of different messages. Try to think of all of the different messages that you can communicate just with your face. How do you communicate anger? Happiness? Sorrow? Confusion?

■ **Figure 2.26** *Staring at one member of the audience is likely to embarrass them and make the rest of the audience feel left out.*

Eye contact is also very important – you can use it to engage your audience and direct questions to individual members of the audience. As a general rule you should try to look at each member of your audience at least once during the presentation. This will make them feel at ease and communicate that your are an honest person who can be trusted. However, if you hold this eye contact for too long and end up staring at people, this can make them feel uncomfortable (Figure 2.26). A couple of seconds is long enough before you move on to another person.

You need to think carefully about all of these aspects of non-verbal communication, and try to control and use them to your advantage.

Spoken communication

Although non-verbal communication is very important, you will also need to say something in your presentation! Speaking in front of a group can be a daunting task and even the most confident of people can get very nervous before making a speech.

Paralanguage refers to the way in which you speak, rather than the content of what you say, and this is another aspect of your presentation that you will need to try to control and use to your advantage.

People often speak too quickly when they are nervous, as if they are trying to get to the end of what they are saying as quickly as possible and then sit down. If you think that you tend to speak too quickly, you need to try to slow down and set the pitch, tone and pace of your spoken language to the right level so that you are communicating in a positive and pleasing way to your audience.

 Theory into practice

Practise different ways of delivering your spoken language, record the results and then listen back to see what you sound like. Be warned. Your recorded voice will sound very different from the one that you are used to hearing!

The **register** of your spoken language refers to the choice of words that you use, and you will have to select a register that takes account of the audience you are presenting to, the context of the presentation and how formal it needs to be. For example, 'Alright mates' might be too casual as an introduction to your presentation, while 'Good morning ladies and gentlemen' might feel too formal. A simple but straightforward 'Hello and welcome to my presentation' might be a good place to start.

You should also be wary of using technical terms, jargon or abbreviations that some members of your audience might not understand.

■ **Figure 2.27** *Technical jargon can confuse your audience.*

Visual aids

When planning your presentation you also need to think carefully about the use of any visual aids that you want to include. You might want to use overhead transparency (OHT) or PowerPoint slides to help structure your talk. These will provide something different for your audience and will divert some of the pressure from you.

If you are using PowerPoint be wary of using too many visual and sound effects, as an audience can easily get bored of such gimmicks. They can also make your presentation look rather superficial and can get in the way of the message that you are trying to communicate.

Remember

The effective use of OHT and PowerPoint slides is a skill that you need to practise. The slides should provide a brief summary of what you are saying (Figure 2.28), rather than a running commentary. A common mistake is to cram too much information onto each slide.

Quantitative research

- **Facts and information that can be measured or counted**

- **Produces numerical and statistical data**

- **Tables, charts and diagrams**

■ **Figure 2.28** *Brief bullet points will get your message across more clearly than reams of text.*

You might also want to consider using posters and flip-charts to help to summarise your main points, or make handouts for your audience, either to read during the presentation itself or to take away after it has finished. You might also want to include some activity for your audience to do rather than just listen to you. A simple way of breaking up the presentation is to ask the audience some questions or to discuss one of the points that you have made with the person next to them.

In the case study below, Alice had to take care to control her verbal and non-verbal communication so that she presented herself in a professional and organised way.

Content of your presentation

Of course you do not have to do an oral presentation of your findings or record them in an audio-visual medium. You can choose to include all of the required material in the form of a written report that is handed in with your research file.

Case study

Giving a presentation

Alice is a student doing the First Diploma in Media and decided to present her research findings in the form of a presentation to her classmates.

Her tutor was also in the audience so he could assess what she had done, and he had arranged for one of the other members of the class to record the presentation on video tape so that he had a record of the work that he could then show to the moderator at the end of the course.

Alice was quite nervous about the presentation because she had never really talked in front of an audience before. However, she had prepared what she was going to say beforehand and had done a runthrough at home in front of her parents.

She decided to structure her talk using PowerPoint slides so that she always knew where she was in her presentation and what came next.

She handed out some of the graphs that she had produced from her survey results and asked the

Alice using PowerPoint slides in her presentation.

class, in pairs, to look at the graphs and try to work out what they were showing.

Despite a nervous start, Alice soon grew in confidence and actually started to enjoy the presentation towards the end. It went very well, and the rest of the class said that they had learnt a lot from her talk and liked the way she had presented the information to them in the form of the graphs.

If you are writing a report there is still a need to communicate professionalism and organisation and you need to ensure that your spelling, punctuation and grammar do not let you down.

There is no set way of writing up your final report, but you do need to make sure that it is clearly and logically laid out. Make sure you use appropriate headings and sub-headings and that you check your spelling and grammar.

Whichever format you choose to present the results of your research, you need to make sure that you include all of the required content.

Remember

However good your research has been, you need to present the results of that research in an effective manner using fluent language and correct terminology if you are hoping for a distinction grade.

- The first thing you need to include is an introduction to your research project in which you explain clearly what the purpose of the reseach is. In other words, what exactly you are trying to find out and why you are doing it.

- You then need to describe and explain the research methods and techniques that you used in your research project and the procedures that you carried out.

Remember

It is always best to describe **what** you did and then explain **why** you did it.

- You should summarise the data that you obtained and present this in a form that is easy to understand. You might want to use a selection of graphs, charts and tables to help you do this.

- You then need to explain and analyse the results that you obtained and draw some conclusions. What did the results of your research show? Did you expect these results or were some of them a surprise to you? Did these results change your views on what you were researching? How will you use these results? All of these questions are important ones to ask yourself and to help you to write up your conclusions.

- Finally you need to include a summary of the sources that you have used, including a **bibliography** of any published works.

What does it mean?

Bibliography – *a list of books that you have used in a particular research project*

You should reference the books in the following way:

Hart, J: *Storyboarding for Film, TV and Animation* (Focal Press, 1999)

Start with the author's surname followed by his or her initial, then the title of the book, which is often written in italics or in bold. Put the name of the publisher and the year of publication in brackets.

You should also include a list of other sources you have used, such as newspapers, magazines and websites.

Assessment task 4

Present the findings of your research project by writing them up in the form of a report, as a presentation to the class or in a suitable audio–visual format. You will need to discuss with your tutor the best way of presenting your information.

Assessment evidence

✓ Present the results of the research that you have carried out. This can either be in written form or in an oral or audio–visual format.

✓✓ Ensure that you present the results of your research competently and with use of appropriate language and an appropriate structure.

✓✓✓ Ensure that you use the correct terminology in your presentation and that the language is fluent and used in the right context. Your meaning will need to be clear at all times and you will need to maintain the attention of the reader or audience throughout.

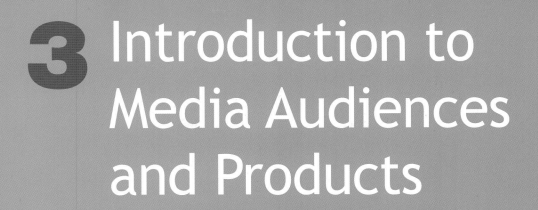

3 Introduction to Media Audiences and Products

Introduction

This unit is about media products and how they are made for particular audiences. It also explains how these audiences understand the media products they choose to read, watch or listen to. You will have to show your understanding of products and audiences, and the assessment tasks will help you to do this.

Learning outcomes

On completion of this unit you should:

- understand how media industries identify audiences for media products
- understand how media products are created for audiences
- be able to show how audiences make sense of media products.

3.1 How the media industry identifies audiences for media products

The audiences of media products are the people who consume them: television viewers, radio listeners, newspaper readers and computer game players, for example. The media industry tends to group the people who might consume a particular media product together so that they can target products to this audience.

You need to describe and discuss how the media industry thinks about the audiences for its products. You should choose *one* sector from the media industry to study, to match your own practical work in another unit. Your work for the practical unit will help you understand this one, and this unit will help you improve your practical work. Two assessment tasks in this section will help you present your work in the correct way.

Classification of audiences

In the media industry, it is important to make products that audiences will enjoy and want to keep coming back for. This is true of media products that are sold in shops or over the Internet, as well as products that are paid for by advertising – the bigger the audience, the more money the producers can make from advertising. Not all audiences are the same, and producers have to target their products at groups of people who have something in common. People who have the same interests often want to read the same magazines or watch the same television programmes. While some magazines are intended for a wide range of readers – such as the *Radio Times*, which lists television and radio programmes that would interest all sorts of people – most of them aim for a specific **market niche**.

Knowing what their audiences like is very important for media producers. They understand that not everyone is the same, and not everyone of the same age or living in the same town is the same. However, they do know that men may be more interested in football and cars, for example, and that women may be more interested in child care, fashion and beauty. It is not surprising, then, that several magazines aimed at men feature cars and football.

One of the most recent market niches discovered by magazine publishers is young males. Magazines such as *Loaded*, *Front* and *Maxim* target their market with lots of pictures of young women and articles about fast cars and gadgets. Of course, men have always bought magazines specialising in such topics as computing, motoring, fishing, racing and football. However, until the arrival of the 'lads' mags' in the 1990s there was no

What does it mean?

Market – *the group of customers a media product can target*

Niche – *a specialised, and sometimes very narrowly defined, segment of the market – the smaller the niche, the more difficult it may be to make money from it*

■ **Figure 3.1** *Newsagents cluster magazines aimed at different niche markets, so customers can easily find the ones that interest them.*

 ## Did you know?

When a new magazine is successfully introduced into a newly discovered market segment, other magazine publishers are quick to follow the successful formula. When Hello! launched as a women's magazine focusing on celebrity and royalty (instead of the traditional fashion, recipes and relationships) it was an instant success. OK! soon followed and now there are many magazines that concentrate on the rich and famous.

 ## What does it mean?

Demographics – *ways of describing groups of people, based on their characteristics such as where they live, age, how much they earn and what they spend their money on*

direct male equivalent of the women's interest magazines, which range from *Woman's Realm* to *Cosmopolitan*.

How do media producers know who their audiences are, what they are like and what they will be interested in? There are a number of ways in which they divide people into **demographic** groups, so that different audiences can be identified and products made just for them.

The ways the media industry divides people into easily identifiable groups include the following:

■ social class
■ lifestyle
■ where they live

- age
- ethnicity
- gender
- sexual orientation.

Most or all of these terms will already be familiar to you. We are going to investigate each one in turn.

Social class

Social class is difficult to define but tends to be linked to type of occupation and level of income. As recently as 30 or 40 years ago in the UK, the term 'lower class' – or more politely 'working class' – was used for people who did the more manual, dirtier and more physically demanding jobs, such as working down mines or in heavy manufacturing industries, including steelworks and shipbuilding. Now the classes are not so easy to define because there is less heavy industry, education has improved and more people work in banking, call centres and shops. The children of working class parents are growing up to be more like the middle class of 30–40 years ago.

Today, audience research (and the media industry in general) uses Standard Occupational Classification to categorise their audiences. For more information on this, see the section on social class on pages 81–82 including the table in Figure 2.20. This way of classifying people can be very useful for media producers and also advertisers.

■ **Figure 3.2** *What will be the next niche market to be discovered?*

Did you know?

Classic FM knows it attracts more ABC1s than C2DEs, and the businesses that advertise on the radio station know what kind of products this audience is most likely to buy. Classic FM also publishes a magazine, on sale through newsagents, with articles about music, concerts and other subjects of interest to ABC1 people.

Some commercial radio stations that play more modern music know that their listeners are more likely to be in the C2DE groups, and people in those groups tend to buy tabloid newspapers rather than broadsheets or compacts. So the presenters on these radio stations talk about stories in the tabloids, rather than classical musicians and composers.

Theory into practice

Work out your own family's Standard Occupation Classification (SOC), referring to the table in Figure 2.20 on page 81. Then do the same for your friends and neighbours. Are you surprised at the results? What do you think knowing someone's SOC could tell you about the media products they are most likely to want to consume? Now choose a selection of media products and match them with SOC groups. For example, which SOC groups would be most likely to read the *Financial Times* newspaper?

	Positively Represented	Negatively Represented
White males		
Old people		
Women		
People with an obvious disability		
Lesbians, gay men, bisexual		
Working-class men		
Non-white people		
People born in different countries		
People from regions other than the south-east of England		
People wearing religious clothing or insignia		

■ **Figure 3.3** *A checklist you can use for monitoring the media representation of people from different social groups. Some people represented may fit more than one category.*

Lifestyle

Lifestyle and **psychographics** include the way people have to live, but also the way they choose to spend their time. As a way of classifying people, lifestyle is very closely related to occupation. This is because wealthier people have more money to spend on expensive hobbies and pastimes – a yachting magazine is more likely to interest people who have the money and the time to go yachting.

It isn't just wealthier people who can afford to enjoy themselves, though. Football is a big lifestyle indicator and its fans include many C2DE men. Radio presenters talk about football in order to interest this group.

Did you know?

The types of advertising that media products attract closely matches the lifestyle of the target audience. Sky Sport can sell advertising during its football coverage for products that appeal to men – such as beer. Beer drinking and watching football are closely related lifestyle activities that help media producers work out what some of their audiences like.

What does it mean?

Psychographics – *the science of measuring people's likes and dislikes. This can be done by asking people questions about their lifestyles, what they do in their spare time, what they are most interested in and what they would like to do if they had the chance.*

Theory into practice

Visit some specialist websites or read some magazines for particular interest groups – for example, people who are interested in cars, antiques or computers. How many different media products could be made to interest each group?

Where people live

Where people live can affect the way they think and what will interest them. An example of this in the UK is the difference between life in rural communities and in cities. People living in the countryside will have lots of things in common with each other that do not apply in cities: transport can be very difficult, especially for the young, the old and the poor; and events that affect the farming community, such as the outbreak of foot and mouth in 2001, can affect whole communities – not just farmers.

Planning content by postcode – or at least by the region or the locality in which people live – can make the content much more relevant to the audience. Local newspapers and radio stations cover news stories that are relevant to people living nearby but are not of national interest (Figure 3.4). In times of crisis, such as an unexpectedly big snowfall, people often turn on their local radio station to find out what is happening and whether the local school is closed.

Age

With age groups, planning content according to people's interests is often a little easier. A whole generation of people who grew up at the same time, had their first date in a particular decade and witnessed particular milestone events, for example the first astronauts on the moon or England winning

■ **Figure 3.4** *A local newspaper can be sure that its audience will be interested in local issues.*

Case study

BBC Radio 1

Target audience

This radio station targets its audience of 15–24 year olds very carefully. If anyone who is outside this core audience does not like the programmes very much, this is unlikely to worry the network controller. Of course, other people do listen, and some of them are much younger than 15 or older than 24. They are very welcome to listen, but their views on programming will not be taken much into account.

Main product

The station concentrates hard on serving its core audience with a mix of mainly current and new music linked by presenters who have lots of 'street cred'. Because of its public service obligations, Radio 1 makes sure there is a well-resourced news team providing regular bulletins that are strongly targeted at the audience, as well as documentaries that are mainly about music. Radio 1 features

some unsigned bands and session recordings in order to promote the development of new music and ensure that as a station it remains at the cutting edge of the music scene.

Associated products

The station's popular website features background information about the programmes and audio downloads so listeners can listen to certain programmes again, or catch them online if they mised them on air. There is advice for the target audience on issues that concern them.

A second radio station, 1Xtra, is targeted even more finely at black audiences within the age group, because the main network has to cater for a wider range of tastes in music. This niche audience has to access the station via digital platforms, because the station does not have an FM transmitter network to broadcast from.

the World Cup (in the 1960s), will share memories and a feeling of nostalgia for this time. Radio stations that play oldies from certain decades exploit such nostalgia in order to target particular age groups. Radio 1 and Saga Radio, which targets the over 50s, are certainly not competing for the same audience.

All the different sectors of the media use age as a way of ensuring that content matches the target audience's interests and expectations. We have already looked at the huge range of printed magazines that are available. The TV channel BBC Three has a target audience of young adults which is tolerant of bad language, whereas BBC Four is targeted at older, more culturally minded people. Both channels are able to plan their content intelligently as a result of knowledge of their audiences. The producer of every successful DVD, newspaper and website considers the age of the audience when planning content.

Theory into practice

In the sector you are going to cover for your coursework, identify a number of different products and decide what age ranges they are targeting. Explain what it is about the products that should appeal to that age group. The differences might lie in the style, content or even the way they present the content.

Ethnicity

Ethnicity is not about lifestyle choices or social class. It is about our origins – where we come from and where our parents and grandparents came from. Everybody has origins in one or more ethnic groups. Although grouping people according to ethnicity can be one way of

Theory into practice

Suggest which ethnic groups are most likely to be the main audience for the following media products. Some will be easier to match than others, and you might need to use the Internet.

The Jewish Chronicle	1Xtra	The Scotsman
BBC Asian Network	B4U	Pobol Y Cwm
The Catholic Herald	Ebony	Sunrise Radio
The Tablet in Britain	Searchlight	

Now research some more products from your chosen sector.

identifying people's interests, it is important to remember that we should all respect people from every ethnic group, no matter how different they are from ourselves.

Ethnic groups can be divided in a number of different ways. We live in a society where many people have moved around the country and even the world before settling where they live, so some people fit into more than one grouping. We can group people according to ethnicity in the following ways: skin colour, country of birth, region of birth, race, religion.

Gender

We have already seen how gender can be a useful way of dividing people into likely audiences for products. Gender is a relatively simple way of classifying people because there are only two groups: male and female. Most people are obviously in either one or the other group and most people do not object to saying which group they belong to in questionnaires, letters or emails.

Every year a tiny number of people are in the process of making the difficult change from one gender to another, but although important as individuals, there are too few such people to make much of an impact on the size of most media audiences.

Having only two genders to think about can be misleading, of course. It is far too easy to assume that all women think the same way as each other, and the same goes for all men. Media producers also need to remember that many activities are enjoyable for both men and women, in just the same way that some media products are enjoyed by whole families. Television soap operas and situation comedies can be enjoyed by people of both genders and all ages (Figure 3.5). Some wise media producers realise they might be able to double their audience if they can appeal to both males and females.

Sexual orientation

Not everyone is heterosexual and some media products exploit differences between people's sexuality in order to attract audiences. Early television portrayals of gay men were very stereotyped and concentrated on how their appearance, dress, speech and behaviour seemed to differ from straight men. They were openly called offensive names. Lesbians were also misrepresented, either in erotic roles to appeal to heterosexual men or as very unattractive characters, rather than in positive roles depicting them as playing a part in society.

■ **Figure 3.5** *Soap operas can appeal to both genders.*

Today, such portrayals are increasingly rare, not least because the rights of gay men and lesbians have improved in recent years. Another reason is economic common sense: offending people who could be part of your audience does not help sales or ratings. In *Little Britain* the character Dafydd, who is 'the only gay in the village' can be understood as less of an attack on gay lifestyles than an attack on his hypocrisy, pretending to be something that he isn't.

Media products aimed at members of the lesbian, bisexual and homosexual communities are now quite common. One of the leading newspapers for this community is the *Gay Times*.

Assessment task 1

Describe the ways in which your one chosen sector of the media industry identifies its audiences. Be methodical, clearly showing how this sector differs from the others. Explain the methods used by the industry and why it uses them.

Assessment evidence

✓ Describe the methods used to classify audiences, showing how they are used.

✓✓ Use examples to show the methods in use *and* explain why they are used.

✓✓✓ Use correct terminology in your explanations, making sure they are detailed and supported by strong evidence of your conclusions.

Audience research

The media industry – that is, the people who work in it and run it – thinks about its audiences in particular ways. When making media products of whatever kind, we all have to think carefully about who will want to consume these products. We also have to make sure that they really will like them and want to keep coming back for more. As we have seen, if audiences do not want the products, the organisations which produce them will soon go out of business.

Imagine a film that earns very little money at the box office, a television channel with very few viewers or a radio station that hardly anybody listens to. Or a commercial website that rarely gets hits or a multimedia product that collects dust on the shelves. These are all disasters for the people who produce them because of the wasted investment and, sooner or later, the lost jobs.

It is not very surprising that media producers try very hard to know as much as possible about their audiences. One major problem, though, is that most of the audiences are invisible when they use the products. Some audiences can be physically counted – attendance at a football ground, the number of people who pass through an art gallery or how many cars pass by an

■ **Figure 3.6** *Some audiences can be seen, and others cannot.*

advertising billboard, for example. Some sectors of the media industry can get fairly reliable data about their products from ticket sales or how many copies are sold. Cinemas make returns to the film distributors, based on how many people pay to watch each showing of a film. This then feeds income back to the producers at the studios – they will make the biggest profits on the films that attract the most people into the cinemas to see them.

Newspapers, magazines and disk-based products are also sold in quantities that can be counted – and if a lot are returned unsold it means lost income for the producers. Pay-to-view television and Internet downloads are also measurable, as are hit counts on websites.

It is broadcasters who face the biggest problems when measuring audiences and trying to find out which of their products are the most popular – we simply do not know how many people are tuned in to a television or radio programme. Likewise we cannot know how many people read a single copy of a newspaper – it may be bought and read by one person or it may find its way into a waiting room where it is read by dozens of people. Consumption of multimedia products can be measured to a certain extent, but once an item has been sold or downloaded from a website or over a mobile phone, it is difficult to find out how many people it is used by.

Ratings and audience measurement

The media industry relies on surveys to find out information about the audiences for different products. It simply cannot afford to regularly ask everyone what they have watched, listened to or read, so it asks a sample instead. Choosing a sample of people to represent everybody in the

Did you know?

The four audience surveying organisations use the following methods to gather audience data:

BARB – *the Broadcasters' Audience Research Board. They use set-top meters in a sample of homes to measure what everyone who lives there watches on* **television** *and for how long.*

RAJAR – *Radio Joint Audience Research. They find out what their sample listen to on the* **radio** *and for how long.*

ABC – *Audit Bureau of Circulations. They check how many* **newspapers** *and* **magazines** *are sold, how many are given away free, and how many are returned unsold (so they do not count the number of people who might read the same copy of a publication).*

NRS – *National Readership Survey. They interview their sample in order to ask if they have read any* **newspapers** *or* **magazines** *(so they do count people who have read a publication but not necessarily bought it themselves).*

population means huge cost savings in collecting the data. The samples are usually carefully chosen in the hope that the people in them are going to be fairly representative of the whole population.

So, what did you think of this year's Format Academy contestants?

■ **Figure 3.7** *Some types of audience research are more reliable than others.*

The four most important audience surveys are carried out on a regular basis by the following four organisations: **BARB**, **RAJAR**, **ABC** and **NRS**.

A major problem with these surveys is that nobody knows how accurate they really are. NRS and RAJAR rely mainly on interviewing people about what they have read, or asking them to complete a 'listening diary'. This depends entirely on people's powers of recall, and some people may be too forgetful or too careless to provide very accurate data.

You might think that electronic meters (such as those used by BARB) are very accurate, but sometimes people fall asleep in front of the television and they are still counted as viewing the programme they are tuned in to. People who have one of the set-top boxes are supposed to key a personal code into a handset when they enter the television room, to tell the meter they are present, and then to sign out when they leave the room for whatever reason. If they forget to do this, the data will be inaccurate.

It is not only the methods used that cause problems – the sample of **respondents** can be equally problematic. If there are too many people from one demographic group and too few from another, their responses will distort the data collected. And because each person in the sample represents many other people, even one person making unusual or uncharacteristic choices actually misrepresents large numbers of people.

Despite all the problems with audience research, it is much better to have some fairly reliable information about audiences than to have none at all. Most people in the media industry are prepared to spend large sums of money collecting and processing audience data, so that they can demonstrate the size of their audiences to their advertisers.

The most easily accessible audience research data uses certain key terms that you will have to learn to understand. **Reach** and **share** relate to the size of the audience. In addition, broadcasters want to know how long their audiences are watching or listening to their output. The longer they are listening, the bigger the share of the market the station or channel has – and that is partly because when someone is listening to Radio 1, for example, they probably are not listening to another station at the same time!

So that means more hours for Radio 1 and fewer for everyone else. This makes the industry very competitive. Every time a competitor increases its share, someone else's goes down to make room for it, because the total share always adds up to 100 per cent. When a product increases its share of the market at the expense of one of its competitors, it will rise in the **ratings**.

Audience research organisations provide their paying customers with much more detailed information than they release to the public on their websites and in publications such as *Media Guardian, Screen International, Broadcast*, and *The Radio Magazine*. Television producers can get

What does it mean?

Respondent – *someone who provides responses in a survey*

Reach – *how many people the product 'reaches' – this could refer to a single issue or a single programme or to a whole radio station or television channel over a fixed period, such as a week or a month.*

Average hours – *how long the station or channel is consumed over a fixed period – this figure indicates how long audiences are listening or viewing*

Share – *how large a slice of the market a product has – the bigger the share, the better!*

Ratings – *how well different products do in the audience research – for example, the number one television show is rated higher than all the rest*

'overnight' figures from BARB, showing how popular – or unpopular – yesterday's programme was. By comparison, audience figures for print products take a long time to arrive.

Just before they receive the figures can be a very tense time for media producers, as unpopular programmes or presenters can be quickly shunted into off-peak parts of the schedule or cancelled altogether. Sometimes the management of the organisation will be replaced, if the parent company or the shareholders feel the results are bad enough. Newspapers and magazines also suffer financially if their circulation figures fall, or if their readership drops significantly. Advertisers buy both space and air time on the basis of the cost per thousand viewers, readers or listeners – so a drop in the audience will make advertisers less likely to buy space in that product.

The danger for producers of only basing their programming on audience ratings is that they may just copy the most popular programmes and formats, never trying anything new. The fashion for 'reality TV' programmes was created by a small number of initial successes. Suddenly, because they proved a hit with audiences, every main channel had its own 'reality' shows and 'makeover' shows, as well as variations on the Big Brother theme.

Focus groups

The type of audience research carried out by BARB and the other organisations does not tell the whole story. A lot of important information is left out. A newspaper editor, for example, might want to know what readers think of the letters page, the

■ **Figure 3.8** *Measuring audiences electronically can sometimes present problems.*

horoscopes or some other feature that appears regularly. If they do not like the horoscope, the editor might want to change the astrologer who writes it or put a different feature in its place. This kind of information is vital when planning or improving a media product.

When people working in the media industry want to try to find out more about what audiences think, one method they use is focus groups. All the problems we have already discussed about samples used in audience research also apply to focus groups, particularly how representative they are. Focus groups are usually much smaller than the panels used for audience ratings and so it is important to try to get the balance of people right. The less representative they are, the more misleading the data collected will be.

It is also unusual for people to be able to say what they would like to see being produced by the media. They usually cannot imagine a new format or approach until they have seen or heard it for the first time. But used carefully and appropriately, focus groups can provide valuable information that would be unavailable using other methods.

You can find more about focus groups in Unit 2 – see page 76.

Questionnaires

Questionnaires are often used in audience research. For example, the NRS survey uses questionnaires to ask people what newspapers and magazines they have read. Before they give them a listening diary or an electronic meter to wear, RAJAR use a questionnaire to find out more about each respondent.

There is a lot more information about questionnaires in Unit 2 – see pages 69–74.

Face-to-face interviews

Interviews can also provide media producers with detailed information about what individuals think. It is wise to conduct a large number of interviews and to think carefully about who to interview, in order to get as representative a sample as possible. One benefit of the face-to-face interview is that you can usually see if someone is telling you the truth. A big disadvantage is that interviews can be time-consuming to carry out and therefore very costly. Focus groups and questionnaires provide lots of results for less cost.

Assessment task 2

Describe the ways in which your one chosen sector of the media industry identifies its audiences. Be methodical, clearly showing how this sector differs from the others. Explain the methods used by the industry and why they use them.

Assessment evidence

✓ Describe the different ways of carrying out audience research, showing how the sector uses them.

✓✓ Use examples to show the results of audience research for a number of different products *and* explain why they use them.

✓✓✓ Use correct terminology in your explanations, making sure they are detailed and supported by strong evidence of your conclusions.

3.2   How media products are created for audiences

You need to identify, describe and discuss how *one* sector of the media industry creates products. That means how people working in that sector decide on the nature of a new product – its style, structure and content. In this section, four more assessment tasks will help you present your work in the correct way.

Categorising products

One of the first ways to begin understanding media products is to put them into categories. This helps us to identify what some products have in common and what makes them different from other products – it also helps us when we make our own products. There are two main ways in which we can categorise media products:

- by genre
- by audience.

By genre

The word **genre** is the French word for 'type'. In media studies it is used to refer to all the media products of one type, in order to help us to discuss and understand them. Television news is one genre. Other television genres include game shows, makeover shows, weather forecasts, dramas and sit-coms.

A genre can be very broad, in which case it may be further divided into sub-genres. For example, television drama has the following sub-genres:

- **Comedy drama** – drama that is meant to be funny (but not like a sit-com). The stories may be quite long and detailed – such as *Cold Feet*, which ran over several series.
- **Period drama** – drama that is set in a particular historical period, such as the Victorian period.
- **Soap opera** – a long-running series with a large number of different characters involved in different plots that intertwine, twist and turn over time, some stories beginning while others are ending.

Some types of media product will mix different genres together – in film, radio and television it is quite common to find docu-drama, in which a real event is re-enacted in the way the producer thinks it happened. A responsible producer will go to great lengths to check facts in order to avoid presenting fiction as fact – but this isn't always successful. Reconstructing a crime for *Crimewatch* on BBC1 depends on piecing together the known information about the crime – but there may be vital facts that are not known at the time.

Did you know?

Reality TV is a genre that many people think began in the 1990s, but in the 1970s a 'fly-on-the-wall' documentary (as the genre was first known) broke a number of the traditions of documentary making – a camera crew was placed in a family's home and the most interesting bits of the family's daily lives were then edited together. The Family *had only limited success on BBC2, and it was a long time before the experiment was repeated.*

Each area of the media industry has its own set of genres – and as people come up with new ideas, new genres are formed. For example, makeover shows were not particularly common until the 1990s but are now an established genre.

So, what makes a genre? A media product belongs to a particular genre if it shares a large number of characteristics with others in that genre. In other words they use the same – or very similar – **codes** and **conventions** in order to make meaning. We will look at codes in greater detail later in this unit.

What does it mean?

Code – *a way of conveying meaning to audiences without having to use words to explain what is happening*

Convention – *a feature of a particular type of media product – it will be used in most or all of that type of product*

Products within a genre also tend to be structured in similar ways. For example, the 'whodunit' is a common sub-genre of radio and film drama. Whodunits almost all feature a murder or some other crime and an investigator, such as a police officer, a private detective or an enthusiastic amateur who likes to solve a mystery. There are usually a number of suspects, and at the end the investigator unmasks the real criminal.

Theory into practice

Choose a range of media products from your chosen sector and categorise them according to their genre. Some of them might seem to come from more than one genre or to mix genres.

Television genres with examples

News programme – *Channel 4 News*

Documentary – *Panorama*

Comedy sketch show – *Little Britain*

Situation comedy – *Two Pints of Lager*

Science fiction – *Doctor Who*

Reality TV – *Big Brother*

Period drama – *Bleak House*

Chat show – *Parkinson*

Soap opera – *EastEnders*

Drama series – *Waking the Dead*

Children's magazine – *Blue Peter*

Teen magazine – *T4*

Cartoon – *Scooby Doo, Where Are You?*

Radio genres with examples

News programme – *Newsbeat*

Documentary – *File on Four*

Comedy sketch show – *Dead Ringers*

Situation comedy – *Clare in the Community*

Science fiction – *The Hitchhiker's Guide to the Galaxy*

Soundscape – *The Twin Towers: A Memorial in Sound*

Period drama – *Classic Serial*

Chat show – *Midweek with Libby Purves*

Soap opera – *The Archers*

Drama series – *Afternoon Theatre*

Print genres with examples

Compact newspaper – *The Times*

Tabloid newspaper – *The Sun*

News magazine – *The Economist*

Free sheet – *Metro*

Regional newspaper – *Western Daily Press*

Local newspaper – *Liverpool Echo*

Print genres with examples (continued)
Womens' magazine – *Cosmopolitan*
Lads' magazine – *Nutz*
TV listings – *Radio Times*
Music magazine – *Smash Hits*
Classified advertising – *Exchange & Mart*
Special interest – *Boat Owner*
Fiction – *True Romances*
Children's magazine – *Bob the Builder*
Pre-teen magazine – *Girl Talk*
Comic – *Beyblade*

Interactive media genres with examples
Website – *amazon.co.uk*
DVD – *Van Helsing*
CD-ROM – *World Atlas*
Computer game – *The Sims*
Console game – *Crash Bandicoot*

By audience

Earlier we discussed the many ways in which media producers think about their audiences. We looked at occupation, lifestyle, where they live, age, ethnicity, gender and sexual orientation. Every sector of the media industry tries to appeal as much as possible to the shared interests and outlook of particular groups of people – their audiences. In order for a product to be successful, its producers need to do four things well:

✓ identify the market segment (or niche) that they are going to target

✓ find out what people in that segment are most likely to be interested in

✓ make a product that people in that market segment (or niche) will find attractive and interesting in some way – so much that they will want the product

✓ communicate to the market segment that the product is available, and how to get it.

Communication to the target audience is called **marketing**. Marketing products is a specialised activity, and often it is not the media producers who do it, but separate marketing departments within organisations – or even external agencies which have the necessary skills to do this important job well.

Target audience	Some of their interests	Product intended to satisfy at least some of those interests	Marketing
Young (perhaps single) men	Cars, having fun, daring activities, young women, weird phonomena	Bravo (television channel)	In magazines and on other TV channels owned by the same company – for example FTN
Young women	Celebrity lifestyles and gossip, fashion, keeping fit, shopping, beauty, dating	*Cosmopolitan* (magazine)	Television advertising, other magazines owned by the same company
Middle-aged men	Rock music, going to gigs featuring classic rock artists	Planet Rock (digital radio station)	Specialist press
Middle-aged women	Real life stories, cooking, fashion and beauty, health, TV soaps	*Woman's Own* (magazine)	Television advertising, other magazines owned by the same company
Book buyers of all demographic groups	Buying books for study, entertainment and finding out information	amazon.co.uk	Internet pop-ups and banner advertising and radio advertising

■ **Figure 3.9** *Different products single out particular interests within their target audiences and aim to satisfy them. Some target audiences are very narrow, while others are very broad.*

The key to successful marketing is knowing the market segment and how to reach the people in it (Figure 3.9). Media products can be marketed in many different ways, including:

■ advertising in print, on radio and television, in cinemas, via websites and on DVDs and videos

■ trails between or during programmes on radio and television and trailers in cinemas

■ features within programmes on radio and television or included within copy in print and on web pages.

You will have noticed that guests on television chat shows and radio programmes are often only there in order to promote their latest book, album or film.

Assessment task 3

Describe the ways in which your one chosen sector of the media industry makes products to suit its audiences. Be methodical, clearly showing how this sector differs from the others. Explain the methods used by the industry and why they are used.

Assessment evidence

✓ Describe the way that products are categorised within the sector and how these categories are used.

✓✓ Use examples to show how a number of products from your chosen sector each fit different categories *and* explain why they fit them.

✓✓✓ Use correct terminology in your explanations, making sure they are detailed and supported by strong evidence of your conclusions.

Elements of construction

When planning a media product, it is important to think carefully about how it should be made – what should go in it, how it should be put together, and what style it should have.

Selection

When choosing material to go in a product, think about the genre and the audience. What do the audience want to see, hear or read about? The genre is important because the audience will have certain expectations. They will not for example, expect to see a television newsreader doing a dance in the middle of a news bulletin. They might, however, find it very funny if a newsreader appears on a comedy sketch show and does a dance.

Does the audience want more of the same kind of material that they usually see in products of the same genre, or do they want something a little different? Audiences can become tired of the same old material and often welcome change if it is well thought out and works well. That is why some media producers gain their reputations by being experimental or innovative. However, beginners should first show that they can produce products following the traditions of a genre, or people might think they are not able to.

Selecting material often means carefully balancing serious and light-hearted items – light and shade. Too much of one may make for a dull or upsetting programme or publication, while too much of the other may make it seem frivolous or lightweight and not worth taking seriously. You will have to plan for this balance in the pre-production stage, as do most media producers.

Composition

This term relates to structure. In what order should different elements of a production be placed? It also means thinking carefully about framing elements, such as opening titles in television, typographical features in print or stylistic features in interactive media.

Did you know?

The BBC's first female television news reader, Angela Rippon may have been most famous for showing her legs in a dance routine on the Morecambe and Wise *comedy show in 1976. This surprised and entertained viewers who were more used to seeing her seriously reading the evening news.*

Combination

Finally, it is important to think about the ways in which different elements in a product are assembled. Sometimes putting one item after another can damage the effectiveness of one or both of them. For example, the Rockpile song *Crawling from the Wreckage* would fit well in a golden oldie show on the radio. But playing the same song after the news bulletin has just reported a fatal accident on the motorway would be seen as offensive, and the presenter or producer responsible could face the sack. Radio stations which use computer automation to run their programming overnight make very sure that this song and others like it will not be played straight after the news, just in case.

There are many ways in which material in media products can be combined in good, entertaining ways, that will improve the product. The use of a very appropriate song as a soundtrack to some visuals, for example. The press use images and captions extensively to create an impact on the printed page – a clever headline used with a strong image can make a powerful impression on readers.

Theory into practice

From the sector you have chosen, identify some good and some bad combinations of different elements used. Explain their positive and negative aspects.

Assessment task 4

Describe the ways in which your one chosen sector of the media industry makes products to suit its audiences. Be methodical, clearly showing how this sector differs from the others. Explain the methods used by the industry and why they are used.

Assessment evidence

✔ Describe the elements of construction used to target audiences and how they are used.

✔✔ Use examples to show the different elements in use in a number of products from your chosen sector *and* explain why they are used.

✔✔✔ Use correct terminology in your explanations, making sure they are detailed and supported by strong evidence of your conclusions.

Modes of address

The way media products address their audiences can have a big effect on how audiences understand them. This is important when planning a media product.

Did you know?

Until the 1980s all the serious programming on radio and television featured 'received pronunciation', a kind of English that was, and still is, spoken in the most prosperous suburbs of London. People from other regions, and even Cockneys (also from London), rarely heard voices like their own, unless they were being made fun of in comedies. Today, many people still speak in a way that could be described as 'received pronunciation', but you can now hear a wide range of other accents on radio and television in a variety of positive, authoritative roles.

Mode of address includes the accents or dialects used, but it is also much more than this. It is primarily about the way a media product communicates with its audience – and this happens in a number of different ways. These include:

- content
- language
- genre
- narrative
- imagery
- style.

We will look at each of these in turn.

Content

What does it mean?

Intertextuality – *where content crosses from one product to another*

The choice of content in a media product speaks volumes about it – whether the content is serious or funny, true or fictional. Audiences pick up on such things very quickly. Media products often include content that refers to other products – like putting a newsreader on a comedy sketch show. *The Simpsons* often does this – for example, it featured scenes from the film *Citizen Kane* in one episode. This is called **intertextuality**.

Language

Language is not just about accent – it can also be formal or informal. For example, a news article could be written in the formal style of a compact newspaper, using long sentences and a wide range of vocabulary.

Alternatively, it could be written in informal language as in a tabloid, with simpler words, colloquial expressions and shorter sentences. The language used in tabloids would look very out of place in *The Times*, unless it was being used in a humorous way, perhaps to make fun of tabloid newspapers.

Theory into practice

There are many more differences between tabloid and more serious newspapers than the layout and the pictures used. Compare some newspaper stories and find out for yourself what these differences are.

In film and in broadcasting, much of the language used is dialogue, but commentaries and narration, as well as news reports and documentaries, use a different way of addressing the viewer or listener. Writing for the ear is quite different from writing for the printed page, as you will find out later in this book. A friendly style will sound very different from a formal or jokey style, and writers have to be careful to use the most appropriate one for the product and the audience.

■ **Figure 3.10** *A still from 1950s children's TV programme* Muffin the Mule. *How does it compare to a modern children's TV programme?*

You may have noticed differences in the way presenters on your favourite programmes have spoken to you as you have grown older. The way most children's television presenters speak to their audiences is just right for children of the target age. Speaking to an adult audience in the same way would not be such a good idea!

Language is also about tone. Speaking softly or harshly can change the mode of address, in the same way that writing in capitals in emails is considered to be shouting and, therefore, rather impolite.

Theory into practice

Select a number of media products from your chosen sector and decide which ones are formal and which are informal in tone. How does the language change to match the tone? Explain the differences in the use of language to help your understanding.

Genre

Genre is important in deciding on the most appropriate mode of address. For example, a comedy show or a printed comic would be most likely to address its audience in an informal, even jokey way. Serious genres and sub-genres, such as the world news pages of a broadsheet or compact newspaper, adopt serious modes of address. If they did not do this, their readers might not know whether to believe them or not.

Theory into practice

Choose some examples of different genres from your sector of the media industry and see how the genre affects the way the product speaks to its audience. Explain why.

Narrative

Narrative structure is the way the content of a media product is put into order. The narrative structure of a product tells the audience a lot about what it is they are looking at or listening to. Each fiction or non-fiction product is organised using one of the following narrative structures:

An **open** narrative structure leaves matters uncertain at the end, with more content to follow – such as the next episode of a series, or the replay of a football match that has ended in a draw. A news article might end with the suggestion that there will be more to report the next day.

In a **closed** structure, there are no loose ends left – for example, the final whistle is blown and the football coverage ends or a criminal has been sentenced and that is the end of the news story.

Multi-strand narratives are typically soap operas and long-running serials, which do not use the more conventional approach of beginning/middle/ending. Instead, several storylines run at the same time, some ending and others beginning. There is no obvious end point to the story.

Alternative narratives tend to be more difficult for audiences to follow – for example, they might jump about through time, without offering a clear sense of the order of events.

Investigative narratives are found in encyclopaedias and dictionaries, websites, CD-ROMs, DVDs and some Internet radio stations (which, through on-screen interactivity, permit listeners to choose the order of what they hear). None of these products are usually read or used continuously from start to finish. Instead, people select items that interest them and move around the product in their own way.

Theory into practice

Identify the narrative structures in a range of products from your chosen sector. Explain what it is about the narrative structure in each one that tells the audience what kind of a product it is. For example, on picking up a dictionary, what would tell a reader that it was a dictionary? (Apart from the description on the cover, of course!)

Imagery

The use of imagery in media products allows us to communicate a lot to our audiences. There is a lot of information later in this unit, which explains how meaning is encoded into media products, and how, in turn, audiences understand them.

Theory into practice

Once you have studied section 3.3 of this unit, come back and investigate how imagery is used in some products from your chosen sector.

Style

There are all sorts of different styles for different media products. The choice of style is important. Some styles will not be right for some genres or sub-genres. For example, television news is presented in a particular style which does not really change much from channel to channel. One of the biggest changes in the style of news presentation in recent years was when Channel Five (as it was then called) began with Kirsty Young sitting *on* a desk, rather than sitting *behind* it.

Theory into practice

Identify a range of style features of products from your chosen sector. You may need to consult the practical unit you have chosen to follow in this book for extra help.

Assessment task 5

Describe the ways in which your one chosen sector of the media industry makes products to suit its audiences. Be methodical, clearly showing how this sector differs from the others. Explain the methods used by the industry and why they use them.

Assessment evidence

✔ Describe the different modes of address used to target audiences, and how they are used.

✔✔ Use examples to show the modes of address in use in a number of products from your chosen sector *and* explain why they are used.

✔✔✔ Use correct terminology in your explanations, making sure they are detailed and supported by strong evidence of your conclusions.

Constraints

Media producers have to work within the wide range of different constraints we explored in Unit 1. You will remember that some are regulatory, relating to the regulatory bodies which oversee some sectors of the industry. Others are legal, meaning that they relate to the laws of the land. You may want to refer back to Unit 1 as we consider how these constraints affect the ways in which media products are created for audiences (see pages 29–45).

Codes of practice

Codes of practice come from either regulatory or self-regulatory bodies. Ways in which they affect media production include the following:

- The film sector must make sure that its products will get the certificates they need to be shown to the target audiences.

- Radio and television broadcasters must make sure they do not get fined over matters of taste and decency – or worse still, lose their licences to broadcast.

- The press must sure that the Press Complaints Commission does not make too many harsh judgments against them.

- Many journalists who are members of the NUJ feel a responsibility to abide by its code of practice (although many others do not).

- Advertising has to abide by the Ofcom code and the rules of the ASA.

Theory into practice

Look on the PCC, ASA or Ofcom websites for results of any decisions over complaints made about products from your chosen sector.

Did you know?

Below are some examples of media products which fell foul of the law.

- *A radio station in the Midlands organised a competition in which some listeners were burned by ice, suffering injuries.*
- *A newspaper was sued for libel by the politician and writer, Jeffery Archer.*
- *A stunt in a television game show went wrong, and a contestant died during the recording.*
- *A website offered free music downloads through file sharing and was closed down for breach of copyright.*

■ **Figure 3.11** *The Royal Courts of Justice in the Strand, London. Most big libel cases are heard here, in the High Court.*

Legal restrictions

While some media producers break some of the codes of practice when they feel they can get away with it, it is rather more difficult to break the law and get off scot free. When media producers break the law they often incur fines, and in some cases the consequences can be more tragic. The huge impact of the media on people's lives means that media producers have to be very careful to act within the law.

Theory into practice

Use the information on pages 29–45 of Unit 1 to make a list of the ways in which media products in your chosen sector could fall foul of the law. What should media producers do to avoid such problems?

Assessment task 6

Describe the ways in which your one chosen sector of the media industry makes products to suit its audiences. Be methodical, clearly showing how this sector differs from the others. Explain the methods used by the industry and why they are used.

Assessment evidence

✔ Describe the ways in which constraints already affect how the sector targets its audiences, showing how the constraints affect the products.

✔✔ Use examples to show how the constraints could affect a number of products from your chosen sector *and* explain why.

✔✔✔ Use correct terminology in your explanations, making sure they are detailed and supported by strong evidence of your conclusions.

3.3   How audiences make sense of media products

You need to describe and discuss how audiences make sense of media products. In this section we will look at different ways in which meaning is created by the industry and understood by audiences. Another assessment task will help you present your work in the correct way.

Decoding

We have already spent some time investigating the ways in which the media industry thinks about its audiences. Now let's consider what happens when audiences consume media products. That is, when audiences read, watch or listen to some of the industry's output.

Media studies uses a number of key terms in order to help understand and describe what is happening when audiences make meanings from what they consume. For example, every media product is considered to be a **text**, in the same way that in English lessons, novels, plays and poems are called texts. In media studies consuming a text is often called **reading** it – even if it is a film, a DVD, a website, a radio programme or a television programme.

What does it mean?

Text – *any media product that is **read** (or consumed) by an audience. The text may include written words or it may consist entirely of sounds and/or images.*

Reading – *making meaning from a media text. For example, forming an understanding of what is happening in a radio play, or making sense of events in a news report.*

General codes

If you have ever watched an obscure film and been unsure what it was all about, or even just argued with friends about what the ending of a film meant, you may have realised that meaning in media texts is not always the same for everyone. Some film directors set out to leave endings ambiguous, to encourage each member of the audience to think about what might happen next. At other times, media producers may try to make sure everyone in the audience understands the text in the same way.

■ Figure 3.12 *Different people are likely to make different readings of the same text, no matter how hard producers try to make them react in the same way.*

Another way to explain this is using the example of a novel. Using the detailed descriptions and dialogues in the text for clues, readers have to imagine for themselves what all the characters and scenes look like. Lots of clear descriptions will mean that each reader is more likely to imagine scenes that are similar to the ones the author had in mind when writing the book. If the descriptions are not very detailed or clear, it is more likely that every reader will form different images. Each reader will have a completely unique reading of the novel.

In the case of a radio play, there are actors' voices speaking the words aloud, as well as sound effects and perhaps music. Each sound in the play provides the listener with a little bit more information to use when building up a mental image of what is happening.

If the play is then adapted for television, images will be added and each viewer will receive a lot more information about what is happening. They do not have to imagine the images because they are already there. Likewise, in other areas of the media industry such as the press and interactive media, audiences are given images to look at, so they have fewer gaps to fill using their own imagination.

The more information given to each member of the audience (and so the less each one has to imagine), the more likely different people are to read a text in similar ways – that is, to make very similar readings of it. Some media producers want individuals in their audiences to make different readings of a text, while others want them to understand the text in the same way. However hard producers may try to impose their own **preferred readings** on their audiences, they do not always succeed. Audiences have a tendency to come up with their own **alternative readings**.

What does it mean?

Preferred reading – *the meaning the producer intended the audience to make from the text*

Alternative reading – *a meaning that is different in some significant way from the producer's preferred reading*

Anchorage – *a means of 'tying down' the meaning of some part of a media text*

Anchorage

One way of fixing a particular meaning to part of a media text is to use **anchorage** – this means adding some extra information designed to make the audience understand it in a particular way. Throughout this book, for example, the images have captions underneath them. They have been added to explain the meaning or to make sure the image tells you something in particular in order to develop your understanding.

In many cases, changing the caption would change the way you think about the image – in other words, you would make a different reading. Look at the way the different captions under the image below alter the meaning of the same picture. Even though the picture is unchanged, the second caption encourages you to think about it in a completely different way.

■ **Figure 3.13** *Animal conservationists assist endangered species to reproduce in safety.*

■ **Figure 3.14** *Life in captivity often causes distress and anxiety to animals.*

Now try to imagine other captions which could alter the meaning again. The possibilities are endless, because your imagination and the imaginations of other people reading this can bring a huge variety of different ideas to the task. Because this activity can be good fun, newspapers and magazines often run caption competitions, inviting readers to suggest new captions for photographs that are already quite amusing. The funniest in the opinion of the editor is the one that wins.

Theory into practice

Explore anchorage in some products from your chosen sector. Choose a range of different products and find examples of how the producer has tried to anchor meaning in some way. Has the anchorage worked?

Signification

Anchoring meaning with a caption is just one of the ways meaning can be produced in media texts. What you have been doing with the images in this book is **decoding** them. Just like someone receiving a secret message, you have been using your own knowledge of the way books are laid out in order to make sense of the images. After all, you already know that a line of text under an image is meant to be read in connection with that image. Someone who has never read a reference book before might not realise that at first.

The way people learn to decode media texts (by experiencing lots of them over time) is very like the way someone learns a code, such as Morse code or semaphore. In some parts of the world, people have communicated effectively using smoke signals or drums, which are also types of code.

Media producers **encode** meanings into their products, just as we have written captions for all the images in this book and divided the writing into sections, adding headings to help you find your way around the book. We also chose which information to tell you about the world of media and – because of the shortage of space – which information to leave out.

In making the decisions about what went into the book and how we put it together, we were encoding large amounts of information for you to

decode. For example, by now we hope you will have realised that inside some of the boxes you will find interesting and useful further information to help your understanding and develop your knowledge of the subject even further.

There are all sorts of ways a media text can make meaning. A printed product can consist entirely of writing (as novels often do), relying on the words alone to tell the reader everything the author wants to encode. A radio programme might

■ **Figure 3.15** *Does this picture show something good happening – or something bad? Look on page 130 to find out!*

consist of only words spoken in a flat monotone voice. A television programme could feature a single person reading aloud from a book.

Such unadventurous use of these different media would quickly become boring because they do not make the most of the opportunities of the media. Adding a picture to a page, some sound effects to a radio play and moving images to a story reading will make the text more interesting. In addition, the combination of different elements within the product work together to create meaning. By putting two elements together – like the picture and the caption – new meanings can be created and others become impossible.

For example, the sound of a lion roaring could make radio listeners think it is in a jungle – until they hear a loudspeaker announcement warning visitors that the zoo is about to close. A scene with a young man running towards an old lady might make television viewers think he is going to rob her – until another shot reveals that he is running to catch a heavy object falling towards her. In the print media, many different typefaces can be used for text of any kind – from traditional to scary to futuristic. Choosing the right one for the type of headline or story can add extra meaning.

All the different elements used to create images in media texts are in fact **signs** which carry meaning. Audiences recognise the signs and understand some of the meanings they are intended to communicate. **Signification** refers to the way in which signs work in media texts.

One of the key academics to have studied signification, Roland Barthes, suggested that this sending of messages happens in two different ways: one on a very basic, obvious level, and the other on a higher, much more sophisticated level. He called the first level **denotation** and the second **connotation**. For example, the word 'red' denotes a colour most people can visualise. If someone says 'red', another person might just imagine the colour itself, as if thinking of a colour to paint a room. So in this case the word 'red' simply *denotes* a colour.

On the second level, the same word 'red' may also suggest a number of less obvious things. These include such things as facing danger, being in debt or being angry. The word 'red' can also make people think of communist or socialist political systems. The interpretation will depend on any anchorage of the word's meaning – such as the way in which it is used and what is said before or after it.

There are many different ways in which elements within texts can work to create meaning. The tables in figures on the next few pages show just a few examples for each sector of the media industry.

■ **Figure 3.16** *Making the sound of horses' hooves with coconuts works well on radio because listeners cannot see how the sound is being made.*

■ **Figure 3.17** *This picture shows the same smoke as on page 128. Now what do you think about the smoke?*

 Theory into practice

Choose some examples of signification from your sector of the media industry and show how meaning is being encoded into these texts. Explain how that meaning is made – does it remind the audience of something else, for example.

Generic codes

Even words can be signifiers. Onomatopoeic words are those which sound like what is being described. For example, 'whoosh' sounds like the noise it is meant to describe. But most words have no obvious link with the thing they are describing and they rely on both encoder (the producer) and decoder (the audience) agreeing on their meaning. For example, the word 'dog' neither looks nor sounds like a four-legged animal, but English speakers all agree it refers to such a creature, and so the word means the same thing to all of us.

The word 'dog' has other meanings, too, which work for people who understand them. They will be lost on anyone who does not. For example, it may be difficult for a non-English speaker to understand that the expression 'you can't teach an old dog new tricks' is used to refer to a person who is set in their ways.

When signifiers work together, each one acts as part of a code – just as in the Morse code (which uses a set of symbols to stand for letters) each symbol would be of little use without the rest. Without a complete set to work with, it would be impossible to spell out a word in Morse, because several letters would be missing.

In the same way, media texts rely on whole systems of signifiers working together in order for producers to construct them, and in turn for audiences to read and understand them. Codes in media texts have evolved – that is, they have developed over time. They were not created from scratch in one sitting. Codes can be **symbolic** or **technical**.

■ **Figure 3.18** *During World War II, Morse code was used to send top secret military information across long distances. By agreeing in advance to swap the letters and the 'dots and dashes' representing them around, a sender and receiver could encrypt messages in a way only they could understand.*

What does it mean?

Symbolic codes *suggest meaning through the choice of content. For example, using the colour red might suggest danger in a vampire movie, because it is the colour of blood. In another context, red can suggest passion or love, and so an article about St Valentine's Day may have a red border or a red background. Facial expressions on actors in a drama, or on presenters, interviewees or contestants in a game show are also symbolic codes as they suggest the emotions that the people are feeling. Voice can portray emotion, too, and this is particularly important on radio, where faces cannot be seen and have to be imagined.*

Technical codes *are ones that use structural elements in a media product to make meaning. They include the way a picture like Figure 3.15 is cropped, the way a television shot is framed, or boxes are drawn around certain parts of a text – as in this textbook, for example. You soon learn what is meant by the boxes, and it does not take long to work out that a newspaper headline tells the most important point in the story below it.*

Radio

Radio has been called the 'blind' medium because listeners have only the sounds available to work out what is happening. This can be very confusing if the sounds are unfamiliar or unexpected. For this reason, radio producers have to be very careful to use sounds in a way that helps, rather than confuses listeners.

Below is a list of signifiers in radio and what they are usually understood to mean.

Signifier in radio	What it can signify
A car horn in a jingle	A traffic and travel report is beginning
The words 'Where in the world?' sung to a certain tune	An advert for PC World
Fade down of speech in a drama	The end of a scene
Fade up of speech in a drama	The beginning of a new scene
Jingle	It's time for the weather forecast
Coconut halves being knocked together	A horse walking or trotting
A siren gets louder, then quieter, in a drama	A police car is passing
Crunching gravel	Someone is walking on a gravel drive
The 'pips' (also known as the 'Greenwich time signal')	It's time for the news on the hour

Television

A good example of how a media code develops over time is the way news is presented on television. Many of the very first news broadcasts on television did not feature a newsreader in vision. Instead scripts were read out while still images or a newsreel were shown on screen.

Once newsreaders began to appear on screen, their dress, seating position and 'look' towards the camera all became important. The first audiences watching television newsreaders had to make sense of what they saw. Now we are all so used to the way television news is *usually* presented, that we subconsciously read those codes without having to think about them.

We usually know we are watching a news programme the moment we tune into a channel because we immediately recognise the various signifiers that are working together to encode meaning into the programme. We see a desk, one or two presenters, some on-screen headlines and sometimes a screen showing a reporter at the scene of an event talking to the presenters. If we tune in before the programme begins, the opening title sequence tells us immediately what kind of programme is going to follow. The theme music is fast-paced and important-sounding, and a series of images show us glimpses of the world: people and places that are often in the news.

Even a foreign news programme in a language we do not understand will be instantly recognisable because a similar code will be used.

Technical codes include the use of graphics on screen and in print and interactive media products, the framing of an image, the use of soft focus to romanticise a scene or to hide someone's true age. Filters, lighting, camera angles, special effects and also sound processing are other examples of ways in which technical aspects of a production can be put to work to create particular meanings.

Did you know?

Some television programmes try to convey a moment in history. In order for the illusion to be convincing, all the different elements have to be right. The scenery or the backgrounds in any images have to reflect the time period. The costumes, tools, transport, buildings, what the people are doing and even the way they speak all have to seem authentic – otherwise there will be conflicting meanings in the text. If everything in the picture – and of course the sound – fits the time period, the most likely audience reading will be that the events shown are actually taking place then, rather than today. This is why film and television producers make great efforts to make sure there are no electricity pylons or satellite dishes visible when they are shooting a scene from the days of Charles Dickens.

Below is a list of signifiers in television and film and what they are usually understood to mean.

Signifier in television and film	What it can signify
Large words on screen	The beginning of a programme/film
Small words on screen	The end of a programme/ film
Suspenseful music is played while an otherwise unremarkable place is shown	Something dramatic or frightening is about to happen
Fast-paced music is played while a car chase is shown	The action on screen is very exciting
Long shot of a location	This is where the action you are about to see takes place
Close up of a frightened face	Something scary is happening
A cowboy on horseback rides towards the setting sun	That is the last we will see of this character
A fast-moving sequence of images, sound and the word 'next'	These are highlights of the next episode or the next programme in a series

The press

You would not need to look for very long at a foreign newspaper before you realised what it was! The similarities between it and our own newspapers are likely to be much greater than the differences.

Print products use signifiers to help their audiences make meaning from the collection of images, text and artwork they see. In a newspaper, for example, the main words on the front page are large and eye-catching, so readers' eyes are drawn towards them. In this way, the main headline on the front page is shown to be one of the most important parts of the day's newspaper. It is certainly meant to persuade people to pick up a copy and buy it.

Below is a list of signifiers in the press and what they are usually understood to mean.

Signifier in the press	What it can signify
Large words covering half the page	The 'lead' or most important story today is below
Small-sized text under an image	Further information about the image
White words on a red panel	The name of the newspaper
Thick, glossy paper	An expensive or luxury item
An image by a reporter or a columnist's name	This is what the reporter of columnist looks like

Signifier in the press (continued)	What it can signify
Words printed in a box within a magazine article	This is some further information about the subject
Words from an article, repeated in much larger type among the rest of the words	This is a highlight which will encourage readers to read the whole article
A single image on the front cover of a novel	This is a highlight or the main theme of the story told inside
A large gap between lines of words in a novel	A change of scene or a flashback follows or time passes

Interactive media

Interactive media products require their audiences to navigate around them so some of the most important signifiers are those that show where to click your mouse or the buttons on a DVD player. As with film and television, sound can work with images and text to produce sophisticated meanings in the audience's readings.

Below is a list of signifiers in interactive media and what they are usually understood to mean.

Signifier in interactive media	What it can signify
Words underlined	This is a hyperlink to another web page
Images on an inlay card	These are scenes from this film or programme
A still background with several images and words arranged around it	You can choose between these menu items
A pop-up box with an image and a message within it	This is an advert for goods or services and by clicking on it you may find more information
The words 'special features' on an inlay card	There is extra material available on this DVD, which you can access interactively
A logo showing Uc, U, PG, 12, 12A, 15, 18 or R18	This is an age restriction relating to the suitability of the content for children
A small box with a cross through it	An image intended to be shown here is missing
The sound of a click is heard	The computer has registered your mouse click

Reasons for preference

There are so many ways in which people differ that different audiences tend towards certain interpretations, depending on their own attitudes and experiences. For example, to a middle-aged or elderly audience the word 'garage' will probably mean a place to park a car. The same word may make a teen audience think of a particular musical genre before they think about anything else – especially those among the audience who do not yet drive.

Theory into practice

Preferred meanings can be due to a person's age, gender, ethnic background, sexual orientation, etc. How many more words with dual meanings, like 'garage', can you think of that could affect audience readings in this way?

Assessment task 7

Describe the ways in which audiences can understand the codes used in your one chosen sector of the media industry. Be methodical, clearly showing how this sector differs from the others. Explain the methods used by the industry and why they use them.

Assessment evidence

✔ Describe the codes that audiences might find in media products, showing how they might make sense of them.

✔✔ Use examples to show the codes in use in a number of products from your chosen sector *and* how they might be understood by an audience.

✔✔✔ Use correct terminology in your explanations, making sure they are detailed and supported by strong evidence of your conclusions.

4 Video Production

Introduction

In this unit you will learn about video production techniques and how to plan and make your own video products.

Video production encompasses a wide variety of moving image products, including television commercials, small promotional programmes for a manufacturer, wedding videos or footage to be used by a football team for training purposes. One of the best known uses of video production is the prime-time entertainment programmes produced by major television companies. The one thing all these different types of product have in common is the use of video technology and techniques to record and edit material.

Learning outcomes

On completion of this unit you should:

- understand pre-production, production and post-production techniques
- be able to contribute to each stage of the creation of a finished video product
- be able to review your own video production work.

4.1 Pre-production, production and post-production techniques

In the media industry, video production covers a wide range of activities, from making full-length feature films to shooting short clips for inclusion in interactive media products.

In this section you will have an opportunity to look at a range of pre-production, production and post-production techniques. You will be able to see how pre-production – the planning stage – allows you to make sure you have all the resources you need for production – the making stage. You will then be able to see how the skills required for post-production – the editing stage – enable you to make a finished video product.

Producing a finished product is not necessary for this section – instead, you will be experimenting with different techniques and learning about the paperwork you will need for working with video. Section 4.2 involves working in a team to produce a complete video product.

Figure 4.1 is a schematic diagram that will help you to understand the video production processes. The amount of red in the diagram shows just how important the pre-production stage is.

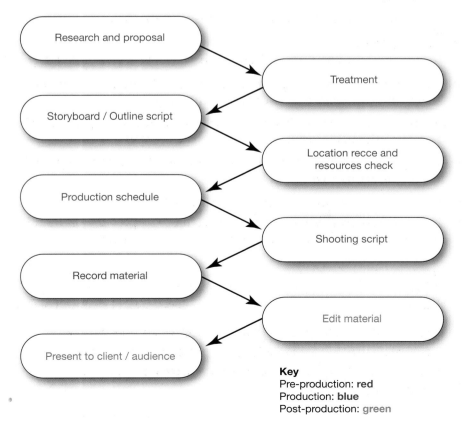

Key
Pre-production: **red**
Production: **blue**
Post-production: **green**

■ **Figure 4.1** *The video production processes.*

Case study

Media productions

In this unit we will be following the pre-production, production and post-production undertaken by Media Productions – a video and new media production company.

Media Productions have been approached by a company called Recycle.It to produce a programme for young people. The aim of the programme is to encourage young people to recycle their waste materials.

Pre-production

Pre-production is the planning stage of any media product, including video. It is the stage where you decide what kind of video product you want to make and the resources you will need to make it. It is also the time to consider what your product will cost to make and the time scale in which you have to produce it. It is an extremely important part of video production and doing things properly at this stage will make the difference between a successful and unsuccessful product.

Resources

First you will need to identify the resources available to you.

Video equipment
There is a wide variety of video formats currently available, including:

- **VHS format** – an analogue format that is still currently in use but is rapidly being replaced with digital technology
- **digital video (DV)** – this format uses digital technology to record the video signal and is lightweight and very portable
- **hi-8 video** – an early version of digital video that is being replaced by better-quality digital
- **DVCAM** – a professional digital video system
- **high-definition video** – the latest technology, produces extremely high-resolution picture and sound of a very high quality.

Theory into practice

Identify the video equipment formats that you will be able to use in your school or college. Make a list of all the cameras available. Identify which of these use analogue technology and which use digital technology.

Audio equipment

The next step is to identify the audio resources you have available to use. A video programme is only as good as the quality of the images and the sound track. Try to imagine watching a video for a new band in which the sound is really poor. The pictures might be excellent but the poor-quality sound will mean that most people do not watch the video.

Audio resources include:

- **microphones** – rifle microphones, necktie microphones, radio microphones, etc.
- **recorders** – cassette, reel-to-reel, MiniDisc, hard disk recorder.

Theory into practice

Identify the audio recording resources available for your use and make a list of them. Identify which of these use analogue technology and which use digital technology.

Did you know?

A major job in the video production industry is to be in charge of pre-production. The person managing this crucial stage has to ensure that all the resources needed for a production are in the right place and at the right time.

Without someone doing this job, a production would not run smoothly, if at all.

You have now identified the resources you have available for recording moving images and sound. Let's move on to the other resources you will need for your video projects.

Personnel

It is unlikely that you will be able to undertake and complete a video product on your own. Instead you are likely to be working as a member of a team. There are many roles you can take in a video production, including director, producer, camera operator, sound recordist and production assistant. All of there roles are important for the successful completion of a video product.

■ **Figure 4.2** *Team work is crucial in successful video production.*

The personnel required for your team will depend on the project you are going to undertake. However, there are a number of roles that you can identify that occur in all video production work.

Theory into practice

Carefully watch the end credits of a video production. Make a list of all the jobs you see listed on the credits. Identify what each of these jobs involves.

If you find that there are too many job roles for you to investigate on your own, ask one of your friends or colleagues to help you.

Pre-production documentation

During the pre-production process you will need to produce a range of documents that will help you in the production stage. These documents are:

1 **Proposal** – initial ideas that sell your ideas to a client.
2 **Treatment** – a detailed development of your proposal.
3 **Production schedule** – dates for things to happen.
4 **Storyboard** – a visual representation of your idea.
5 **Shooting script** – details of camera angles and sound.

6 **Location reconnaissance record** – a plan of the location to be used.

7 **Risk assessment** – details of any potential problems when recording and editing.

8 **Budget** – details of how much the whole thing will cost.

All of these documents are vital in the pre-production planning process and we will look at each of them in turn.

1 Proposal

The proposal is a document in which you set out to sell your ideas to a client – its purpose is to whet the appetite of a potential client and encourage them to invest in your production. The proposal should include sufficient information for the reader to understand what you intend to do.

Before you can prepare a proposal, you need to explore your ideas for your video product. One way of doing this is to produce a mind map – this allows you to put all your ideas in schematic diagram. You can then see where your ideas are leading. You can cross out ideas that are not appropriate and finally you will arrive at an appropriate idea.

Figure 4.3 shows the mind map prepared by Media Productions in response to a request from their client Recycle.It to produce a video programme encouraging young people to recycle their waste material. It includes all their ideas for what to include in the programme. Your mind map might have a different shape, but the format could be the same.

Figure 4.4 shows the proposal Media Productions prepared to present to Recycle.It. They have included many of the ideas from their mind map and discarded others. You can use this example to help you set out your own proposals for video productions.

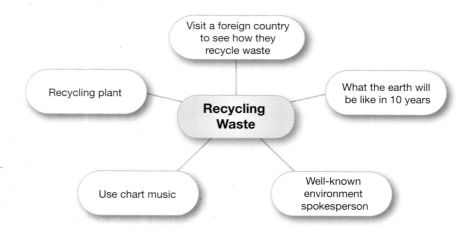

■ **Figure 4.3** *Media Productions have made a mind map with the ideas they would like to include in their recycling video.*

Proposal
for
a video programme

Recycling and YOU

Prepared by
James Subrami

Media Productions
james.subrami@mediap.co.uk
21st March 2006

Client
Recycle.It

copyright © 2006

PROPOSAL

Prepared by James Subrami

Media Productions proposes to produce a ten-minute video programme aimed at encouraging young people to consider how they can recycle waste material. The programme will be aimed at an audience of 11–14 year olds and will be informative and educational. The programme will provide evidence of the effects on the environment of not recycling waste material.

The programme will feature material shot on location at a large school, a waste recycling plant and a large landfill site. It will be fronted by a well-known environmental spokesperson and will be accompanied by music from a chart band. We have approached Coldplay to provide an appropriate track and their initial response has been positive.

The programme will feature four young people who are all students at West Smethwick School. They are not concerned about the environment but after being shown what might happen to the planet they reconsider their views. We have contacted the school and they are willing for their pupils to take part in this programme.

We will include facts and figures concerning pollution levels and the effects of waste on the planet will be shown. We have obtained figures from Greenpeace and local authorities on the effects of waste material on the environment.

The spokesperson will appear on screen when interviewing the four young people about the choices they are about to make. Graphics will be used to reinforce the facts and figures about the effects of pollution on the planet.

The programme will be produced on digital format cameras and edited using the latest digital editing technology at our Birmingham editing facility.

The programme budget is subject to discussion but will be approximately £20,000.

■ **Figure 4.4** *Your proposal should be concise but contain enough detail to make the client want to find out more.*

2 Treatment

Once you have decided on your idea and produced your proposal, the next stage in the pre-production process is to develop a treatment. The treatment is the development of your idea from the proposal and is an integral part of the pre-production stage, allowing you to plan the production.

The treatment should include:

- An **introduction** with details of the size and content of the video.

- An **outline script** – sometimes called a 'scene script', this gives an outline of each scene without going into detail about each shot. It can indicate whether daytime or night, the characters used and dialogue or narration.

- A **storyboard** – this is a paper visualisation of the media product.

- An indication of the proposed **production schedule**.

- An **outline budget** giving the approximate cost of the product, including pre-production, production and post-production costs.

- A **contingency plan**, indicating what you will do in the event of unexpected delays, poor weather on location, staff shortages, etc. The contingency plan should inform the budget and allowances must be made in the budget to cover unforeseen costs.

- An idea of the **personnel** and **talent** involved in the project.

- Details of the **research** you have carried out for the production.

A treatment should be produced using DTP and look professional. Figure 4.5 shows the treatment format used by Media Productions. You should complete all the sections of the treatment – some sections will be quite short but others may take up one or more pages.

3 Production schedule

If you are to produce your video product successfully you need to plan effectively. The next stage of pre-production involves producing a production schedule. This important document will include all your plans for production, together with the details of what will happen and when. It will help you to ensure that you can get all tasks done within the timescale available and that all your resources, crew and materials will be available in the right place at the right time.

The first part of your production schedule will include all the key dates for your production. Media Productions' schedule for their Recycle.It project is shown in Figure 4.6.

As well as providing a framework for when all the pre-production, production and post-production tasks should happen, the schedule also allows you to monitor and keep a record of your progress throughout the project. You can tick off tasks as they are completed and amend any dates which have to be changed for whatever reason.

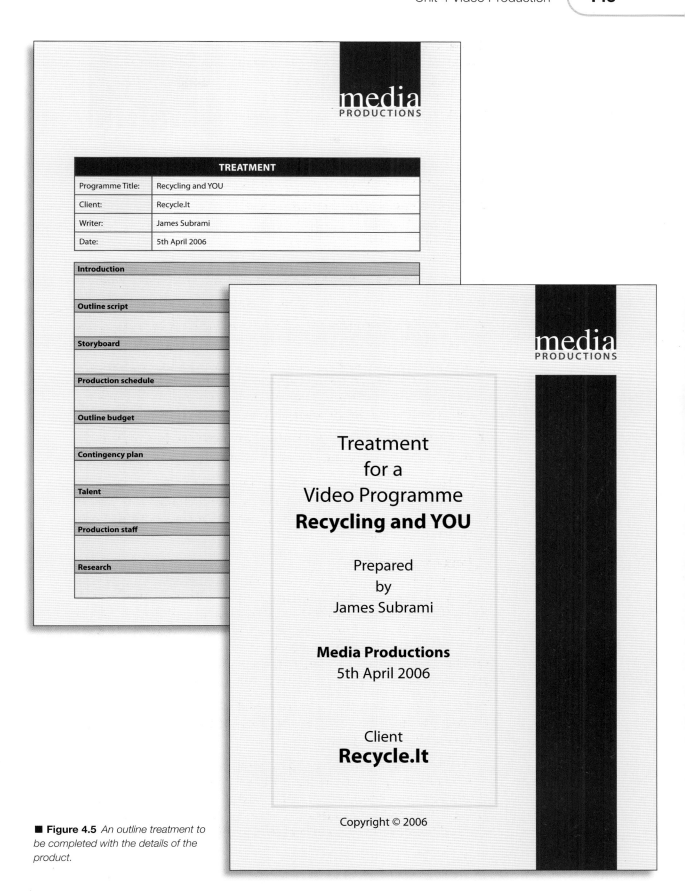

TREATMENT

Programme Title:	Recycling and YOU
Client:	Recycle.It
Writer:	James Subrami
Date:	5th April 2006

Introduction

Outline script

Storyboard

Production schedule

Outline budget

Contingency plan

Talent

Production staff

Research

Treatment
for a
Video Programme
Recycling and YOU

Prepared
by
James Subrami

Media Productions
5th April 2006

Client
Recycle.It

Copyright © 2006

■ **Figure 4.5** *An outline treatment to be completed with the details of the product.*

PRODUCTION SCHEDULE PART 1	
Programme Title:	Recycling and YOU
Client:	Recycle.It
Writer:	James Subrami
Date:	21st April 2006

	Date		Date
Programme start:	**20/05/06**	**Programme completed:**	**22/08/06**
Proposal start:	20/05/06	Completed:	21/05/06
Agreement from client:	23/05/06		
Treatment start:	24/05/06	Completed:	15/06/06
Agreement from client:	16/06/06		
Shooting script start:	21/06/06	Completed:	30/06/06
Storyboard start:	04/07/06	Completed:	08/07/06
Production start:	23/07/06	Completed:	06/08/06
Post-production start:	09/08/06	Completed:	12/08/06
Rough cut to client:	13/08/06		
Agreement from client:	15/08/06		
Final version to client:	22/08/06		

■ **Figure 4.6** *Part 1 of the production schedule lists all the key dates for the production of the video, including start dates and completion dates.*

The second part of the production schedule should provide a clear picture of all your requirements for your production, including equipment, personnel, talent, transport, props and post-production requirements such as sound effects and music. Figure 4.8 shows the second part of Media Productions' production schedule for their recycling video project.

4 Storyboard

A storyboard is a paper visualisation of the video product that represents both the overall structure and the details of the product. It includes an image of how each shot will look, as well as information about timings, camera angles and dialogue. Creating a storyboard will help you to develop your ideas about the way that the visual and sound elements of your product will work together. It is really useful when developing ideas for a video or multimedia product.

Remember

The way to get a really good grade in this unit is to demonstrate a high level of ability in pre-production, production and post-production. You must keep careful records of your own pre-production work. Photocopied documents of other people's work will not be acceptable as evidence.

■ **Figure 4.7** *A good production schedule will help you organise your work throughout the project.*

PRODUCTION SCHEDULE PART 2

Programme Title:	Recycling and YOU
Client:	Recycle.It
Writer:	James Subrami
Date:	21st April 2006

Production equipment required

cameras
lights
microphones
tripod

Crewing requirements

camera operator
sound recordist
production assistant
lighting technician
props technician

Actors

1 male actor
1 female actor
3 extras

Transport requirements

Transport to 3 locations required for approximately 20 people

Props/scenery

1 large globe of the world

Post-production requirements (format, effects, music, voice-over)

Editing using Final Cut Pro
Graphics for titles and credits
Music throughout programme
Sound effects where necessary

■ **Figure 4.8** *Part 2 of the production schedule lists all the requirements for the production and post-production stages.*

Teams working on feature films and television programmes develop a comprehensive storyboard before a single frame is shot. This is done to ensure that all of the scenes are feasible before expensive equipment is hired and staff employed.

5 Shooting script

The shooting script is a more detailed version of the outline script you prepared for the treatment. It needs to contain all the words to be spoken in your video, together with instructions for the actors/presenters about their positions and movements.

In addition, it should contain details of the location, any background noise or sound effects you would like and details of the types of shot you would like.

6 Location reconnaissance record

Before undertaking a project that involves filming on location, you should carry out a location reconnaissance, usually known as a 'recce'. This involves you visiting the location to find out if it is suitable for filming and to check such things as the lighting, power supply and accessibility for your crew and talent. It also allows you to identify where potential problems might occur and any health and safety issues.

Always make sure you gain permission to film on location and notify the police if you are planning to film in a public area. It could ruin all your plans if you turn up to carry out your shoot, only to find out that the location is closed or the owners do not allow you to film there. And make sure you do not plan to film in a place where you could cause an obstruction.

Use a location reconnaissance record sheet to record all of the information you gather during your recce. Figure 4.10 shows the record sheet produced by Media Productions when planning a location shoot for their recycling video.

■ **Figure 4.9** *Gaining permission in advance to film on location can prevent all kinds of problems!*

Did you know?

There have been cases of students filming mock hold-ups outside bank premises without obtaining permission or notifying the local police. In one case, a team of armed police arrived at the scene as they thought a real robbery was taking place. This was not only a waste of police time but also put the students and the public at risk.

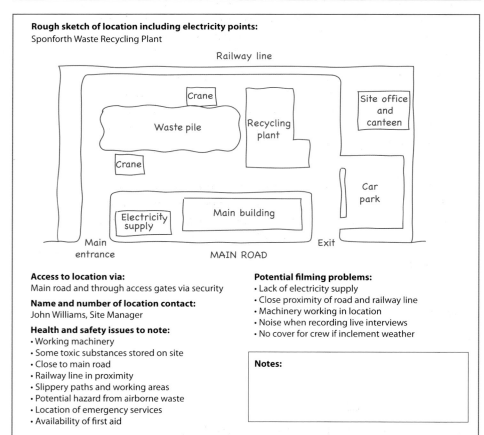

PRODUCTION SCHEDULE LOCATION VISIT SHEET

Programme Title:	Recycling and YOU
Client:	Recycle.It
Writer:	James Subrami
Producer:	Amanda Phillips
Director:	Barry Norman
Date:	16th July 2006

Rough sketch of location including electricity points:
Sponforth Waste Recycling Plant

Access to location via:
Main road and through access gates via security

Name and number of location contact:
John Williams, Site Manager

Health and safety issues to note:
• Working machinery
• Some toxic substances stored on site
• Close to main road
• Railway line in proximity
• Slippery paths and working areas
• Potential hazard from airborne waste
• Location of emergency services
• Availability of first aid

Potential filming problems:
• Lack of electricity supply
• Close proximity of road and railway line
• Machinery working in location
• Noise when recording live interviews
• No cover for crew if inclement weather

Notes:

■ **Figure 4.10** *The location reconnaissance record sheet created by Media Productions for one of the locations used in their recycling video.*

7 Risk assessment

You must follow safe working practices at all stages of work on your media product. You need to take particular care when working with equipment, other people and sometimes with an audience. It is your responsibility to try to minimise the dangers in any situation you are working in. The following are examples of things you need to be particularly aware of when undertaking your recording:

- handling recording and editing equipment safely
- being aware of trailing cables
- handling hot lights
- organising teams to work together in a safe environment
- recognising the dangers of prolonged use of VDU screens
- working in a sensible way and responding to directions.

In addition, you need to be aware of any issues in the studio or location you will be using. During your location recce, you will have identified potential hazards and you can use the record sheet of your visit (see Figure 4.10) to help you to produce a risk assessment. You will then use your risk assessment document during the production stage to help you to work safely and to minimise any risks to yourself and others.

Figure 4.11 shows the risk assessment sheet produced by Media Productions for their location shoot at the recycling plant. As well as identifying the risks and how to minimise them, it includes a list of contacts and emergency services so that the appropriate people can be contacted if anything does go wrong.

8 Budget

Once you know all the requirements for your media product, you can begin to formalise a budget. Your budget should include all the costs of your pre-production, production and post-production work and should be as realistic as possible. Remember to include costs for:

- hire of equipment
- cost of materials
- crew payments
- actors' fees
- location charges
- travel
- subsistence (i.e. meals, hotels)
- contingency (e.g. equipment failure, bad weather delays).

You will need to research realistic costs for your project based on the current industry rates. For the equipment costs, you could contact a local media equipment hire company and ask for their rates – remember to include a computer to edit your work as well as a video camera.

RISK ASSESSMENT SHEET	
Programme Title:	Recycling and YOU
Client:	Recycle.It
Writer:	James Subrami
Producer:	Amanda Phillips
Director:	Barry Norman
Date:	18th July 2006

FILMING AT SPONFORTH WASTE RECYCLING PLANT

Possible hazards

Risk	Level of risk
1. Waste material on floor making it dangerous for crew and equipment	High
2. Machinery operating in the area	High
3. Visibility of crew when on site	High
4. Contamination of equipment by waste materials	Medium
5. Close to dual carriageway and access road	Low

Solutions

1. Ensure someone checks that area is clear for filming.

2. Have a look-out person to ensure that crew are aware of operating machinery.

3. Crew to wear high-visibility vests at all times when on site.

4. All equipment to be covered, where possible, by protective covers.
    All equipment to be cleaned before being returned to base.

5. Film well away from the roads.

Contacts

• Site Safety Manager   Bill Brown xxxxxxxxxxxxxxx

Emergency Services

• On-site services   xxxxxxxxxxxxxxxxxxxxxxxxx

• Local police xxxxxxxxxxxxxxxx

• Local fire xxxxxxxxxxxxxxxxxxxxx

• Local hospital xxxxxxxxxxxxxxxx

■ **Figure 4.11** *You should consider all the risks before starting your production work and produce a risk assessment document like this one.*

BUDGET	
Programme Title:	Recycling and YOU
Client:	Recycle.It
Writer:	James Subrami
Producer:	Amanda Phillips
Director:	Barry Norman
Date:	25th June 2006

MATERIALS	COST	TOTAL
3 x DVCAM tapes	£20 each	£60
Equipment		
Hire - Sony DVCAM camera	£150 per day × 3 days	£450
Hire of 1 tripod	£20 per day × 3 days	£60
Hire of lighting kit	£50 per day × 3 days	£150
Hire of microphone kit	£75 per day × 3 days	£225
Actors		
1 male actor	rehearsal £50 × 3 days	£150
	shooting £150 × 3 days	£450
1 female actor	rehearsal £50 × 3 days	£150
	shooting £150 × 3 days	£450
3 extras	shooting 3 × £50 × 1 day	£150
Props/scenery		
1 large globe of the world	purchased price	£30
Post-production		
Editing suite	£150 per day × 3 days	£450
Editor	£100 per day × 3 days	£300
Graphic designer	£100 per day × 1 day	£100
	TOTAL	**£3175**
Contingency @ 10% of budget		£318
	Total Budget	**£3493**

■ **Figure 4.12** *This budget is for the Media Productions video Recycling and YOU. The production crew are not included because they are on the company payroll. Remember to adapt this budget template to fit the requirements of your own video project.*

To get an idea of the cost of the personnel you need for your project, you could contact an organisation such as BECTU, which is the union for the moving image, radio and information design industries. They will have a rate card for various roles within the industry.

Making your budget as realistic as possible will help you to gain an understanding of the sort of costs involved in media production. It is usual to add on about ten per cent to the budget to allow for contingency. Figure 4.12 shows the Media Productions budget for their recycling video.

Communication

It is vital that you keep in communication with your team and your teacher. Everyone needs to know what is going on and what they have to do next. Hold regular meetings with your team so that decisions about pre-production can be made. These meetings will carry on right through the pre-production process to production and post-production.

Case study

Why communication matters

Media Productions has always kept careful records of its planning. But when the company first started it did not realise how important communications were to the successful completion of a project.

One of its first projects was a TV documentary that involved filming in Spain. Media Productions arranged for the film crew to fly to Spain, but did not check that all of the crew had the necessary documents. In fact, two of the crew members did not have passports and were not able to leave the country. The project was delayed by several weeks while alternative arrangements were made.

The company now has a proper system of communication for each project, including production schedules and checklists of items needed. It makes sure that everyone involved in a project knows where they will be going and any special requirements well in advance.

The lesson they learnt was that clear and regular communication is a crucial part of planning a production.

■ **Figure 4.13** *Proper planning and communication can help to avoid some embarrassing situations!*

Think it over

Imagine that you have made plans to film a scene in a local cinema. You have asked for the manager's permission to shoot and she has allowed you just thirty minutes to film when the cinema is closed. You arrive at the cinema with your camera but your crew and your actors do not arrive. You realise that you forgot to tell them the exact place and time of your shoot.

What would you say to the manager?

Do you think you would get another chance to film this vital scene?

Never leave things to chance – always communicate with your team and keep records of all communications. One very effective way of keeping records is to take minutes of all your team meetings. Figure 4.14 shows a template you could use for this.

Meeting Record Sheet

Date:	Time:	Place:

Present:

Apologies for absence:

Minutes:

1.

2.

3.

■ **Figure 4.14** *A template for taking minutes of team meetings. Each item discussed should be numbered so it is easy to refer to later.*

One way of making sure that everyone knows where they need to be and when they need to be there is to produce a call sheet for your location or studio shoot. As well as including details of date, time and location, a call sheet lists all the people and equipment required and information about transport and catering arrangements. It also provides a useful checklist of everything (and everyone) that is needed on the day.

Figure 4.15 shows the Media Productions call sheet for their video shoot at the waste recycling plant. You can see that they have included all the details needed for their crew and performers. You can adapt the call sheet shown to include all the details of your own video shoot.

 Remember

- You do not need to produce a finished product at this stage – use this as an opportunity to explore all the relevant pre-production techniques and develop your skills.

- You can work either individually or as a member of a team at this stage.

- You must keep your own records of your investigations into pre-production, production and post-production techniques.

- You must carefully store all the evidence you produce so that your teacher can use this as evidence for your assessment.

PRODUCTION SCHEDULE CALL SHEET	
Programme Title:	Recycling and YOU
Client:	Recycle.It
Writer:	James Subrami
Date:	15th July 2006

Crew	
Camera:	Robin Williams
Sound:	Rory Smith
Lighting:	Jill Sparks
Production Assistant:	Kate Azhami
Technicians:	John Brown/Bill Bailley
Transport:	Just Cars
Props:	Gary Musazawksi
Meeting at:	Sponforth Waste Recycling Plant, Sponforth, Kent Meet at front gates
Location Venue:	Interior of reclamation plant

CALL DATE:	**25th July 2005**
CALL TIME:	**6.30 am**
Transport:	Leaving from Media Productions offices at 6 a.m. prompt
INSTRUCTIONS:	Crew to wear sturdy boots or shoes

Actors:	Bill Foreman	Jane Smith	Extras: to be confirmed
Wardrobe:	Bill: 7 a.m.	Jane: 7.30 a.m.	Extras: from 8 a.m.
Make-up:	Bill: 7.30 a.m.	Jane: 8 a.m.	Extras: from 8.30 a.m.

Location catering:	Breakfast required for 30 people from 7 a.m. Lunch required for 30 people from 12.30 p.m. Evening meal for 10 people from 6 p.m. Coffee/tea available at all times Chuck Wagon caterers on site at all times
Properties:	1 large globe of the world – Day 1

■ **Figure 4.15** *An example of a call sheet used by Media Productions for the first day of the Recycling and YOU video shoot.*

Assessment task 1

Describe the pre-production stage of a video product and explain why it is so important.

Provide evidence that you have carried out a wide range of pre-production tasks and that you have experimented with the pre-production techniques covered in this section.

Assessment evidence

✔ Identify and undertake pre-production techniques.

✔✔ Demonstrate competence in pre-production techniques.

✔✔✔ Demonstrate a high level of ability in pre-production techniques.

Production

Production is the stage when you use equipment, materials and resources to actually make your video product. All the planning and paperwork you produced in the pre-production stage will help you to achieve this successfully.

You have now planned the production and you will have firm ideas about the content and look of your finished video product. The next step is to turn your ideas and planning into a reality. In this section we will be looking at the techniques and technology you will use to produce material for your media product.

Recording material

Before you can start to record the material for your video, you must ensure that you have the right equipment for the job.

- For video you will need: studio or location equipment – this might be cameras, tripods, lights and microphones.

- For any additional sound you will need: studio or location equipment – this might be cassette/minidisc recorders and microphones.

You need to consider how to record on location. Generally video on location is shot on one camera with the camera being moved around to look like two cameras have been used. If you use two cameras you will have many problems to overcome, such as balancing the colour of the different cameras. In sound recording it is a good idea to use just one recorder and one microphone to ensure that the quality of the sound recorded is consistent throughout.

In order to successfully record material on location or in a studio you must plan carefully to ensure everything runs smoothly. You should ensure that:

■ crew and cast are aware of the time and location of the recording

■ materials are available on the day of the recording

■ equipment has been booked in time

■ recording material – tapes, minidiscs, CD-ROMs, memory sticks, data disks, etc. – have been purchased or borrowed

■ batteries have been charged

■ props are available on the day.

Keeping a record

Once you start to shoot it is useful to keep a careful record of all recorded material. This job is normally undertaken by a production assistant, where one is available.

The record should indicate a brief description of the action and the timing of the action. It could also indicate whether there was more than one **take** (this means the actual footage recorded) of each shot and which take you will be using for the finished media product.

Many digital video cameras have 'time code' recording, in which the running time is included in the recording and can be displayed in the monitor. Audio recorders using cassettes have limited ability to log the takes on tape. However, digital recorders do allow you to log the start and finish of recordings.

Figure 4.16 shows the record (known as the 'shot material log') from the Media Productions location shoot. Next to each scene number, the production assistant has kept careful records of the number of takes for each scene, as well as a brief description of the scene and a comment to indicate whether each take is good or not.

These records will be invaluable when the producer goes into the edit suite – they could help her to save valuable time by only looking at the takes that have been marked as good.

Location considerations

In your pre-production work you will have looked at factors that might influence the material you record. Factors involving location work are sometimes the most problematic. You will have obtained permission to film at your chosen location, but you might need other permissions, too.

If you are filming in a public place and people appear in your recording, you should ask their permission before you can use the shots in which they appear in your product. You may need to produce release forms for people to sign, granting you permission to use the footage you have

SHOT MATERIAL LOG	
Programme Title:	Recycling and YOU
Client:	Recycle.It
Writer:	James Subrami
Producer:	Amanda Phillips
Director:	Barry Norman
Date:	2nd August 2006

SCENE NO.	TAKE NO.	TIME CODE IN	TIME CODE OUT	DESCRIPTION	COMMENTS
1	1	00.01	00.09	L/S of crane	good shot/clear sound
2	1	00.10	00.25	M/S of crane	slightly out of focus
	2	00.26	00.35	M/S of crane	good shot/good sound
3	1	00.37	00.55	M/S 3 men digging waste	good shot
4	1	00.57	01.10	C/U digging	good shot – poor sound
	2	0 0.16	01.25	C/U digging	good shot – sound better
5	1	01.26	01.59	M/S digging	good – waste site in back
6	1	01.60	02.45	interview with worker	OK – poor background
	2	02.46	03.59	interview with worker	better background
7	1	04.00	04.50	L/S workers	good
8	1	04.51	05.58	M/L/S workers	good – large crane in shot
9	1	04.59	07.35	interview with manager	good – sound good

■ **Figure 4.16** *The records kept by the production assistant on the location shoot at the waste recycling plant. The abbreviations C/U, L/S and M/S stand for types of shot. Look at the list on page 165 and see if you can work out what they mean.*

Case study

Gaining permissions

Media Productions were filming a sequence for a programme for young children. The scene required footage of children playing on the beach.

The producer initially planned to simply go to the south coast and find a location. She would then ask the parents' permission to film their children playing on the sand and jumping throught the waves. This could of course be problematic, as the parents might not have agreed for their children to be filmed or they might have wanted payment. Some parents might even have phoned the police if they were not sure what the film was to be used for and were suspicious.

After careful consideration, the producer decided to hire several child models and take them to the beach. Although this might seem like an expensive option, it meant that no money was wasted in turning up to the location and not being able to shoot. This option meant that all the expenses were already in the budget and the parents' permission could easily be obtained.

Media Productions still had to get permission to use the beach for filming and had to take care to avoid filming other people who were using the beach.

taken of them. You may also need to pay a fee. For example, there may be a busker playing in the background of your shot. Would you pay him a fee for his performance and what about the copyright of the music he was playing?

When recording on location, make sure that you have all the angles covered. If you prepare a release form in advance and take a few copies along to your location recording, it will help ensure that everyone who appears in your project has agreed to it. You could include a brief description of the programme you are making so that the people concerned understand what it is they are appearing in.

Producing material

By now you have identified appropriate recording equipment, booked out the equipment and ensured that the batteries are charged, purchased sufficient recording material and made sure that everyone knows where to go and at what time, as well as ensuring a safe working environment and safe working practices.

You now need to ensure that the material you record is of the highest possible standard, and this section deals with production techniques.

Using cameras

One of the first decisions you will have to make is which camera to use. You will probably have a camcorder available in your school or college. A camcorder is a camera and recorder combined. You may also have the use of a television studio to record your video programme. You must get used to using the camera and be able to use all of the controls.

■ **Figure 4.17** *You need to know how to use all of the controls of your chosen camera.*

Camcorders are generally lightweight and are ideal for location recording. You will need support for your camera – using a tripod will ensure that you get a steady shot. When working in a studio, the studio camera might be heavy as it will have a large viewfinder attached. You will therefore need to use a tripod or other stabilising system that also allows you to move the camera across the studio floor in a smooth operation. In a studio-based recording you may want to use more than one camera. In this case, you will have to use a vision mixer to generate a picture from the cameras and to be able to switch between them.

■ **Figure 4.18** *A television studio with a multiple camera set-up.*

Shooting techniques

When shooting video, it is important to remember that the image you see in the viewfinder is the image that is being recorded. You will need to make sure that the image is in the correct position in the viewfinder.

There are a number of basic visual codes you will need to use when you plan and record your video material.

Camera angle: The position of the camera is very important to the viewer. If it is positioned at a low angle then the subject appears to dominate the scene. If, however, the camera is positioned at a high angle then the subject appears to be weaker or smaller.

Camera movement: When the camera moves with the subject, known as a tracking shot, an intimate feel is created, almost as though the viewer is part of the action. Moving from a wide-angle shot to a close-up directs the viewer's attention to a particular point. Generally, camera movements are made slowly to avoid jarring the viewer.

Theory into practice

Try recording a small scene on video and zoom the camera in and out quickly. Try panning the camera from right to left and back again quickly.

Sit down with some of your colleagues and try to watch the video. How does it make you feel?

There are several types of camera movements:

- the camera pans from left to right and back again
- the camera tracks the action
- the camera tilts up and down from a fixed position
- the camera is raised above the subject, on a jib, for an overhead view
- the camera is hand-held.

It is standard practice in film and television production to move the camera rather than alter the zoom. If you use your camera on full zoom (close-up), then every shake or wobble is exaggerated. If you use an ordinary lens setting and move the camera in, you can avoid the shakes and also retain a good depth of field.

Depth of field: This refers to subjects in the picture that are in focus. Using a wide-angle lens you can normally achieve a good depth of field and all the subjects in both the background and foreground are in focus. A telephoto or long lens will magnify the image into the frame but this results in a poor depth of field. The image in the foreground may be sharp but the detail in the background will be blurred and fuzzy. However, this technique can be used to good effect when you want the subject in the foreground to be emphasised.

Framing: The image in the viewfinder is important to the viewer whether it is a still or moving image. The position of the subject within the frame can make the scene look interesting or boring.

There is a simple technique called the 'rule of thirds' that breaks up the frame into three equal horizontal and vertical bands. You compose the shot so that the main subjects sit on these lines or where they cross (Figure 4.19). This rule can be broken intentionally or by necessity, but if you try this technique, eventually you will begin to use it naturally when composing your shots.

Camera shots: There are a variety of camera shots that you could use when making your programme, as shown in Figure 4.20.

Theory into practice

Take a piece of black cardboard and cut a rectangular aperture in the centre of it with the proportions 5:4 (5 units long by 4 units high). Make sure that you have enough card left around the aperture to block out any extraneous light.

Use the card to view the room you are working in.

What does the limitation of the aperture show you about framing for a standard television screen?

What will you have to be aware of when recording your video?

Move close into a subject and then move out for a wide-angle shot.

Theory into practice

Now repeat the exercise, but this time use the proportions 6:9. These are the proportions of a widescreen television.

How much more can you see now?

What are the implications for filming in widescreen?

■ **Figure 4.19** *Using the 'rule of thirds' helps to create a pleasing composition.*

Extreme wide shot (EWS). This type of shot shows as much of the scene or location as possible and is often used as an establishing shot.

Wide shot (WS) or **Long shot (LS).** Here the subject is shot from a distance so that all of the subject can be seen as well as the location that they are in.

Mid-shot (MS). Here only about half of the subject is seen and you can see less of the surroundings.

Close-up (CU). With this type of shot, a part of the subject such as the head fills the whole frame and very little, if any, of the surroundings can be seen.

Extreme close-up (ECU). A very close shot of the subject, or some part of them, that is often used for dramatic effect.

Two-shot. A shot of two people framed like a mid-shot.

Over-the-shoulder shot (OSS). This is a shot of a subject taken from just behind a person who is looking at that subject. This shot helps to establish the positions of each person and is used a lot in interviews.

Point-of-view shot (POV). This is a shot that shows what a character is seeing, as if you are looking through their eyes.

■ **Figure 4.20** *Eight commonly used types of camera shot.*

Lighting

If you are using a studio or shooting a scene in poor daylight you will need some form of extra light. This might be:

- a hand-held spotlight – sometimes called a 'sun gun' or 'hand basher'
- a set of portable lights – usually three or four lamps on stands
- overhead lamps on a studio track system – these can be moved around the room to suit the set being used
- a set of filters or 'gels' – these are used to change the colour **temperature** of the light source.

What does it mean?

Colour temperature *is measured in degrees Kelvin. It refers to the colour of the light source and is indicated by the following scale:*

Lighting	Approximate temperature in degrees Kelvin (K)
Candle	1,800 K
Indoor tungsten	3,000 K
Indoor fluorescent	4,000 K
Outdoor sunlight	5,500 K
Outdoor shade	7,500 K

The lower the Kelvin rating, the 'warmer' or more yellow the light. The higher the rating, the 'cooler' or more blue the light.

Colour temperature might seem quite complicated at first, but you need to know about it, as the camera you will be using will have a white balance control. This allows the camera to decide which is the correct colour to record based on the Kelvin scale.

The lighting of a scene, whether natural or artificial, can add or detract from a subject. Dramatic lighting can give real depth to a subject and soft lighting can give a sympathetic feel.

Studio lights tend to be secured to a lighting rig attached to the ceiling or walls of the studio. On location you may be able to use a set of portable lights. The types of lights you may use are:

Broad – a light that gives a very wide light spread.

Spot – a light that gives an intense pool of light that can be varied.

Redhead – a multi-purpose light that gives off around 800 watts of light – this light can normally be varied from spot to broad.

Blonde – a multi-purpose light that gives off around 2000 watts of light.

Did you know

Dramatic lighting is used to good effect in many feature films. For example, in a scene from Close Encounters of the Third Kind *(Steven Spielberg,1977) a young boy finds his toys coming to life, and is then surrounded by shafts of bright light from a spaceship.*

Hand basher – a small portable light used to infill small areas that need some light – generally used by news crews when filming interviews.

Using reflectors
You can control light without using additional lamps by using reflectors to alter the lighting for your video. Reflected light is softer (more diffuse) than direct light, particularly if the reflecting surface is slightly textured. It will reduce harsh shadows from a direct light source.

You can use sheets of polystyrene from a DIY store to make very adaptable and lightweight reflectors. These will create a soft fill light (due to the textured surface, which scatters the reflected light in different directions). Soft light is more flattering as it flattens imperfections in skin, and generally smoothes out a surface.

A smooth reflective surface (e.g. aluminium foil glued to a sheet of cardboard) creates a harder, more focused reflection. Coloured reflectors will add a colour cast to the scene. You can use them to create special effects.

Reflectors need to be held in position, either by a stand or a pair of hands.

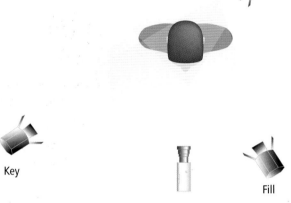

■ **Figure 4.21** *A three-point lighting set-up.*

Did you know?

Three-point lighting

There are many lighting set-ups for a variety of recording techniques. The most commonly used set-up in video production is three-point lighting (Figure 4.21).

- *The main light, or key light, is positioned slightly above and to one side of the camera. This is normally a spotlight to give a hard lighting effect.*
- *A broad light, or fill light, is positioned on the opposite side of the camera to light the shadow areas.*
- *A back light is placed behind the subject and angled down to bring the subject forward from the background. Extra broads can also be used to light the background area.*

This is a good set-up for interviews.

Gels and filters
Sometimes you have to change the colour of the light being emitted from lamps. To do this you can use lighting 'gels' or filters. These come in a wide variety of colours and are used to control the colour of the lights.

For example, on location it can be very hard to control the lighting as daylight can be so variable. At different times of the day, from sunrise to sunset, the colour of daylight can change. Light coming in through a window has a daylight (bluish) tint while lamps have an orange tint. To make the two lights match, you could place a piece of blue gel over the lamp to match the daylight blue coming through the window.

Theory into practice

Find as many colour filters as you can. These may be simple filters, such as transparent sweet wrappers, or actual lighting gels.

Look at the world through these filters and describe the atmosphere they create. For example, does red give you a warm world and does blue give you a cold world?

Sound

No video programme would be complete without sound, unless you are deliberately creating a silent film! Sound can enhance a production or it can detract from it if the sound quality is poor. The marriage between sound and vision should be so balanced that neither element should overtake the other. There are three basic sound codes:

Music – an important part of moving image products since the early days of cinema, when musical accompaniment was played by a pianist or an orchestra. Music can add an extra dimension to your programme. Horror films are a prime example of the use of atmospheric music. The ferocity of the music can enhance the horror or give a sense of impending doom.

Sound effects – sound is not normally recorded as part of the programme but is added at the post-production stage to enhance the viewers' perception of what is happening on screen. Sometimes sound effects are recorded as 'buzz tracks' or 'wild tracks'. They might be the natural sounds of the interior of a building or traffic noise. These effects can also be purchased on CD or on the Internet but it is much more fun to create your own.

Theory into practice

Think about some of the films you have seen.

Make a list of at least three types of films that use music sound tracks.

For each film type try to list the ways in which music has been used to create a sense of atmosphere.

Theory into practice

It is interesting to simply close your eyes and listen to the sounds around you. Why not try this in the classroom or outside in the car park?

Take a notepad and make a list of all the sounds you can hear.

Listen carefully for the background sounds that are not always obvious to the human ear but could be picked up by a sensitive microphone.

Case study

Sound considerations

Media Productions had to film some of their programme at a very noisy waste recycling plant. They knew that there would be problems when interviewing personnel on site. They arranged with the management to switch off all the site machinery while they filmed the interviews and then recorded some wild track sounds of the machinery running. They were able to mix the two sounds together at the post production stage.

- What would have been the result if Media Productions had simply interviewed people in front of machinery with no sound effects added? Would it have sounded strange to have no sounds in the background?

- What do you think the interview would have been like if they had not switched off the noisy machinery?

Dialogue – this can be delivered by an actor on screen or off camera as a voiceover. In the early days of film there was no dialogue as the technology to record it and play it back in sync (where the words match the mouth as it opens and closes) did not yet exist. When you record on video you generally record the sound at the same time as part of the video signal. This means that your recording should never be out of sync.

Theory into practice

Record a scene from three different film genres, e.g. a comedy, a horror film and a science fiction film. Include music in your productions.

Play each one in turn to an audence that cannot see the screen and ask them if they can identify the genre from the music.

Remember

- You do not need to produce a finished product at this stage – use this as an opportunity to explore all the relevant production techniques and develop your skills.

Assessment task 2

Describe what the production stage of a video product involves and what the key tasks are.

Provide evidence that you have carried out a wide range of production tasks and produced examples of the paperwork.

Provide evidence that you have experimented with the production techniques covered in this section, including camera work, sound and lighting techniques.

Assessment evidence

✔ Identify and undertake production techniques.

✔✔ Demonstrate competence in production techniques.

✔✔✔ Demonstrate a high level of ability in production techniques.

Post-production

In this section you will consider the post-production process involving the various techniques used to manipulate and amend your original video material. The post-production process allows for flexibility when creating video products from original recorded material. It provides an opportunity to correct or improve the original material to make a finished product. At this stage you can:

- join together sections of video footage in the correct order
- correct errors in recording by omitting them from the finished product
- choose to use alternative shots from the ones you originally thought would be appropriate
- shorten sequences that are uninteresting or repetitive
- control the overall length of the finished product by shortening or lengthening individual scenes or adding more information
- introduce visual special effects and sound effects
- change the colour of images and manipulate them to alter their meaning.

Safe storage

It is very important to keep your recorded material safe. You will need to access this material throughout the editing process so all tapes, memory cards and files should be kept in a safe place. You must always do the following to ensure that you do not lose any of your hard work.

- Label the source material clearly with programme title, date recorded, location/studio, tape/disk/card number.

- If the material has been transferred to a hard drive you must have a clearly labelled folder on the drive where all the source material has been stored and a backup alternative in place.

- Keep the tapes and files in a safe place.

- Ensure that the source material cannot be recorded over by removing the recording tab or making the file 'read only'.

Losing your source material will result in you having to re-record all your material. It may be impossible to recreate some of the original material and it will certainly put you behind your planned deadlines.

Use a material storage log to keep a record of where you have stored all the material for your video. See Figure 4.23 for an example. Keep a backup of all files stored on a computer hard drive – on a CD-ROM for example.

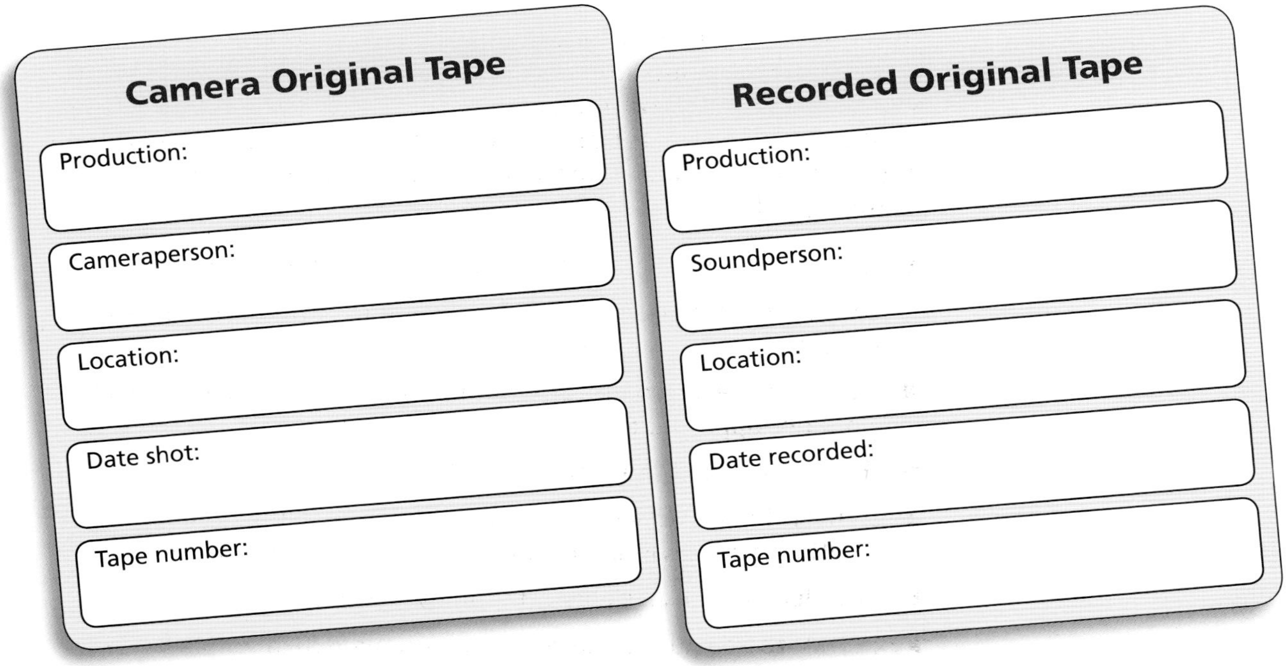

Camera Original Tape

Production:

Cameraperson:

Location:

Date shot:

Tape number:

Recorded Original Tape

Production:

Soundperson:

Location:

Date recorded:

Tape number:

■ **Figure 4.22** *Labels for all your video and audio materials will clearly identify your recorded materials. These could be physical labels for tapes or disks or descriptions attached to computer files.*

MATERIAL STORAGE LOG	
Programme Title:	Recycling and YOU
Client:	Recycle.It
Writer:	James Subrami
Producer:	Amanda Phillips
Director:	Barry Norman
Date:	8th August 2006

Tape number	Located
1	Tape storage locker – Edit Suite 1
2	Tape storage locker – Edit Suite 1
3	Tape storage locker – Edit Suite 1

Computer files	
Graphic designs for titles	Hard drive – folder: Recycle.It / file: titles
Graphic designs for credits	Hard drive – folder: Recycle.It / file: credits
Music tracks	Hard drive – folder: Recycle.It / music
Voiceover	Hard drive – folder: Recycle.It / voiceover
Backup files	CD-ROM labelled Recycle.It stored in filing cabinet

■ **Figure 4.23** *Some of the material for the Recycling and YOU programme is stored in lockers and some as computer files. You can adapt this log for your own product.*

Editing your source material

The editing process involves reviewing all the material you have created and putting together the pieces you will be using in the final product. Your shot material log will be invaluable in this process, as it will allow you to locate the relevant material quickly and easily. (Look at the shot material log shown in Figure 4.16 for an example.)

You should make sure that all your materials are logged in a similar way, including any audio material you have recorded for sound effects and background sound and any photographic images you have taken to use in the programme or on the cover of the DVD box.

It is advisable to use a consistent style of logging whatever the product you have chosen to make. The log should include:

- scene/take/image no.
- time code, where appropriate
- brief description
- comments (including whether it is a good or bad shot).

If you did not make a detailed log at the time of the video shoot, now is the time to do it. In any case, you will want to have a look at all your recorded material. It is always interesting to go back and look at material you shot days or even weeks earlier. You may see or hear things you had forgotten and this can be useful when starting the editing process. It may give you new ideas about the best way of putting the different elements of your product together.

■ **Figure 4.24** *Your shot material log will be invaluable in the editing process as it includes all the details you need about each scene you have recorded.*

Video editing

There are various ways in which you can shape your video product during the editing process.

- You may want to change the order of the visual material from the camera original material. Perhaps you want to make the sequence more logical or remove poor footage.

- You may need to edit the sound you recorded on location or in the studio, perhaps to take out unwanted passages or instructions from the director.

- You may wish to add a title at the front of the product or credits at the end.

- Maybe you are going to add graphics, such as animations or pictures. The editing process will allow you to make room in your product for these to be added.

- You might need to correct the colour of your images or the level of your sound recording.

In video, the initial editing process is called the **off-line edit**. This process involves editing together the sequences and making a version that can be viewed by colleagues and the client so that they can suggest changes. The final editing process is called the **on-line edit** and this is where the final effects and finishing details are included.

Paper edit

It is good practice to prepare for editing by undertaking a **paper edit** exercise. This will give you a clear picture of the shape, size and form of your video product. It will also save you time in the editing suite.

Figure 4.25 shows the paper edit produced by Media Productions for one section of the Recycling and YOU programme. You can see how this has been developed from their shot material log sheet from the location shoot – see Figure 4.16. The best takes have been selected based on the comments recorded at the time of the shoot. The Effect column has been added to show how the scenes link together, and the type of sound to be used with each scene has been listed in the final column. You can see how the paper edit can be done quite easily by using details from the shot material log sheet and amending information as necessary.

Reviewing your editing

Once you have completed the initial edit of your video product, you should show the resulting **rough cut** to your client and a sample of your target audience. It is important that you understand that even at this stage you can still make changes to your product if it does not meet the needs of your client or audience.

Many major feature films have to be re-edited because the feedback from an invited audience has been negative. Imagine that you have spent several millions of pounds on making a film only to find that audiences stay away because they cannot understand the film or because the editing has left them confused. It is much better to get their comments before release when there is still time to make some changes.

One way of getting feedback from your client and target audience is to hold a focus group in which you show all or part of the product in order to get valuable feedback. Do not be offended or discouraged if people suggest changes – it is all part of the process of producing a successful media product that is fit for purpose and popular with its audience.

It is a good idea to develop a questionnaire to use in the focus group that allows your participants to review your product in an appropriate way. You may want them to focus on certain aspects of the product. A questionnaire is useful because it provides you with some written feedback that you can analyse afterwards and will help you to identify any changes you need to make.

You might like your focus group to consider the following aspects:

- the length of the product
- the quality of the visual and sound elements in the product
- how well the product gets the storyline across
- consistency of style
- the suitability of the product for the target audience.

Remember

It will not help you if you choose people to review the product who would not want to offend you. You must include a cross-section of people from your target audience.

media
PRODUCTIONS

PAPER EDIT	
Programme Title:	Recycling and YOU
Client:	Recycle.It
Writer:	James Subrami
Producer:	Amanda Phillips
Director:	Barry Norman
Date:	9th August 2006

TAPE	SCENE NO.	TIME CODE IN	TIME CODE OUT	DESCRIPTION	EFFECT	SOUND
2	1	00.01	00.09	L/S of crane	fade in and cut to	atmos
2	2	00.26	00.35	M/S of crane	fade to	atmos
2	3	00.37	00.55	M/S 3 men digging waste	cut to	atmos
2	4	00.16	01.25	C/U digging	cut to	atmos
2	5	01.26	01.59	M/S digging	cut to	atmos
2	6	02.46	03.59	interview with worker	cut to caption (name)	live interview
2	7	04.00	04.50	L/S workers	fade to	atmos & music
2	8	04.51	05.48	M/L/S workers	fade to	atmos & music
2	9	05.49	07.35	interview with manager	fade out caption (name)	live interview

■ **Figure 4.25** *The paper edit is closely based on the shot material log shown in Figure 4.16.*

Assessment task 3

Describe what is involved in the post-production stage of a video product and what the key tasks are.

Provide evidence that you have carried out a wide range of post-production tasks and produced examples of the paperwork.

Provide evidence that you have experimented with a variety of editing techniques.

Assessment evidence

✔ Identify and undertake post-production techniques.

✔✔ Demonstrate competence in post-production techniques.

✔✔✔ Demonstrate a high level of ability in post-production techniques.

4.2 Contributing to each stage of the creation of a video product

We have already looked in detail at the techniques and paperwork involved in creating a video product, from planning your product in the pre-production stage, through recording in the production stage, to editing and getting feedback during post-production.

In this section, you will actually create a complete video product, working as part of a production team. Whether your role is producer, camera operator, sound recordist, editor or director – or a combination of two or more roles – you will have an important contribution to make to your team's product.

Ideas

You will need to produce your own ideas for a video production and then present your ideas to your team. Together with your team, you will choose the idea that will be taken forward for production – this might be one of your ideas or somebody else's.

Pre-production process

As part of the team you will have to prepare the pre-production documentation needed for your video product. It is advisable for you to keep copies of any pre-production paperwork you produce and to clearly label all your own paperwork with your name.

You must take an active part in the planning of the video product. Try to make a positive contribution to the team. Use the sample pre-production paperwork we looked at in section 4.1 to make your own documentation.

Checklist of pre-production documents:

- Proposal
- Treatment
- Production schedule
- Storyboard
- Shooting script
- Location reconnaissance record
- Risk assessment
- Budget

Production process

You must play an active part in the production process of your team. Make sure you keep a record of all your contributions to the work of your team, including:

- all the paperwork that you produce
- all the creative decisions that you have made
- the responsibilities that you have within the team
- any extra responsibilities you have taken on, for example, if one of your team is absent or needs help.

In section 4.3 we will be looking at some more ways of monitoring and reviewing your production work – such as using a production diary (see page 181). Try to use these techniques to record your own production process.

Checklist of production documents:

- Call sheets
- Shot material log
- Production diary

Post-production process

The post-production process involves editing the material you have recorded. At this stage, you will be able to set the timing and pace of the finished video product by how you edit the scenes together. Post-production also involves adding extra material, changing the order of the material and adding sound and graphics.

You should undertake the post-production work as a team, making sure that you keep a record of all the positive and significant contributions that you make to the post-production process.

Checklist of post-production documents:

- Storage labels
- Paper edit
- Questionnaire (for focus group)

What does it mean?

Aesthetic – *refers to something that is beautiful – so contributing to the aesthetic aspects of a video product means helping to make it look good*
Technical – *relating to the use of equipment and the specialist practical skills involved in an activity*

Assessment task 4

Work with your team to produce a finished video product.

1 *Produce an idea for a video product.*
2 *Meet with your group and decide which idea will be most suitable for your group to make.*
3 *Prepare your own proposal for the chosen idea and pitch this to your teacher or client.*
4 *Produce your own treatment for the chosen project.*
5 *Make plans for your product, including preparing all the pre-production documentation you will need for the project.*
6 *Work with your team mates to record the material for your project.*
7 *Edit your product and present it to your client and a sample of your target audience.*

Assessment evidence

✔ Contribute to each stage of the creation of a finished video product.

✔✔ Provide evidence of your positive contributions to the **technical** and **aesthetic** aspects of the finished video product.

✔✔✔ Provide evidence that you have made significant contributions to the technical and aesthetic aspects of the finished video product.

Remember

■ For this section of the unit you will need to work on a complete video project as part of a team.

■ You must keep your own records of your contribution to pre-production, production and post-production processes.

■ You must provide evidence that you have played a significant part in the pre-production, production and post-production stages within your team.

■ You must carefully store all the evidence you produce so that your teacher can use this as evidence for your assessment.

4.3 Reviewing your video production work

Keeping a log or diary

You should keep a comprehensive diary or log of the work you have undertaken during the pre-production, production and post-production phases of your work. This diary or log will help you to reflect on the work that you did and the help you had from colleagues. The following is a list of the points you could cover in your diary:

- how you thought of your idea
- how you developed the idea into a proposal
- how the proposal developed into a treatment
- a breakdown of the primary and secondary research methods used
- notes of meetings with team members
- notes on the way that your team members worked
- notes on the work you undertook for others
- ongoing notes of the skills you are developing
- reflections on the quality of your work
- an analysis of your video product as compared to a professionally produced product of a similar nature
- your understanding of the fitness for purpose of your product
- an analysis of how well your media product meets the client's brief and audience needs.

 Case study

Keeping a production diary

The producers at Media Productions always keep a comprehensive diary of their work. This helps them when they are reviewing the finished product with their client and provides evidence should any disagreements arise.

The producer's diary was very helpful on one occasion when the client decided, at the last minute, that they did not like a particular sequence in the video. They tried to claim that they had not given approval for this scene to be included.

The producer was able to find the date and time of a discussion with the client when the content of this scene was agreed. Of course, if the client wants a scene to be deleted then that is fine, but it is good to be able to prove that the scene has been agreed in the first place.

You might choose to keep a written diary or to use an appropriate format such as a PowerPoint presentation or a video or audio evaluation. Whichever method you use for your diary or log, you should use appropriate media language.

PRODUCTION DIARY	
Name:	Amanda Phillips (Producer)
Production:	Recycling and YOU

Date	Action Taken
17th July	Met with client to discuss the location shoot at Sponforth Waste Recycling Plant (SWRP). Client agreed to contact SWRP to clear the location shoot.
19th July	Met with cameraperson to discuss issues with camera safety when working on waste recycling sites. Agreed that the camera must be protected against waste material and that this was the responsibility of the camera crew.
23rd July	Met with the director to discuss the location shoots. There was agreement on the length of time required for each location shoot – this was set at one day for each location.
30th July	Met with camera crew to brief them on the locations we will be using. Discussed the health and safety hazards when working on a waste recycling site. Each member of the crew took a risk assessment document and agreed to read and follow the instructions on the form.
2nd August	Location day at SWRP – weather good. Camera crew arrived thirty minutes late at the location. The management at SWRP were expecting us but were unsure just what we were doing. Contacted client to ask them to confirm with SWRP the nature of location shoot and what the footage would be used for. This was carried out and confirmed by SWRP senior management.

■ **Figure 4.26** *In your production diary it is important to keep a record of all the discussions that you have had regarding the production, and what decisions were taken.*

Figure 4.26 on the previous page shows an extract from the production diary of Amanda Phillips, the director of the Recyling and YOU video for Recycle.It. This extract shows the entries she made regarding the location shoot at Sponforth Waste Recycling Plant.

■ **Figure 4.27** *Making time to keep a production diary is important – even when you are very busy with other tasks involved in your production.*

Reviewing your video product

As part of your product evaluation, try to get a number of people to see and comment on the finished product. In the case of the Recycle.It programme, it would be a good idea to get some 11–14 year olds to comment on the effectiveness of the product for the target audience. You should also get feedback from your client, in this case it may be your teacher, and ask them to comment on its effectiveness.

If you want to get a wider range of feedback, consider making multiple copies of your video product and giving or sending it to people outside your school. This might include finding a group of 11–14 year olds from another school who could give you some good and impartial feedback. If you send your product in the post, include a stamped addressed envelope to make sure they return it to you.

Include a questionnaire with your product so that the audience can provide structured feedback to inform your evaluation. Put some thought into the design of your questionnaire. Providing options with tick boxes makes it much easier for people to respond than asking them to write answers to each question. However, you may want to include some questions that require short written answers in order to gain more detailed feedback. It is good practice to have a mixture of the two question types in the same questionnaire. For more information on writing questionnaires, see Unit 2, pages 69–75.

Do not be disheartened by any negative views of your work. See them as a pointer to doing better next time. You could always use their comments to re-edit the programme or even re-record some of the material.

It can also be useful to sit down with an audience after a viewing of your product and ask for their immediate responses. You could record their views on video or audio and transcribe them (write or type them out) later. Some people will be more forthcoming in a face-to-face situation than in a written questionnaire.

What next?

Once you have obtained sufficient feedback, you will need to analyse and record this information in a way that gives a representative view of what the audience thinks of your video product.

Maybe the video is too short or too long, the sound might be indistinct or the pictures might be blurred. All of these things can be corrected if you know about them.

Did you know?

It is interesting to note that the makers of feature films go to great lengths to obtain audience feedback – and the films often have to be edited as a result.

In one of the Star Trek films, Captain Kirk was shown dying a horrible death after an alien attack. The initial reviews showed that the audience reacted very badly to this scene, so the film makers decided to re-shoot the whole scene, this time showing Captain Kirk returning to fight alongside the new captain, Jean-Luc Picard.

Imagine the cost of doing this! But if the film was to be a success it was essential that the audience and film critics would be happy.

You won't have to go to such great expense to make changes to your video, but wouldn't it be really good if as many people as possible liked your finished product.

Evaluating your work

As the final stage of your project, you will need to carry out a comprehensive evaluation of your video production work. In order to do this try to answer the following questions.

- What did I do?
- What skills did I learn?
- What went wrong?
- What went right?
- What would I do if I could start again?

Remember

- Try to sell yourself in your evaluation. If you have done really good work, then say so. If you had problems, remember to say how you overcame them.

- There is more than one way of recording your evaluation. You could use:
  - a video recording of your thoughts and comments
  - an audio recording
  - a PowerPoint presentation
  - a discussion with your teacher – make sure you record this conversation, perhaps in written or audio form

- Whatever format you use, make sure you keep your review for assessment and store it safely.

Assessment task 5

Produce a review of your video production work. Use the following points and questions to help you.

1 *Check that the product matches the intentions you set out in your proposal and treatment.*
2 *Is the product appropriate for the audience?*
3 *What about the technical qualities of your work?*
4 *How did you work with your team?*
5 *How well did you manage your time?*
6 *How was your work received by the client and/or audience?*
7 *Did you have to make any changes to your work?*

Assessment evidence

✔ Describe clearly the work that you did, giving examples of what went wrong, what went right and what you would do if you had the opportunity to work on this project again.

✔✔ Discuss your own video production work in detail, giving a range of relevant examples of the factors involved in producing your video.

✔✔✔ Explain clearly the work that you did, giving a range of relevant examples and using correct technical language.

Remember

- Your review must be your own work.

- Try to use correct technical language in your review.

- Give examples of how you completed your work.

- Give examples of what the audience or client thought of your work.

- Explain how you worked with your team. Did you take a leading role? Did you have to undertake other team members' roles?

- What have you learnt from doing this work?

- What would you like to do now?

- How could you further develop your skills in video production?

5 Audio Production

Introduction

This unit is all about production in the audio sectors of the media industry. You will learn about the kinds of audio product that are made, who they are made for and how they are made. Then you will learn a number of skills in audio production and go on to make your own audio product. Finally, you will review your work, deciding what went well and how you could have improved your final product by doing things differently.

Learning outcomes

On completion of this unit you should:

- know about broadcast and non-broadcast audio products and audio formats
- understand audio recording and digital editing technology and techniques
- be able to produce an audio product
- be able to review audio production work.

5.1 Broadcast and non-broadcast audio products and audio formats

The audio sector within the media industry comprises two main branches: broadcast and non-broadcast audio.

You need to describe and discuss a number of different audio products and the different formats they use. You do not need to study each one in great detail, but a good overview is essential and some in-depth knowledge of a few products and formats will help you achieve a better grade. Three assessment tasks will help you present your work in the correct way.

Broadcast audio

Most broadcast audio is on the radio. It is now over 100 years since the very first radio programme was broadcast, by a Canadian called Reginald Fessenden on Christmas Eve 1906. Even though there are many more forms of home entertainment available now than at the beginning of the twentieth century, radio listening is as popular as it has ever been. This is partly because there are more kinds of radio programme than ever before, and partly because there are many more ways of listening to the radio.

Today, you can listen to radio in many different ways:

- using analogue radio receivers (FM and AM)
- using digital radio receivers (DAB and DRM)
- through digital television platforms (Sky and Freeview)
- over the Internet (live streams and podcasts).

 Theory into practice

If you visit RAJAR's website, you can see the latest audience figures. At the time of writing this book, FM was still by far the most popular way of listening to the radio.

You could call television sound 'broadcast audio' as well, but Unit 4 covers video production, including sound, and so this unit concentrates on products that are intended just to be listened to. **Convergence** means that different parts of the media industry are beginning to seem like each other, and many radio stations now broadcast text and pictures as well as their websites. Here we are going to concentrate on radio programmes, though, because simply making radio can be both enjoyable and rewarding – as can listening to the radio.

Form and genre

Radio programmes can be either live or recorded. Sometimes they are recorded in such a way as to *sound* like they are live. You cannot pre-record a news bulletin much before it is broadcast, because after a short while it will no longer be the latest news. Audiences would get used to hearing the latest news on rival radio stations and they would quickly decide that those other stations were better to listen to for news and information. But there are many radio genres that can be pre-recorded without the audience's enjoyment being affected – in fact, they might never realise that they are listening to a recording.

These radio genres are usually broadcast live:

- news bulletins
- weather forecasts
- traffic and travel reports
- phone-ins
- magazine programmes
- commentaries
- music sequences.

Commentaries tend to be sporting events, such as football, cricket or tennis, but any important event can be described on radio so that listeners can hear for themselves what is going on. Music sequences are music programmes, usually featuring presenters who play songs, do live links between them and introduce other items, such as competitions, at regular fixed points in the programme. Sequence programmes can be pre-recorded 'as-live' – and some are even automated with the links being recorded separately from the music. Playout software on a computer literally plays out the links, songs and jingles in the correct order at the correct times, usually without anyone knowing the difference.

These radio genres are usually recorded:

- drama
- documentary
- commercials.

Drama and documentary programmes are usually recorded because of the large number of different voices, music and sound effects used in them. In post-production they can be edited to run much more smoothly than if they were performed live.

There are many other radio genres which can either be recorded or broadcast live, such as round-table discussion programmes, panel games,

■ **Figure 5.1** *Many people listen avidly to commentaries on the radio, even though they cannot see for themselves what is happening.*

quizzes, comedy and light entertainment. We will concentrate on some of the most popular ones – ones you will find it most practical to produce yourself later in this unit.

Theory into practice

Use a good listings magazine, such as the *Radio Times*, to identify as many different genres of radio programme as you can. You could also use websites, such as www.bbc.co.uk. Explain in class how you can tell the different genres apart.

News bulletins

This genre is found on almost all radio stations and most stations broadcast news bulletins 'on the hour'. They can range from around one minute on a music station, such as Radio 1, Kiss or Galaxy, to five or ten minutes on a talk station, such as Radio 4. The main purpose of the bulletin is to inform: it is meant to provide listeners with a quick, regular update on the news – which may well have changed in whole or in part since the last bulletin. It is the job of the bulletin editor to freshen the material whenever possible, so people listening for longer periods do not get bored by hearing the same bulletin again and again.

Case study

Rob Harris

Rob has been a reporter on the County Sound Radio Network since 1995. His nine-hour shift begins at 5 a.m. and he is responsible for compiling and reading news bulletins until early afternoon. On opening up the newsdesk he will check with the local emergency services in case a story has broken overnight. He will read through national stories sent to County Sound by Independent Radio News in London and decide whether there are any local angles to them that might be worth following.

Then he will begin to put the stories in order of importance for the early morning listeners to the

breakfast show, which is about to begin. Some of the local news copy (**scripts**) will have been written for him the evening before, by the evening news staff. There may be audio with them in the form of voiced reports (**voicers**) or short packages (**wraps**).

Each news item is identified by its **catch** or **catchline** – an item about a dangerous building collapsing on children playing inside would probably be given the catchline BUILDING. A second item about the same story – for instance, reactions from a parent – would be called BUILDING 2.

After reading the first bulletin of the day, Rob Harris receives a call from the traffic news spotter-plane Sky Eagle One. A chemical tanker has overturned on the A31 and traffic is building up in both directions. A check call to the police reveals that the spillage is toxic and the area is going to have to be evacuated. Rob alerts the studio and reads a brief newsflash on air, giving the details he has. The incident is to become the lead story in the station's bulletins for the rest of

■ *Rob Harris at the County Sound newsdesk.*

CRIMINALS
An urgent inquiry's been launched by the Home Secretary after revelations tabs haven't been kept on hundreds of serious criminals convicted abroad.
John Reid says it will be completed within six weeks.
Shadow Home Secretary David Davis says the buck must stop with Mr Reid:
[CLIP]
***

CHOPPER SNAP
Two helicopters have collided at an RAF base in Shropshire,
We'll bring you more through the afternoon
***

MOLLY
A girl at the centre of an international tug-of-love insists she won't go back to Scotland.

Misbah Rana's mother's ending her custody battle – in return for regular access.
Her daughter, who's also known as Molly Campbell, is likely to stay in Pakistan with her father.
***

Bogus 1
It's a message police around the country try to push all year round, but the problem repeatedly causes distress to the elderly.
Bogus callers continue to succeed in tricking their way into homes, and Surrey Police have launched a new poster campaign in the hope of halting the crime.
We spoke with Detective Chief Inspector Neville Blackwood.
[CLIP]
***

WEATHER

■ *The running order for the 06:00 bulletin.*

Case study continued

the day, as it develops and different reactions come in – from police, the hospital, the fire brigade and the public. Luckily another reporter arrives at 06.15 and she takes over reporting the story, while a third reporter is sent to the scene to send back live audio using the radio car.

At 09.15 Rob Harris attends an editorial meeting with the rest of the duty news staff. The station receives calls and press releases from different sorts of organisations wanting publicity. These include clubs and societies, companies and pressure groups. At the meeting decisions are

made about which upcoming stories to cover, and plans may be made to send a reporter to an event or to do a phone interview.

Different people and organisations often like to respond to news items that affect them, too. Broadcast journalists are expected to be unbiased in the way they report news and what they cover – especially with politics. Sometimes groups and individuals feel their point of view or their particular cause has been under-represented, or not covered at all. Any story in any bulletin may raise issues of representation.

This is a typical hour in Rob's day:

07:15 Make check calls to all local emergency services

07:25 Write brief news headlines

07:30 Read headlines and sport on air

07:35 Follow up lead in the station's news diary and record telephone interview

07:42 Edit telephone interview down to a good 13-second 'soundbite'

07:47 Write a **cue** (or introduction) to accompany soundbite

07:49 Rewrite the top line of the lead story in the bulletin

07:51 Decide final running order of the 0800 bulletin

07:54 Scan through new copy to check for errors and practise difficult sentences

07:58 Enter news booth and get ready to present the news

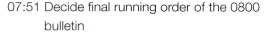

Theory into practice

During one day, listen to a number of news bulletins on Radio 4 and on a local commercial station. Compare bulletins as stories develop and then disappear to be replaced by new ones. Compare bulletins at the same time on the two stations.

Identify issues of representation in the bulletins. Are all viewpoints represented on the topics covered or are some ignored (for example, in an item about the 'war on terror')? Are all possible social groups represented fairly or has the shortage of time meant some are ignored?

You will probably notice that local events are likely to be reported on the local radio station but not on national stations. For example, an overturned lorry is unlikely to make the national news – however large the traffic jams – unless the crash was particularly dramatic, making the story of interest to a wider audience than just those in the local area.

When compiling any bulletin, the news editor pays attention to the interests of the target audience. This means making assumptions about who they are and what is important to them.

Editors usually assume that 'upmarket' listeners to Radio 4 are more interested in international news than listeners to Radio 1, for instance. Local radio audiences want to hear about what is happening in their own areas, and, unless it is something very unusual, they probably do not want to hear about other areas of the country. The target audience will affect the style of delivery, too: the news may be fast and upbeat, as on Radio 1, or read at the slower, more careful pace that Radio 4 listeners prefer.

Theory into practice

Record a radio news bulletin from a station of your choice. Who do you think the target audience is? (Look at the groups mentioned in Unit 3 for ideas about different target audiences.) Where is the target audience located? Does the time of day of the news bulletin affect the target audience? (For example, a bulletin broadcast at 8 a.m. might be listened to by commuters, while a bulletin at 2 p.m. might be listened to by office workers.)

Describe how the target audience has influenced the content and style of the bulletin.

On each station, the **structure** of a bulletin is usually the same, hour after hour. It may begin with headlines and even end with a recap of the 'top' or lead story. The length and number of stories depends on the house style of the radio station. Each story can be dealt with in a number of ways:

- copy read only
- copy + audio   the audio may be a brief clip of a relevant interview
- copy + **voicer**
- copy + **wrap**   the wrap may consist of one or more interview clips, all linked by the reporter

What does it mean?

In the newsroom, journalists use different terms to describe the different elements in a bulletin.

Cue – *copy that is used to introduce audio, a voicer or a wrap*

Wrap – *a mini-feature item of perhaps 20 seconds or so*

Billboard – *a longer feature of over a minute*

Package – *the term used in the BBC for a wrap*

Voicer or **voice piece** – *a report from a reporter covering a story*

The different ways of reporting stories are all conventions used by journalists. So are the use of jingles, the positioning of headlines and the weather, and the way most stations begin their bulletins with a time check.

Bulletins often end with out-cues that will be easily recognised by the next person due to speak or start a jingle – newsreaders on Radio 4 say 'BBC Radio News' to signal that the bulletin has ended.

As well as being a convention, the manner in which journalists speak is also a code. The tone is always authoritative – it implies that what the listener is hearing is important and that it is to be believed because it is proven fact that the news organisation knows to be true. Few people would bother to listen to news that sounded made up or was not taken seriously even by the news reader. A news jingle is also a code: it symbolises the start of the news and says 'listen carefully, here is the news!'

The narrative structure (see Unit 3, page 120) of a whole news bulletin is usually **multi-strand** because several different stories, or narratives, are being covered – as in a soap opera. Individual items may be considered to be **closed** if they report something which has happened and the facts will not change. If a new development may be expected on a live story, the narrative is **open** because listeners are left wondering what is going to happen next. If they keep listening, they might find out!

Phone-ins

People love to talk – and many people love to hear others talking on the telephone, particularly when they can hear *both* sides of the conversation! There are two main uses of phone-ins on radio. They can be part of a sequence programme, alongside a mix of music, interviews, chat and competitions, or the whole programme can be a phone-in.

Most sequence programmes, such as breakfast shows, use phone-ins to get listeners' opinions on the news of the day, to run competitions or simply to add variety to the content. Some programmes will phone out to listeners who have sent in their telephone numbers, while others will simply announce the studio number and wait for people to phone in. A producer can often see how popular a programme is by the speed and the size of the response from callers – although if nobody calls in for a competition it is always possible the question was too tricky! On sequence programmes such as the Radio 1 breakfast show (Figure 5.2), a phone-in competition is just the thing to add some lively extra interest in the form of a jokey conversation between the presenter and a caller.

■ **Figure 5.2** *Chris Moyles on air in the Radio 1 studio.*

Dedications are a popular type of phone-in used in sequence programmes. The caller gets the chance to say hello to family or friends who might be listening, as well as chatting with the presenter. Whether the friends hear it or not does not always matter – many callers are thrilled just to have been on the radio.

Theory into practice

Listen to a number of sequence programmes and note down how the presenters use phone-in material to make the programmes more interesting. Explain in class what you find, and suggest some new ways of using the phone on air.

Did you know?

Programmes that feature the phone-in more than any other type of programming usually fall into one of four categories:

1 *The open line – callers can talk with the presenter about anything they want.*
2 *The specific subject – calls are taken on a subject chosen by the producer.*
3 *Problem counselling – callers want help with emotional or health problems.*
4 *Expert help – the expert gives advice to callers on gardening, consumer affairs, etc.*

Programmes with a high proportion of phone-in content are mainly used on talk stations, such as national BBC Radio Five Live and TalkSPORT, as well as LBC in London and Talk 107 in Edinburgh. They feature phone-in programmes of all four types (see Did you know? box on page 195) right round the clock. BBC Radio 4 has a few short phone-in programmes – for example, the current affairs discussion *Any Answers* (type 2), the financial advice line *Moneybox Live* (type 4) and *Veg Talk* (type 4), which is all about vegetables!

When TalkSPORT began broadcasting it was called Talk Radio and it was about much more than just sport. The launch publicity spoke of 'shock jocks' in the style of the ranting, raving, talk show presenters in the United States – where all-talk is one of the most popular formats. There were many complaints about bad language and inappropriate programming on Talk Radio, particularly during the daytime, when children might have been listening. The station featured a phone-in on sexual and emotional problems in the middle of the afternoon – many stations would consider this type of programme more appropriate for late night broadcast.

The style of presentation and the choice of callers sets the tone for any phone-in programme. Even without the shock jocks, TalkSPORT still aims to be lively and exciting, while Radio 4's political phone-in *Any Answers* is much more formal in approach. The producers of each programme are making assumptions about *who* is listening and *what* will interest them.

The structure of a phone-in depends very much on the content and the style. If it is to be an open line programme, with callers deciding what they talk about, all the presenter may do at the beginning is to give the telephone number and invite people to call. If there is to be a specific subject, there may be some scene-setting first – for example, the presenter might quote some current newspaper headlines or discuss the topic with a studio guest. The guest may be called upon to make further comment as the programme progresses, or even talk with the callers.

 Theory into practice

Listen to two different types of phone-in on different types of radio station, and analyse what makes them different. Identify the target audience and find reasons for the style of programme chosen. What is the approach of each phone-in and how are their styles different?

Describe the structure used in each phone-in, and explain why it is used. How would *you* plan the structure of a phone-in for a student-run radio station of your own, bearing in mind the target audience you would have?

If the studio guest is doing most of the talking in a phone-in programme, it may be that there are not many callers – or not many that the producer wants to put on air. However 'open' the programme may sound, someone is likely to be filtering the callers, chatting to them first to find out what they are going to say. The producer will want to know whether they are going to be good talkers, and may have to warn them to keep language decent and avoid naming other people for legal reasons (see the section on libel in Unit 1). The programme is the result of someone making choices – who to put on, when to cut them off, whether to question them about their views and whether or not to agree with them.

There are issues of representation here, as elsewhere in the media. Are only certain types of callers getting access to the airwaves? Are the views being expressed representative of *all* the listeners or *all* of society or just certain groups? A producer might decide to feature certain social issues that seem interesting or likely to cause a heated discussion – and to ignore others because they seem dull or not controversial enough.

There are several codes in any phone-in. The format itself, whether in a one-off phone-in item or as a whole programme, involves the positioning of the host as the person *in charge* of the proceedings. The callers are allowed to take part in response to the host's kind invitation to phone in. If a listener gets through the crowded switchboard and the producer or assistant who is filtering the calls, they will only be allowed to speak for as long as the presenter wants them to, and then they will be cut off again.

Conventions in phone-ins include the repetition of the telephone number, to encourage people to call. This can also be a code, because it will probably be repeated even if there are already too many callers lined up to fit in the programme. By doing so, the presenter is saying to the listeners that the programme is still keen to hear from them, and they still have every opportunity to get 'on air'. This creates an impression of open access.

The hellos and goodbyes at the start and end of each individual call may be brief or drawn out, depending on the style of the programme. It is a

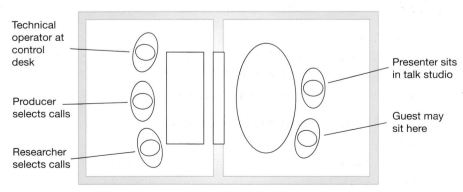

■ **Figure 5.3** *The layout of a control room and studio for a typical phone-in programme keeps the live microphone work separated from the production operations.*

convention of the genre that each call is identified. The identity of a caller is often designed to keep them fairly anonymous (such as 'Julie from Bolton') to reduce the chance of someone being libelled. This works because nobody listening can be certain who exactly was talking and who was being talked about.

Drama

Most audio drama is made for radio, but some is produced for release on other media, such as CDs and audio cassettes. Some 'talking books' for

GIRL:	JOHN, WHAT'RE YOU READING
BOY:	OH, SOME STORY ABOUT A COUPLE LOST ON A PARADISE ISLAND.
GIRL:	WHAT'S IT LIKE?
FX:	WAVES LAPPING ON BEACH (HOLD UNDER)
BOY:	BLUE SKIES, PALM TREES, COCONUTS AND SO MANY FISH IN THE SEA THAT YOU CAN JUST PUT YOUR HAND IN AND PULL ONE OUT.
GIRL:	WHAT DO THEY DO ALL DAY?
FX:	THUNDERCLAP 2"
BOY:	WELL, THEY BUILD THEMSELVES A SHELTER AND . . .
FX:	HEAVY RAIN AND WIND (HOLD UNDER)
BOY: (SHOUTING)	. . . IT BLOWS DOWN WHEN A TROPICAL STORM COMES, SO THEY GET SOAKED TO THE SKIN UNTIL . . .
FX:	HERD OF ELEPHANTS STAMPEDING 3" (QUICK FADE)
BOY:	. . . THEY GET TRAMPLED TO DEATH.
GIRL: (SARCASTICALLY)	MMM . . . SOUNDS LOVELY! BUT DON'T YOU NEED PICTURES TO ENJOY A GOOD STORY?

From *Radio in Context* by Guy Starkey

■ **Figure 5.4** *This script for a radio play shows how creative sound on its own can be.*

listening to in the car or by blind people are more like dramatic works than simple readings by a narrator.

Some people who have never heard an audio drama have difficulty imagining how it can work as they will not be able to see the characters or scenery. But drama has been successfully produced on radio since the early days of the BBC. One of the first plays to be broadcast on radio was called *Danger*, in 1923. It was a dialogue between two people trapped in a mine.

Audio drama can seem very realistic. In 1938, Orson Welles and his Mercury Theatre Company terrorised America with their dramatisation of the classic tale *War of the Worlds*. They broadcast spoof news reports of strange objects landing from outer space, in between dance band music, as if they were real news flashes interrupting the normal programmes. By the time the 'news flashes' were reporting that the Martians were climbing out of their spaceships, many listeners had climbed into their cars and jammed the streets, trying to escape from the invasion.

The BBC's radio soap opera *The Archers* was first broadcast in 1951, long before ITV was invented and the set for *Coronation Street*'s Rovers had been built. Since then, this five-days-a-week soap set in the fictional village of Ambridge has entertained millions of faithful listeners. For publicity purposes, the cast of *The Archers* do dress up for photographs from time to time, but the programmes are normally recorded without a costume or make-up artist in sight (Figure 5.5).

■ **Figure 5.5** *The cast of* The Archers *recording an episode.*

What makes radio drama believable to the listeners is the large number of codes which operate in it. They can be the sound effects used – either as background **atmosphere** (e.g. waves lapping on a beach) or **spot** effects which are brief and describe an action (e.g. a thunderclap). Music can have a similar effect: an accordion playing mixed with street sounds can evoke a street scene in Paris. The theme music to a radio soap announces the start of the programme and takes the listeners all the way to the fictional location. When it fades in at the end – often on a cliff-hanger – it underlines the emotion or surprise in the closing words.

Other symbolic codes might be used in the dialogue spoken by the actors. Compare the two lines below, and ask yourself which gives you the most information about what is going on – information you would need if you were listening to but not seeing the action.

```
TONY: (shouts)     Hey! What do you think
                   you're doing in here?

TONY: (shouts)     Hey, Constable! What do
                   you think you're doing in
                   my office at this time of
                   the night?!
```

It is a convention in radio drama that the script is written to include a maximum amount of information about what is happening, who is doing what, where they are and so on. In this way, the dialogue and the sound effects combine to create a picture in the mind of the audience. Some people say that the scenery in radio is better than on television or film. They mean that they feel more a part of what is going on because they created the scenery in their own minds.

Another convention is that scene changes are indicated by a fade out of one scene, then a second pause and the fade in of another. The passage of time can be suggested by a longer pause between scenes.

Not every drama follows the same conventions, though. Instead, some radio dramas use a fade in/fade out of music to mark changes in location or time. Sometimes a narrator may be used between scenes – often representing the thoughts inside a character's head. These are all codes, too, in the way that different sounds combine to make meaning.

 Theory into practice

Listen to *The Archers* and another radio drama that is not a soap opera. You will find the *Radio Times* useful for finding out when and where they are broadcast. Identify as many codes and conventions as possible, and play some examples to the rest of the class, explaining how they work.

Did you know?

The television comedies Dead Ringers *and* Little Britain *both began as comedy sketch shows on Radio 4. Today you can hear them and many other classic radio drama programmes on the BBC's digital network BBC 7.*

13:00 The Beagle Diary

Charles Darwin's first-hand account of his epic five-year voyage on board HMS *Beagle* at the age of 22, which provided the material that helped form his theory of evolution. Abridged by Polly Coles.

4/5. Darwin arrives at the mythically famous island of Tahiti, where he finds himself involved in a dispute between the British Crown and the Queen of Tahiti.

[Rptd Fri 12.30am]

14:00 The Archers

Jill reverts to type.
[Rpt of Tue 7.00pm]

14:15 Afternoon Play
Chocolate Frigates
By Juliet Ace.

While Jack prepares a triumphant leaving dinner for his Captain – a magnificent fleet of 12 chocolate frigates – his son is in the thick of action in Iraq. When your son is away at war how can your life just carry on as normal? Jack thinks it can and must, but his wife and son aren't so sure.

Jack ...... Todd Carty
Ella ...... Lindsey Coulson
Eliot ...... Jamie Kenna
Austin .... Nick Sayce
Cheryl ...... Emma Noakes
Captain ...... Sam Dale
Visiting Officer/Steward ......Dan Starkey
Announcer/Newsreader/Padre ...... Peter Donaldson

Produced and directed by Tracey Neale.

■ **Figure 5.6** *These listings include examples of different sub-genres of radio drama: a soap, a single play and a serial with several episodes.*

Source: www.bbc.co.uk

Radio drama has a number of sub-genres. Soap operas are one of them. You will also find one-off or **single** plays and even serials, such as *Sherlock Holmes*. Most radio drama in this country is broadcast on Radio 4, but drama can often be heard where you least expect to find it – for example, in advertisements on commercial stations and in comedy shows, such as on Radio 2. Some more **experimental** plays can be heard on Radio 3, while drama on Radio 4 is usually aimed at a more general target audience. As with all media products, the target audience influences not only what kind of drama is scheduled, but when.

Drama is comparatively expensive to produce as actors and scriptwriters have to be paid for their work. However, it is not necessarily what people want to hear on the radio at peak time. On television, the most expensive drama is scheduled during peak viewing hours, but peak time on radio is when people are on the move: at breakfast and evening drive times. Few listeners are able to concentrate on a 90-minute play while eating breakfast and dashing out of the house to catch the bus.

Advertisements which use drama are so short they can be run at any time, of course. If a radio commercial uses drama, rather than the more

Sound Effect:	*Little scream and strenuous breathing*
Male Voice Over:	Push. Push.
Sound Effect:	*Soft thud*
Male Voice Over:	It's a boy!
Sound Effect:	Soft thud
Male Voice Over:	And a girl!
Sound Effect:	*Soft thud*
Male Voice Over:	Another boy!
Sound Effect:	*Soft thud*
Male Voice Over:	And another girl!
Female Voice Over:	Don't just feel really, really, really, really proud about it. Write about it. If, like many people, you find writing a challenge, ask Learndirect about literacy workshops to develop your skills. Call 0800 100 900, that's 0800 100 900.
Sound Effect:	*Baby goo goo-ing*

■ **Figure 5.7** *This script for a radio commercial uses humour to encourage people to join a course.*

usual voiceover and music, it is because the client, or advertiser, has asked for something more creative to be made. This will often cost more money, too, partly because the scripting and effects take more time to prepare, but mainly because there are more actors to pay.

The style of a drama will depend upon the purpose and the target audience. Drama can be funny, serious, moving, exciting, depressing, inspirational, challenging or many other things, depending on what the scriptwriter intends. The scope for playing to all the different human emotions is also limited by the time available and the time slot: it may be difficult to move a radio audience to tears in a 30-second advertisement for a used car dealership – but there are talented creative copywriters out there who would be willing to give it a try!

Narrative structures do differ, depending on the drama. Soap opera is normally multi-strand, because a number of different storylines are

 Theory into practice

Compare the styles of different radio advertisements that use drama to put their message across. Then write a script for a 30-second advert of your own, deciding what atmosphere, effects and music would be needed to make it come alive.

Do the same for a soap opera and a short play. Present your findings to the rest of the class, using recorded extracts to help make the most important points.

being developed alongside each other in each episode. Of course, the final episode ever of a soap would be closed *if* all the different storylines were wound up, with no cliff hangers or mysteries left as to what happens next. Most single plays will also be closed. The narrative structure of a drama series is serial.

Drama raises many issues of representation and stereotyping. Some producers argue that stereotyped characters are necessary to allow the listeners to imagine them as being like someone they know. In *The Archers*, the Grundys are a working-class family, whose members are often up to no good. Only the mother, being female, tries to keep the men on the right track. *The Archers* does try to be representative – wider social issues are covered as well as farming, and the people of Ambridge have often shown concern for issues that affect people living in towns.

Advertisements

As well as advertisements using drama, there are also other styles of radio commercial. The simplest is the single voice. This is a simple announcement with nothing but the voice and the script to put across the message about the advertiser's product. Used sparingly, it can be very effective, but if every advert used the same style, commercial breaks would be very dull indeed.

Many clients want their message read over music – called a **bed**. A voice over music is a **voiceover** or **v/o**. Even more creative clients (with bigger budgets) might want the advert to feature a jingle to be sung that has been written especially for them. The idea is that people will start singing along to a catchy lyric advertising the product or company's name. Here is a very famous example:

Where in the world?... PC World

Some advertisement scripts require two or more voices. The more people who are involved in the production process, the more it will cost the client to produce. Some very well-known actors and actresses voice radio adverts, and they may charge much higher fees to perform because they are endorsing a product. Many of the other voices you hear are those of the professional **voiceover artists** who each week record ads for several different radio stations. Production houses like S2Blue produce adverts for several stations, sending them from their studios to the radio stations over quality ISDN lines or the Internet, ready for almost-immediate transmission.

The main purpose of advertisements is to persuade (i.e. to sell the advertiser's message to the listener) and so to generate income. They may, of course, also entertain, as listeners are often more likely to remember the message if the advert is amusing.

■ **Figure 5.8** *Production houses like S2 Blue make commercials for many different radio stations.*

In terms of structure, often the simpler the message is, the more effective it is. Usually a product will have a **unique selling point** (USP), and all that matters is putting that across as well as the name of the product and how to get it. The basic formula is:

Create interest – Explain USP – Product name – Where?/How?

Commercial producers will have a library of musical tracks created for just this kind of production – called **library music**. An important part of the creative process is being able to select from hundreds of tracks *the one* which sounds right for the mood the producer wants to create. The various compilations will have names like 'Industrial' or 'Pastoral', to indicate how the tracks will sound and what messages they will convey about the product. For this reason, the beds used are signifiers.

The symbolic codes in radio commercials include the voices used. Are they serious or light-hearted? Do they sound authoritative, as if the people speaking know what they are talking about and can be trusted?

Issues of representation in adverts are really in the hands of the advertisers – the ones who are paying for the message to be produced and broadcast. They are likely to want to be representative of the majority of their listeners, so any under-representation of minority groups may be because the advertisers want to appeal to the widest possible market. However, some advertising targets **niche** markets – for example Kiss 100 FM in London has a high number of listeners among the black community in the capital, and so advertisers on that station will want to make sure they are representative of their listeners.

1. **Amazement** (:30) Techno, confident & winning
2. **Dance All Night** (:30) Dance, solid groove
3. **Funky Banana** (:30) Funk, big bass, energetic and exciting
4. **Get It** (:60) Cool, warm and fun
5. **Get On Up** (:60) Rock, party, up-tempo
6. **Getting Better** (:30) Techno, solid, movement
7. **Got The Message** (:30) Electric, cool guitar and keys
8. **Havin Fun** (:60) Orchestra techno mix, upbeat & fun
9. **Heartland** (:30) Light rock, acoustic guitars, hopeful
10. **Heavy** (:30) Hard rock, big guitars & drums, aggressive
11. **Highway Run** (:60) Rock, grooving, sense of well being
12. **Implode** (:60) Rock, Big drums, bold & confident
13. **In the dark** (:30) Electronic, groovin bass, movement
14. **Kickin In** (:30) Hard Rock, motivational & exciting
15. **Livin Live** (:30) Rock, solid, groovin guitar licks
16. **Mechanical Mama** (:30) Robotic, upbeat & neat keyboards
17. **Moon Walk** (:60) Haunting, fluid & spacey
18. **Mountain Man** (:30) Odd and a bit scary
19. **Move It Along** (:60) Cool, groovin & cool sounds effects
20. **On The Green** (:60) Classical, bright & enthusiastic piece
21. **Ornament** (:60) Rock, mid tempo grooving track
22. **Out Of This World** (:30) Electronic, futuristic with solid energy
23. **Playing Around** (:60) Dance, winning, excellent movement
24. **Priceless** (:60) Rock, upbeat & thought provocative
25. **Rockin Tonight** (:30) Rock, confident & fun
26. **Say What** (:60) Dance, Beautiful & solid
27. **She Is The One** (:30) Techno, fast & furious
28. **Spotlight** (:60) Techno, movement, excitement
29. **The Prince** (:60) Electronic, solid & cool
30. **Turkish Twist** (:60) Ethnic, unorthodox, European feeling

Source: www.zebramusic.com

■ **Figure 5.9** *The track list shows the style of each track and its duration.*

Theory into practice

Record six different adverts from different commercial radio stations, noting down the date, day and time each one was broadcast, as well as the station. For each one, match the style and structure to the target audience for the product.

Now find as many codes and conventions as you can in the adverts, and note your findings. What issues of representation are raised in them. Discuss your findings in class, using your recordings as examples.

Magazine programmes

A radio magazine programme is just what the name suggests – a collection of different items all wrapped together in one single programme. Like print magazines, they can be general in content, or specialised – with a name that indicates what they are about and who they would interest. Below is a list of national magazine programmes on Radio 4.

Magazine title	Content
Today	News/Current affairs
Money Box	Financial matters
Front Row	Arts
Law in Action	Legal issues
You and Yours	Consumer/Family issues

The content is determined by the target audience, and so is the time of broadcast. *Today* is the Radio 4 breakfast show – it has a wide appeal among the network's listeners and it runs for three hours a day, five days a week, with a two-hour Saturday edition as well. *Money Box* and *Law in Action* are for very specialised audiences, which is why they are broadcast at off-peak times, around 9 p.m.

Radio 1 has broadcast magazines, too, and in the One Click series there were weekly film and entertainment magazines designed especially for the Radio 1 audience.

The style of a magazine depends upon the content, because specialist audiences expect to be spoken to as if they know something about the subject. More general audiences are likely to need more explanation about specialist topics, to set the scene and help them understand better what is going to be discussed.

There are a number of different types of items found in a magazine. A programme might regularly use some or all of these:

- feature, package, wrap or billboard – a report linked by a single reporter
- live or recorded interview – by the presenter or a reporter on location
- two-way – presenter talks to a reporter on location
- double-header – presenter chairs discussion between two guests
- debate – presenter chairs studio debate
- review or talk – guest in studio reads prepared script
- music
- competition
- weather, travel, business updates
- news headlines.

Theory into practice

Listen carefully to a national magazine programme. Identify the target audience, based on the station, day, time and content. Use all of this information to explain the style of the programme and why it is broadcast at that time. Explain how the style chosen helps it to attract an audience.

The structure of a magazine depends on its target audience, content and duration. Shorter magazines are unlikely to repeat items because many people listening at the end will have been listening at the beginning. *Today* on Radio 4 runs for a number of hours – and so some early items may be repeated or updated later on. All the items in a magazine are linked together by one or two presenters. The role of the presenter is crucial in keeping the programme flowing and introducing each individual item.

12.02	Introduce programme
	Menu of items
	Cue to item 1
12.06	Back announcement to item 1
	Time check and signpost
	Cue to item 2
12.11	Back announcement to item 2
	Time check and signpost
	Cue to item 3

■ **Figure 5.10** *A typical magazine programme presenter's role, with times.*

Certain conventions apply to magazine programmes – such as the use of a **menu** at the start, to list the items coming up. Regular **signposting** in links provides a reminder of what the programme is called and what items are still to come. **Back announcements** give a quick reference to the item that has just been featured. Often a weekly or daily magazine will end with a brief mention of what is coming up in the next edition.

It is also a convention that the presenter, as the central linking figure in the programme, is identified as a personality – rather than taking the more neutral role of a newsreader in a news bulletin. Friendly, off-the-cuff chat with contributors is very common – even in Radio 4's *Today*, which is listened to by top politicians and academics.

It is usual, too, for items to be around four to five minutes long, although there will always be exceptions within programmes. Jingles or **idents** to identify the programme may be used, too, depending upon the programme style.

The informality of the magazine presenter is a signifier – informality suggests friendliness, which is intended to draw listeners in and to encourage loyalty. After all, the producers do want the listeners to tune in again next time.

Individual items – especially features or packages – use sound codes in the form of **atmosphere** (sound effects to paint audio pictures just as in drama) or music to suggest locations, subjects or mood.

The narrative structure of a whole magazine is **multi-strand** because a number of different items run through the programme. Individual items within the programme may be either **closed** (because the item is finished with) or **open** (because there is more to come later or in a different programme as a follow-on).

Theory into practice

Analyse the structure of the magazine programme you studied earlier. Write down all the different types of item, and identify where the menu and signposting are used. Identify any codes and conventions you hear, noting down your findings. Do the same with any issues of **representation** raised by the choice of presenters, reporters and/or guests. What social issues are covered by the programme, and whose side of the story gets the most favourable coverage? Is there any bias in the programme?

Assessment task 1

Describe the main broadcast audio products, using examples from different radio genres. Be methodical, clearly separating each product from the others. Explain what makes each one different from the others and why.

Assessment evidence

✔ Describe the products, identifying the main features of each genre.

✔✔ Use examples to explain why some products are more popular than others – or more common – and why others are not.

✔✔✔ Use correct terminology in your explanations, making sure they are detailed and supported by strong evidence of your conclusions.

Non-broadcast audio

The media industry's main non-broadcast audio products are talking books and in-store audio, which are what we will be looking at in this section. In addition, the music industry produces music for sale through shops and the Internet, as well as production music for use by the media. The music industry also releases soundtracks to films for film fans to purchase.

Form and genre

Talking books

These are sometimes also called audio books. They are produced for sale in shops and over the Internet. Most are monologues, consisting of a narrator reading a version of a novel or some other written book, but some are dramatisations, rather like radio drama. Some of the longest popular novels can result in talking books that are up to nine hours long.

Theory into practice

Use the Internet to identify a range of different talking book titles currently on sale. What kind of titles sell well and what target markets do you think they are for? Explain your answers.

As well as being of great interest to people who are blind or visually impaired, talking books can keep children and drivers entertained on long journeys. One obvious market for them is in motorway service stations.

In-store audio

At first, in-store audio was distributed to shops on tapes, for staff to play over the loudspeaker systems. The tapes were each usually only an hour or two in duration, so they would have to be repeated over and over again before the next tape arrived.

One famous exception to this was Radio Topshop – this was modelled on a pop music radio station, but run live from the Topshop store in London's Oxford Street. Some of radio's most popular presenters began their careeers on Radio Topshop, because they saw it was a good way to get some experience of performing live to an audience and getting themselves known.

Today, in-store audio has changed a great deal – because now there are alternative methods of getting the audio into the stores all around the country. First, audio channels were used alongside satellite television transmissions to beam live programming to stores with special decoders. Now broadband is used to distribute the audio to stores connected to the Internet. The in-store audio of today is very much like broadcast radio, with presenters chatting about offers and special events, encouraging shoppers to stay in the store longer and to browse products they may not have even thought about buying.

As in-store audio has become more professional, specialist companies have taken over production. TEAMtalk Broadcast produces stations for Asda and all:sports. In-store Radio Productions have run music programmes for PC World, The Officers Club and Manpower Jobshops. Costcutter FM has been running since 1996 and Co-op Radio since 2004.

■ **Figure 5.11** *Shoppers in this store are entertained by in-store audio, as well as hearing about the latest offers and the newest products.*

Theory into practice

Listen to an in-store audio service, either on the premises or over the Internet. What similarities and differences are there with broadcast radio stations? Explain your answers.

Assessment task 2

Describe the main non-broadcast audio products, using examples of talking books and in-store audio. Be methodical, clearly separating each product from the others. Explain what makes each one different from the others and why.

Assessment evidence

✔ Describe the products, identifying the main features of each genre.

✔✔ Use examples to explain why some products are more popular or more common than others – and why others are not.

✔✔✔ Use correct terminology in your explanations, making sure they are detailed and supported by strong evidence of your conclusions.

Audio formats

Recorded audio is stored in a number of different formats, and it is important that you understand the differences between them. Some are more appropriate than others for your production work in this unit. Depending on the resources in your school, you may have some choices to make. You certainly need to show your understanding of all the different formats, even if you do not get to use them.

CD

The compact disc has been used for music and other audio recordings since the early 1980s. When it first arrived, consumers were amazed that over an hour of music could be stored on so small a disk, and compared to vinyl it seemed indestructible. Certainly it was not as easy to scratch, and finger prints could be easily wiped off with a cloth, without fear of scratching the surface.

Because CDs store audio digitally, there is none of the rumble or clicks associated with analogue vinyl recordings. Tracks can be played very loud without such unwanted noise also being amplified. Some people insist that because digital recording techniques use sampling to record only parts of the audio, the sound on a CD is not pure enough. Because the sampling rate used on CDs is quite high, most people cannot tell the difference between sound that has been sampled and recorded onto a CD and sound that has not.

CDs are much smaller in size than the vinyl discs they all but replaced, so storage is easier, and they are much less likely to melt if left in hot sun. The latest CDs are writeable and rewriteable in computers, and used for data storage as well as audio recording. Audio CDs can carry extra information, such as track titles and duration, and access to each track is made easy using a menu system.

However, they are *not* indestructible and scratches, blemishes and stains on the playing surface of a CD can cause the laser beam that 'reads' it to be misdirected. Skipping can occur and badly damaged CDs can become unreadable.

Minidisc

The minidisc was developed as a high-quality recording medium on which recordings can be erased and re-recorded over. It uses a combination of magnetic and optical encoding to record audio and to enable playback using very compact discs housed in a plastic case. They are much smaller in size than the reel-to-reel audio tapes radio broadcasters used for many years, and the recorders are much smaller and lighter, too. A menu system allows individual tracks to be deleted, and tracks may also be divided to allow editing on the minidisc (MD) recorder itself. Playback is menu driven, so the order of tracks can be altered, allowing you to cut, paste and copy parts of a recording in whatever way you choose. This feature has proven very useful for reporters out on location, but it is tricky to edit very precisely, and it is not possible to mix audio on the MD recorder in the same way as you can on a computer.

Such features as track naming, write protection, time displays and automatic level controls are very attractive, and some machines have a single button to start recording after the last track, so you do not accidentally erase something else.

Did you know?

Minidiscs and DATs were very popular recording formats in the media industry in the 1990s, but both may soon be obsolete.

On basic MD recorders, the audio must be played out in real time, which although perfectly acceptable in the 1990s seems rather slow now. Today there are alternative formats allowing audio to be transferred much faster into a computer for more sophisticated editing and mixing. Sometimes the MD itself becomes unreadable, because it is not indestructible either, and imperfections on the playing surface affect its performance. The reason for their compact size is that MD recorders also sample audio, rather than storing every part of a sound – again not very satisfying for 'purists'.

DAT

Digital audio tape (DAT) also became popular in the radio and music industries in the 1990s, because it offered a means of storing large amounts of audio in a compact format at a quality that was high enough for professional use. The menu and time displays allow pinpoint accuracy in finding a particular place on a tape, as well as track naming and write protection.

However, the DAT tape is very fragile and can easily be damaged if the cassettes are not taken care of. Also, the tape has to spool backwards or forwards to the right place, rather than being almost instantly accessible as with disc-based systems. Digital sampling is used to encode the audio onto this format, too.

Video tape

Though not used for commercial audio products, video tape has been used in radio stations to record **logs** of their broadcast output for legal purposes. A requirement of the regulator is that recordings are made of a radio station's output and kept for 60 days in case of a complaint. It is good practice to keep a log in any case.

A four-hour video tape, running at half speed, records eight hours of audio, and the video display can be of a security camera and a time and date imprint if required. This budget solution to the problem of needing to change logging tapes very regularly has been used a lot by Restricted Service Licence (RSL) radio stations, in schools and colleges for example. Today there are even simpler methods of logging and date stamping audio using dedicated software on a computer, so this practice is unlikely to survive much longer.

Vinyl

This is one for the audio purists! Vinyl recording has enabled the storage of audio on flat discs for decades, and because there is no sampling of the audio, all the sound is there, and not just parts of it. The disadvantage is that on quieter analogue recordings even very fine, hairline scratches on the playing surface will cause irritating clicks. So vinyl records have to be handled with great care. No wonder the CD seemed indestructible by comparison when it first came out.

The stylus (or needle) on a record player has to be placed very carefully in the groove, and you have only your sight to guide you to find an exact point in a recording. The weight of a wrongly balanced tone arm pressing the stylus down onto the playing surface causes rumble, which can be heard very clearly under quieter recordings, and it wears the vinyl down, so that the sound deteriorates after many repeat playings.

The stylus will skip if the record player is knocked or unstable – so very few portable vinyl record players were ever made. Leaving a vinyl record in bright sunshine will cause it to warp. Balancing it on a jam jar in the sun will produce a very attractive black plant pot! Stacking large numbers of discs on top of each other will cause the ones at the bottom

■ **Figure 5.12** *Twin turntables in a radio studio before CD players and hard-disc playout became more common.*

of the pile to warp, so they should be stored vertically on a shelf, away from heat and dust.

Vinyl is only recordable in the factory where it is made – vinyl records are still made today for a limited market of enthusiasts and club DJs. A mould is made first, then each disc is physically stamped with the sound groove on both sides. Except in the case of picture discs which include a coloured image under the playing surface, the only track information available is what is printed on the label and the protective cardboard sleeve.

To avoid scratching the disc, there is usually an inner sleeve made of paper – so when radio presenters used only vinyl on air, they had plenty to do, taking discs carefully out of two sleeves, dusting them and then finding the start of the right track before they could be played live!

Tape systems

Reel-to-reel tape is rarely used for audio storage today, mainly because of all the advantages of the other formats described above. Some music recording studios still use analogue audio tape when they want to avoid audio sampling, but they are not common. There is no track listing on analogue tape and editing must be done by physically marking edit points with a soft chinagraph pencil and then cutting out the unwanted material with a sharp razor blade.

It was easy to lose or to crumple a section of tape that was being moved from one part of a recording to another, and it was not possible to write protect recordings, so digital alternatives have been very welcome, especially as portable recorders were heavy to carry around.

■ **Figure 5.13** *Reel-to-reel tape machines were widely used in audio production until the 1990s.*

Digital sound files, e.g. MP3

Storing audio as digital files – although involving sampling – is most people's preferred method today. MP3 is one of many different types of encoding that can be used – it has the advantage of compressing sound into much smaller files than, for example, the .wav format. The more a file is compressed and the less storage space it takes up, though, the greater the sampling – and if the sample rate is too low it becomes obvious to the human ear. Many broadcasting organisations refuse to accept MP3 files because they are not of a high enough quality.

MP3 is used for selling and distributing audio over the Internet because of the faster download times it allows. Download sales have been increasing dramatically since the launch of iTunes by Apple. People convert their own music collections to MP3 for sharing and to use on their own MP3 players – which are small and highly portable.

Professionals are more likely to use less compressed audio files for editing and mixing audio products for distribution to the public. These are still quick to move around from recorder to computer and from work station or laptop to studio. They are also easy to copy and to back-up to avoid losing work. Also, new methods of access control may increasingly allow producers to prevent pirating of their work.

Assessment task 3

Describe each of the recording formats above in your own words. Be methodical, clearly separating each format from the others.

Assessment evidence

✔ Describe the nature of each format, explaining differences in the way they are used.

✔✔ Use examples to explain the advantages and disadvantages of each format. You will find a lot of the information you need on the last few pages.

✔✔✔ Use correct terminology in your explanations, making sure they are detailed and supported by strong evidence of your conclusions.

5.2 Audio recording and editing – technology and techniques

You need to learn how to use equipment for audio production and show you understand how it works and what you are doing. In this section we will describe the technology and techniques and in the next you will use the equipment to make a number of recordings to demonstrate your ability and understanding. The two assessment tasks in this section will help you to keep a record of your investigations.

Recording technologies

For both broadcast and non-broadcast audio production, recording sound focuses on three stages:

- **Capture** – collecting sound, usually through a microphone, which turns it into an electronic signal you can work with.
- **Production** – moving that electronic signal from the microphone into other production and recording equipment. It can be mixed with other sound at this stage.
- **Post-production** – editing sound and mixing or changing it in some way to create a finished product. There may also be some post-production paperwork to fill in.

Before you can capture sound, there will be some pre-production planning to do: deciding what sound you want to capture, why, and where to get it – as well as what to do with it once you have recorded it. We will come back to pre-production in section 5.3, when you start to plan an audio product. The equipment you use must always be suitable for the job.

 Assessment task 4

a) *Read through the rest of section 5.2, trying out as many of the different items of production equipment as you have available. Experiment with the different settings and setups highlighted in bold throughout the section. Keep a record of your work in the form of written notes or recordings of your experimentation with the equipment.*

b) *Investigate different indoor and outdoor recording situations, making brief recordings in a number of different locations using different equipment. Keep a note of where each recording was made and the equipment used.*

Assessment evidence

✓ Describe the different types of equipment in detail, clearly showing how they differ from each other.

✓✓ Use examples to explain what each item of equipment is used for and how it is used.

✓✓✓ Use correct terminology in your explanations, making sure they are detailed and supported by strong evidence of your conclusions.

Microphones

The choice of microphone is very important for any audio capture. Different types have different characteristics, which makes some more suitable for certain tasks than others. For most jobs mono microphones are used. Even in drama, you can create a stereo effect by giving each actor a microphone of their own and **panning** each microphone channel to the left or right on the **mixer**, as we will see later.

Stereo microphones are able to detect whether a sound is coming more from the left or more from the right, and then to feed a stereo signal into the mixer or the recording machine. They can be very useful in recording drama, because voices or sounds coming from different places from left to right can sound very effective when listened to through twin loudspeakers or headphones.

You should choose your microphone by its direction of **pick up**.

- **Omni-directional** means 'all directions'.

- **Directional** or **uni-directional** means the microphone picks up sound mainly from one particular direction.

- A **rifle** microphone is **highly directional** – when pointed in a direction, it is very good at picking out sounds from that particular place.

Radio producers do not often use rifle microphones – they are more often used in video, where a hand holding a microphone up close would be visible on screen.

Omni-directional microphones are used for interviewing and for many location recordings, mainly because of their ability to pick up sounds from all around. If you use an omni-directional microphone, it means there are likely to be background sounds on your recorded interview. Remember that the amount of background is under your control, because the closer you place the microphone to the source of a sound – an interviewee's mouth, for example – the louder it will sound against the background. However, beware of rattle, because the microphone will be sensitive to any knocks against its body or **lead** (the wire attaching it to a recorder or a mixer).

More directional microphones are needed where there is any element of mixing sounds. To pick up audience reaction at a live quiz show, an effects microphone will need to be directional or it will pick up output from the public address system and cause **howlround** (or electronic feedback). Miking up a band or orchestra can be done very precisely, with one microphone per instrument if necessary, but make sure the microphone for the piano does not also pick up other instruments nearby. A drum kit may need more than one microphone.

The basic principle of any microphone is that it converts sound waves into electrical energy. The **dynamic response** is the amount of accuracy in the microphone's translation of sound into electrical signal. **Condenser** microphones have variable pick-up areas that can be set to cover the required area. **Cardioid** microphones have a heart-shaped pick-up area.

It is important to choose the correct microphone for the job. That means deciding exactly what sounds you want the microphone to pick up, and what direction they will be coming from. Using a directional microphone with a particular pattern of sensitivity will allow you to reduce unwanted sounds from a particular direction – the direction of the microphone's **blind spot**. **Bidirectional** microphones pick up sound from two opposite directions and are very useful when recording an interview.

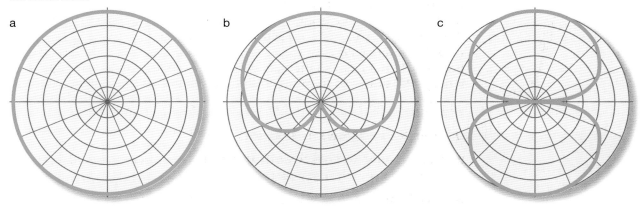

■ **Figure 5.14** *Diagrams showing the pick-up area of three types of microphone: a) omnidirectional, b) cardioid, c) bidirectional.*

Theory into practice

Experiment with different microphones that have different characteristics. Speak into them, changing their position and direction, noting the differences in what they pick up. Do this in noisy locations as well as quiet ones.

Recording devices

The choice of recording machine is just as important as the microphone you use. This choice may well have been made for you, and you now know the advantages and disadvantages of the different recording formats that might be available:

- Computer – recording directly into editing software in a studio, or using a laptop on location.
- Minidisc recorder – available in portable and studio versions.
- DAT recorder – available in portable and studio versions.
- Cassette recorder – available in portable and studio versions.
- Reel-to-reel recorder – still available in portable and studio versions.

Some portable recorders are **solid-state** – meaning there are no discs, tapes or moving parts of any kind. They record onto a chip, rather like in a memory stick, and some of the latest microphones have such a chip built into the stem so there is no need for a connecting lead. The audio is output via a USB plug at the end of the microphone.

Mixers

The **mixer** is the centrepiece of any sound studio (Figure 5.15). Mixers are also used on location whenever more than one individual sound source is to be put into the programme mix. A sound source may be a microphone, a CD or record player, a tape machine used for playback, a minidisc, or even a special effects generator.

Any source of live or recorded sound may be routed into a mixer, and the mixer is where the producer's decisions about what sound should be heard are put into effect. Depending on how a recording or live programme is crewed, the mixer may be operated by a technical operator (**sound mixer** or **SM**), a producer, a **self-operating** presenter or an assistant. A reporter would usually **drive** a simpler studio alone, to produce a wrap, feature or voice piece. The other sound sources which feed into the mixer will be operated by the same person – or, in a complicated production, by another SM or assistant.

A location recording such as a drama or a quiz may well also have a portable mixer at the heart of the technical operations. Where there is a live audience, a second mixer may be used to produce a different version of the proceedings or the

■ **Figure 5.15** *The mixer is the most important set of controls in an audio studio. Sometimes smaller versions are taken on location.*

Did you know?

How to use a sound mixer

The basic principle behind any mixer is that there is one channel for each sound source. Usually each channel will be labelled with the name of the sound source connected to it. Sometimes the production will require the channels to be reorganised – for example, when more microphones are added for a quiz, or outside broadcast feeds from sports grounds need to be connected.

*Each channel has a number of different controls as well as a **fader**. Some mixers have a channel-on switch, but it is the fader which allows you to raise or lower the volume of the sound source to the level required. When two or more different sources are being mixed, the operator must find the correct balance between the sounds. A voice over a musical track should be clearly heard over the music, so the fader for the CD player must be set low enough not to drown the voice. If the CD fader is set too low, the music may not be heard at all.*

second version may be produced on the same mixer as the programme output. Any situation where a large number of different people are due to speak will need a mixer with several microphone inputs, so that each microphone can be turned off and on individually.

In general, each fader should be in the 'quiet' position except when the sound source needs to be mixed into the output. The meter (or meters) on the mixer are used to measure the levels going through the mixer (or **desk** – as in **mixing desk**). Remember that if more than one source is playing through the desk at any one time, the mixer will only be showing the level of the loudest source. When making a recording through a mixer, you should take care to set the level of each source one at a time, so it peaks at the correct level on the meter. A common peak level for music is 4, and for speech 5 (when the meter is a **peak programme meter** or **PPM**).

If, when the fader is pushed up as high as it will go, the level from that source is still not high enough, the **gain control** should be adjusted until it is. If the level is too high, the gain control should be altered once more. The gain is usually at the top end of the channel.

Often you will be using a mixing desk **live** – that is, connected to a transmitter or PA. Here, it will not be possible to set up levels on the desk with the faders open, because your audience will hear the tapes, discs or microphones being **lined up**. A radio programme would not sound very professional if 'testing, testing, 1, 2, 3' was heard each time an interviewee was lined up!

All mixers for live use have a **PFL** (**pre-fade listen**) facility to allow levels to be set before faders are opened. The operator can then actually listen to any different source before it is put on air. For example, a presenter may wish to hear the start or end of a music track before it is broadcast, in order to plan how to **talk in** to or **talk out** of it. Lining up the start of a tape or a track is made possible by the PFL function on the mixer. Normally, the operator selects PFL by pushing a button on the channel to be heard. That channel then **takes over** the headphones and the studio speakers, or both.

Other features on a standard sound mixer are:

- **aux output** – allows you to send a different choice of sources to a particular destination
- **pan control** – moves a source to the left or right in the stereo 'image'
- **talkback** – an intercom system allowing you to talk to another studio or location
- **mono** – can put either leg of a stereo recording onto both legs of the output
- **ducking** – can be set to lower the level of one source for a voice to do a **talk over** over it
- **EQ** – equalisation.

Equalisation means changing the way some audio sounds. That is, if it sounds too woolly, turning up the higher frequencies will make it crisper. If a sound is too tinny, then the high frequencies can be turned down, and the middle and low frequencies turned up. A mixer may have a full range of equalisation controls on each channel, or the facility may only be available on some of the channels. Equalisation – or **EQ** – works the same way as the graphic equalisation on the more expensive stereo hi-fi equipment or car stereos.

Graphic equalisation is available on studio sound-processing equipment, and on some digital audio production software too. The different frequencies are displayed visually, and the amount of each different frequency range can be seen on the screen and turned up or down as required.

Theory into practice

The only way to learn how to operate a mixer is to use it. If you have a studio, experiment with playing different types of audio through the mixer, fading in and out, speaking over music, cross fading from one item to another and mixing different sources together. Later you could be presenting a sequence programme in the studio, so the more practice you get, the better.

Recording situations

The choice of recording location is important for any audio production. You can record indoors or outdoors, and you may be lucky enough to have access to a studio. Even if you do not have a studio, you can achieve excellent results if you are careful, but you should at least know about studio recording. Check the section on health and safety in Unit 1 (pages 34–36) before you go anywhere to record.

Location recording

Recording on location involves making choices based upon research into all the possible locations. If recording indoors, you must consider acoustics. The size of the room and the amount of soft furnishings (carpets, curtains, furniture, etc.) may all deaden the sound. You should also think about how many people will be present during the recording, because human beings can have the same effect.

If recording outdoors, the acoustic may be that of a cave or a tunnel entrance. Using this **ambient** (or natural) sound is an excellent way to begin to create a picture in the mind of the listeners. Background sounds in a location can add to the listener's 'mind picture' of where the action is – or is meant to be, in the case of fiction. An interview about heavy traffic clogging up the roads, or about pollution, can be enhanced if we can hear the heavy traffic. The recording would be called **actuality** – and the background is **atmosphere**.

Consider each possible location in terms of its strengths and weaknesses, and how well suited it is to your recording. As well as ambient and background sound, you must also consider the cost of getting people and equipment to the location – train tickets and car parking will all have to be paid for. If the location is private property, you must get permission to gain access to it. The owner should be told right at the start what you intend to do there. The time it takes to get to your

■ **Figure 5.16** *When interviewing on location, choose the place very carefully and carry out a risk assessment first. Make sure you wear any protective clothing necessary.*

location will affect how much time you will have left to make your recording.

If the cons outweigh the pros, you may well be better off looking for somewhere more convenient to record. Sometimes you can fool the listener into thinking you are somewhere else, simply by choosing a location with a similar **acoustic** and perhaps adding some effects later.

Studio recording

A broadcasting or recording studio is acoustically treated to prevent unwanted sound being reflected back to the microphones. The materials and expertise needed to **deaden** a new studio can be very costly, although some cheap college solutions include foam packaging stuck to walls, or even egg boxes! (Beware of the fire risk when using flammable materials in large quantities.)

Some of the most expensive studios are actually floating on a bed of oil, which prevents sound waves being transmitted by the ground when trains or lorries rumble by. It is unlikely that any indoor location you use will be as effectively treated as a professional studio, so you will need to consider reflections from the walls and unwanted background noise from outside when you choose your locations for recording.

What does it mean?

Acoustics – *the audio characteristics of a particular place. If you record in a washroom, for example, a voice will seem very different from when it is recorded outside.*

■ **Figure 5.17** *Sound is reflected back towards a microphone in a room, but no sound is reflected back when talking in an outdoor location, such as a field.*

Assessment task 5

Record a number of different interviews or commentaries in a number of different locations – both indoor and outdoor. Use your findings from assessment task 4 to decide on the most appropriate equipment for each scenario. Keep a record of the equipment and location used for each recording and why you chose the equipment for each location.

Assessment evidence

✓ Make recordings in different situations, and state how the recordings differ from each other.

✓✓ Use examples to explain *how* and *why* any change of situation affected your recordings.

✓✓✓ Use correct terminology in your explanations, making sure they are detailed and supported by strong evidence of your conclusions.

5.3 How to produce an audio product

Now you should be ready to create an audio product of your own, to the very best quality you can manage. In this section we will look at the different stages involved: pre-production, production and post-production. A single production assessment task will help you carry out your production work in the correct way.

Pre-production

Developing an idea

At the heart of any audio product is the basic idea. In order to develop an idea into a product, it must be fully worked out in terms of the following:

- **Form** – is it a broadcast or a non-broadcast product?

- **Genre** – which of the known genres is it to be in? Perhaps it is to be a development of one or more genres, or something entirely new. (As explained in Unit 3, it may be best to stick to an established genre but try to be creative in the way you develop the idea.)

- **Format** – which of the formats described in section 5.1 will you use to record and submit your product?

- **Content** – what will be in the product itself? Examples include interviews, narration, music, sound effects, dialogue – depending on the chosen genre of the product.

- **Style** – this will depend on the genre but it should also be right for the target audience.

- **Audience** – who is this product aimed at? You should think carefully about the audience and what is most likely to interest them, as described in section 3.2 of Unit 3.

- **Length** – your time and resources may be limited, so you should think carefully about what you can achieve. A 28-minute radio documentary is probably unrealistic, but a very good seven-minute package could help earn a very good grade.

Once you have decided on an idea to develop, you should work it into a proposal (Figure 5.18). You will need to use many of the research techniques covered in Unit 2 to show that there is a demand for your product, and to identify the right kind of content to put in it.

From a basic proposal, you can develop a treatment, giving more detail about the content of your product and what will be in it. The treatment can be short or run to a few pages, depending on how much information you have at this stage. You may identify the interviewees for a radio

Subject	Dangerous dogs
Angle	Muzzling pit bulls in public – is it fair?
Treatment	Interviews: Pit bull owner
	Council dog warden
	Pit bull breeder
	Dog bite victim
	Atmosphere: Barking, snarling dogs recorded at dog
	pound
	Children playing in playground
	Linking script: 'Reporter' links all audio clips
	together

■ **Figure 5.18** *A proposal for a radio package shows key information about its nature and content.*

package, for example, and say why they have been chosen. If you have not yet selected the interviewees, you can say what kind of job or experience they have that makes them suitable for interviewing for your package.

 Case study

Planning a radio package

Suppose you decide to work on a package for a radio magazine programme. You will first have to decide on a subject and an angle. The subject is what the package is about. The angle is how you approach that subject – what aspect of it are you going to explain to the radio audience?

How easily you can gather the material that will form the content affects you as much as anything else. Every part of the content has to be something you stand a realistic chance of getting. Can you really afford to get to Hollywood to interview a film star and get back before the deadline is past?

It may be difficult getting out of school to carry out interviews, and remember the health and safety risks in approaching people you do not

know. There might be interesting interviewees on the school staff. Do not just interview your mates, unless they have something important to say about the subject that will interest your audience.

The content is a vital part of any programme, wrap or package. Once you have thought of a subject you wish to investigate, consider what angle you will explore it from. If you choose dogs as your subject, you could fill hours of radio time covering every aspect of dogs – from what they eat to what to do if you are bitten by one. Choosing one angle for a five-minute package allows you to home in on a particular aspect, and cover it in enough depth to make some impact.

Let's imagine you choose as your angle the law that says certain breeds of dog should be kept

Case study continued

muzzled when out in public. Next you would have to decide on a **treatment**. The treatment is where you explain *how* you are going to cover the angle: who you are going to interview and what is the listener going to hear. You would also have to consider how to record sounds of dogs without getting bitten yourself!

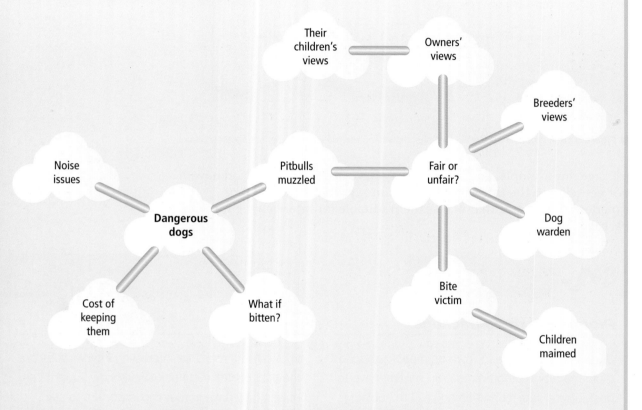

■ *From an initial idea, you can decide on any number of different angles and approaches.*

Most audio products require a script. It should include all the words to be spoken by actors or reporters, and when any pre-recorded material is to be included. Be careful to write for the ear – no long, complicated sentences.

Take care over the duration of all material you want to include – how much interview material can you include in a short package? Should you include, say, 30 seconds of vox pops? How many scenes can there be in a short drama? Who will act in it for you?

Scheduling your production

A production schedule allows you to plan your work and finish in time to meet the final deadline. You should allow extra time at the end in case there is a problem at any stage. Work back from the final deadline, seeing how many weeks you have to get each stage done. You will need time to do:

- research
- scriptwriting
- recording
- editing
- post-production paperwork.

Assessment task 6

Choose an audio product to make from those described in section 5.1 and plan how to make it. Use the information in this section to carry out the pre-production, production and post-production stages to the best of your ability.

Assessment evidence

✓ Plan, produce and post-produce your chosen audio product.

✓✓ Make sure your product is well suited to the target audience and format and that it is technically well-produced.

✓✓✓ Show creativity in your ideas and your choice of material, as well as high levels of technical ability in making your product.

Production

You will need to use many of the skills and techniques covered in section 5.2 to produce your product. Keeping a log of how things went will help you to review your work in the next section.

Studio protocols

When in a radio or recording studio, you need to remember to adopt professional standards of behaviour at all times. The checklist below shows what protocols are important.

- Be silent when mics are live or about to go live.
- Take care of equipment, furniture and soundproofing on the walls.
- Observe electrical safety rules – no drink or food allowed.
- Leave the studio clean and tidy for the next person.

Post-production

Mixing and editing software

There are a number of different software applications available for editing and mixing audio on computer, and it is likely you will have access to at least one of them. It may be expensive, top-end professional software, such as SADiE, which is popular in radio studios, or Pro Tools, which is mainly used in music recording studios. It is more likely to be a less expensive solution, such as Adobe Audition, or even freeware such as Audacity, which can be downloaded from the Internet.

Whichever system you use, they all work in similar ways and certain rules apply to them all. This checklist will help you get the best results.

■ Record audio into the software at the correct level – see section 5.2.

■ Zoom in to edit points to get as accurate a cut as possible.

■ Listen carefully to each edit and make sure it is not obviously a cut.

■ Use your own ears to decide if voices are drowned out in a mix or too loud.

■ Save your work regularly in case the computer crashes.

Storing and labelling audio

There are three important rules about any kind of audio recording. They may seem like common sense, but you would be surprised how many people have lost their work because they did not follow them.

■ Make backup copies at the end of each session. This is easiest on computers, but advisable in any format.

■ Label your work clearly so you will find it again, and store it in the correct folder or keep it somewhere safe.

■ When handing in your work on disk or some other format, clearly label it.

Post-production paperwork

Recordings often need paperwork to accompany them, especially when they are for use on radio. The **cue sheet** shown in Figure 5.19 contains essential information, which the studio producer will need in order to play it live on air. In the case of a package that is going into a magazine programme, the presenter will need a mini script in order to introduce the package.

```
RADIO XYZ    THE LUNCHTIME MAGAZINE
CATCHLINE    PIT BULLS
TX DATE:     16/10/06

INTRO:       Being attacked by a pit bull terrier must be one of the most frightening
             experiences possible. But if you were the owner of a dog that hadn't
             bitten anyone, and a court ordered the dog to be put down, you would
             probably not be too happy - as Simon Partner has been finding out.

IN:          fx DOG SNARLING 4"
             "BUSTER IS A PIT BULL TERRIER...

OUT:         ... MEANS CERTAIN DEATH FOR BUSTER."
DUR:         4'57"

BACK ANNO    Simon Partner reporting. There is a helpline for pit bull owners in
             similar circumstances. I'll give you the number after the next piece of
             music.
```

■ **Figure 5.19** *A cue sheet for a radio package displays essential information for playback.*

5.4 Reviewing audio production work

It is good practice to review your work in order to identify ways in which you can do better in future. This final section of the unit shows you how to review the work you did *and* the product you made. An assessment task will help you to do it the correct way.

Finished product

Comparing it with your original intentions

Now the product is finished, you should compare it with the proposal and treatment you developed earlier. How well have you met your expectations of the product? It is important to remember that the product may be good in some ways even if falls short of your expectations in some other respects.

Ask yourself the following questions:

- How much of the original idea has been changed?
- How much of the proposal has been achieved?
- How much of the treatment has been put into practice?
- What improvements have been made to the original plans?

Technical qualities

Next you should ask yourself some more difficult questions about the technical qualities of the finished product.

- Microphone technique: are recordings clear, without any unwanted interference?
- Location work: have you chosen the most appropriate places to record?
- Acoustics: how appropriate are the acoustics for the recordings made?
- Atmosphere and actuality: are there background sounds which add interest?
- Sound effects: have these been added well to a drama?
- Mixing: are levels correct or are some voices or sounds drowned by others?
- Music: was music used effectively?
- Scripting: was the writing clear and effective?

Finally, you should explain what was creative about your product and why.

Production process

Once you have thought about the good and bad aspects of your product, you need to consider the *process* – that is, the things you did in order to make it. If you have kept a log as you worked, you will find it easier to discuss what went wrong and what went right and give evidence.

You should consider:

- technical ability
- creative input
- how well you kept to your production schedule.

Sources of information

As well as your own opinions about your work and how well it went, you should get the opinions of some other people to add to your review. You should play your product to a small number of people in the target audience, and make notes on what they think about it. You could use some of the research methods covered in Unit 2, such as a questionnaire, to help organise the information you get from the audience. If you have made a product for a client, either real or make-believe, get that person to provide some extra feedback. In any case, feedback from your teacher should be included in your review.

Assessment task 7

Review your own production work and your finished product. Do this systematically and present your findings in a permanent form.

Assessment evidence

✅ Describe the work done and the product you have produced.

✅✅ Discuss the strengths and weaknesses of your work and the finished product.

✅✅✅ Explain the reasons for the strengths and weaknesses in your work, using correct terminology and making sure they are detailed and supported by evidence.

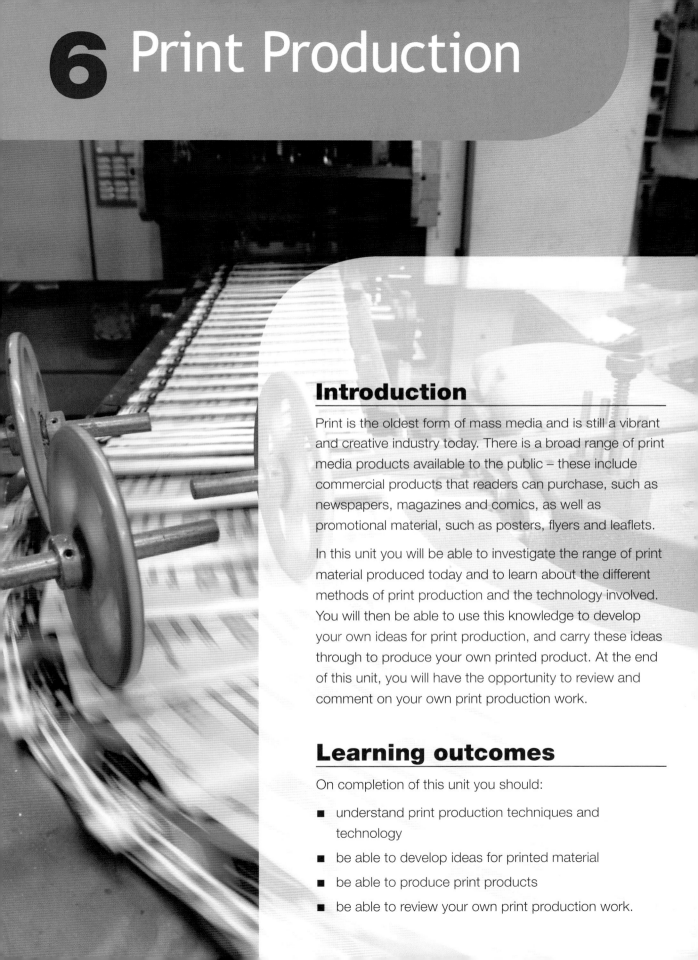

6 Print Production

Introduction

Print is the oldest form of mass media and is still a vibrant and creative industry today. There is a broad range of print media products available to the public – these include commercial products that readers can purchase, such as newspapers, magazines and comics, as well as promotional material, such as posters, flyers and leaflets.

In this unit you will be able to investigate the range of print material produced today and to learn about the different methods of print production and the technology involved. You will then be able to use this knowledge to develop your own ideas for print production, and carry these ideas through to produce your own printed product. At the end of this unit, you will have the opportunity to review and comment on your own print production work.

Learning outcomes

On completion of this unit you should:

- understand print production techniques and technology
- be able to develop ideas for printed material
- be able to produce print products
- be able to review your own print production work.

6.1 Print production techniques and technology

Whatever technology is used, the process of printing remains broadly the same and involves the mass reproduction of words and images onto a **substrate** of some kind, usually some form of paper.

The **artwork** is put onto a printing plate, which is then brought into contact with an ink-covered roller, and it is this ink that reproduces the artwork onto the substrate.

What does it mean?

Substrate – *the material onto which the printing ink is applied – usually paper or card, but can be textiles, plastics, etc.*

Artwork – *all the text, photographs and illustrations that are intended to be printed*

The printing plate itself will have areas on it that carry ink and areas that do not. Printing plates have the printing area either raised (relief printing), in holes (intaglio printing) or at the same level and separated from the non-printing areas by a chemical process (planographic printing). The other main printing technique is through the use of a stencil which marks out the printing and non-printing areas. We will look in more detail at these different processes later in the unit.

■ **Figure 6.1** *A relief printing type showing the raised letters that will carry the ink.*

Case study

Yatin Valand: Printer

Yatin is 21 years old and works at Leicester College as a printer in their National Print Skills Centre. After completing First Diploma and National Diploma qualifications he joined the Modern Apprenticeship scheme and started working in the centre's print department.

He was always more interested in the practical side of media production and operating the equipment – the job he now has is one in which he can use his practical skills to the full.

He enjoys working in an area that uses the latest technology and can now take a design that has been developed on a computer, transfer it to a digital printer and see this work printed on to a variety of different forms and products, including leaflets, posters, T-shirts and mouse mats.

Commercial printing

The printing industry is one of the top ten employers in the UK, with over 12,000 companies employing around 185,000 people in a variety of different roles.

The three main stages of the commercial printing process are called **pre-press**, **press** and **post-press**, also known as **print finishing**.

What does it mean?

Pre-press – *all of the design and preparatory work that takes place to get a product ready for print*

Press – *the actual printing process*

Post-press or **print finishing** – *the processes such as cutting, trimming, folding and binding that take place on the printed material before a product such as a newspaper or magazine can be distributed*

Range of print products

There are print products all around us. In this unit you will be mainly interested in printed media products such as magazines, posters and flyers, but the range of products that a commercial printer will produce is far greater.

Theory into practice

- Do some research into the different types of printed products that you come into contact with.

- Find examples of the different types of printed products and collect them together into a folder.

- Do some further research to find out more information about them, such as how they were printed, who printed them and how many copies of the product were printed, and then write up your findings in a short report.

Most, if not all, of the products that you come across will have been printed by some form of machine, but this has not always been the case. Many traditional hand-operated processes are still in use today, though they tend to be used for producing pieces of art and design work, and for hobby crafts, rather than for producing media products.

■ **Figure 6.2** *Some of the wide range of print products that are available.*

Different ways of printing

There are three main types of printing process that you need to understand. These are traditional **hand-operated** processes, **mechanical** processes that use some form of machinery and new **digital** processes.

What does it mean?

Hand-operated *processes – include the use of etching, linocut, woodcut and screen print*

Mechanical *processes – involve the use of some form of machinery and include offset litho, flexography and gravure*

Digital *processes – include photocopying, laser printing, inkjet printing and the use of desktop-publishing (DTP) software*

Hand-operated processes

One hand method of printing that is still popular today is **screen printing**. This is a way of making multiple copies of a two-dimensional design on to a range of different materials including fabric, paper and card. The screen is made from a material such as silk which has a fine mesh and is stretched on to a wooden frame. A stencil of the image to be reproduced is laid on to the mesh and ink is forced through the mesh and on to the paper or fabric underneath.

Screen printing can be a very creative process but can also be rather time-consuming, so it is only really suitable for small print runs. Mechanised and now digital versions of traditional hand-operated screen printing equipment are now available and are often used for printing posters, T-shirts, fabric and wallpaper.

■ **Figure 6.3** *A screen printer at work, using traditional hand-operated equipment.*

Did you know?

In the 1960s the artist Andy Warhol produced screen prints of celebrities such as Marilyn Monroe and Elvis Presley. He transferred photographic images to a silk screen and then used a rubber squeegee to press different coloured paints through the screen and on to paper underneath.

By repeating the process the image is reproduced, but each one is different.

Did you know?

Some of the earliest examples of printing using wooden blocks have been found in China and date back to the year 581.

Another method of printing by hand is **etching**. Etches (or scratches) are made on a copper plate which is then coated with ink and pressed on to paper to reproduce the image. Many famous artists, including Picasso and Rembrandt, used etching to reproduce their pictures.

In **woodcut**, an image is carved into the surface of a piece of wood in such a way that the parts that will be printed remain level with the surface of the wood, while the parts that will not be printed are removed. This is called **relief printing**. The surface of the wooden block is covered with ink using a roller, and the block is then pressed down on to paper so that the ink is transferred and the image reproduced.

Linocut is also a form of relief printing similar to woodcut, but the image is cut into a sheet of linoleum instead of a block of wood. Linoleum is made from solidified linseed oil and is easier to cut than wood, though it is quite fragile and the linoleum printing plate can deteriorate with continued use.

Remember

The main hand-operated printing processes that you need to understand are:

- etching
- woodcut
- linocut
- screen print.

Mechanised printing processes

The invention of the printing press around 1450 by Johannes Gutenberg in Germany led to a decline in the use of traditional hand methods of printing and the growth of ever more sophisticated mechanical processes as the demand for mass-produced printed material grew.

■ **Figure 6.4** *This Chinese woodcut creates a bold political statement (the text reads 'To revolt is no crime, to rebel is justified') – the block would have been used to create numerous copies without losing detail.*

Before printing was invented, books and manuscripts had to be copied by hand – it could take up to two years to hand-copy a book. The invention of **letterpress** printing, which uses moveable type made from metal characters, meant that whole pages of text could be put on to a press and used to reproduce hundreds of copies of books and manuscripts. At first press runs were quite small and limited to around 200 or 300 copies, but soon much larger print runs were being produced.

Letterpress printing is not often used now, as it is time-consuming to set up the loose type and make the plates, and there is only a limited range of fonts and styles.

■ **Figure 6.5** *An example of letterpress type being set.*

Flexography is a printing process that uses much thinner plates made of a flexible material such as rubber or a special type of plastic. The words and images to be printed are transferred to the plates by a photographic process, and the inks used are quick-drying thin liquids. This means that flexography can be used to print on to materials such as polythene and metallic films, and is used for printing plastic shopping bags and packaging for food products.

Lithography also uses flexible plates produced by a photographic process, which are attached to a cylinder. The process relies on the fact that oil and water do not mix. During the lithography process, parts of the printing plate are kept wet so that the oily ink is rejected by the wet areas of the plate and only sticks to the dry areas, which are the words and images that need to be printed. These are transferred on to the paper that comes into contact with the inky cylinder.

Offset-lithography printing uses the same principle, but the paper does not come into direct contact with the printing plate. The image is first transferred to a rubber roller, called an **offset blanket** or **offset cylinder** (Figure 6.6). Until the advent of digital printing technologies, lithography was a very popular form of commercial printing used for medium and long printing runs of products such as magazines, posters and books. Now it is used for high-quality illustrated books.

Off-set litho presses that are fed paper one sheet at a time are called **sheet-fed** presses and are often used for high-quality work. Paper can also be fed from a large roll, called a web – these sorts of presses are called **web litho presses** and were often used for large print runs such as magazines and catalogues.

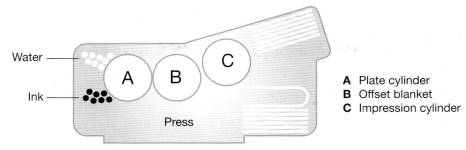

Water ————
Ink ————
Press

A Plate cylinder
B Offset blanket
C Impression cylinder

■ **Figure 6.6** *Diagram showing the off-set lithography process.*

When printing with more than one colour a different plate is used for each of the main colours, with overprinting using translucent ink allowing different colours to be reproduced. **Four-colour printing** derives its name from the fact that four different colours of ink are used – by combining these four colours the full range of colours can be printed.

Did you know?

CMYK *is the term used in four-colour printing for the four ink colours used:*
C*yan*
Y*ellow*
M*agenta*
K*ey (black)*

RGB *is the other important term used for colours and stands for* **R***ed,* **G***reen and* **B***lue. Scanners and digital cameras produce images using a combination of these three colours and the conversion of RGB produced colours into CMYK colours for printing is an important job that commercial printers have to do to make sure that their products look correct.*

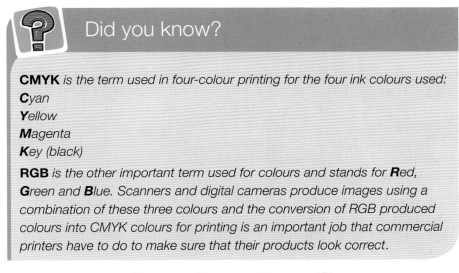

Cyan   Magenta   Yellow   Black

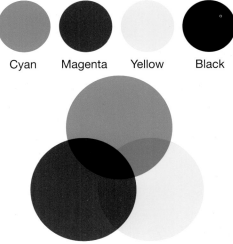

■ **Figure 6.7** *The colours used in four-colour printing. Combining them can produce any other colour in the spectrum.*

Gravure is a web-fed printing process that uses a copper-coated cylinder on to which a reverse image of the print product is engraved.

This cylinder prints directly on to the substrate, with a softer roller applying pressure. It is used for large-quantity runs where the set-up costs are high, but the unit cost is low, such as mail-order catalogues, free brochures, packaging, and printing on to fabric and wallpaper.

■ **Figure 6.8** *A finishing machine gathering and folding the signatures of a publication.*

What does it mean?

There are four main printing techniques:

Relief *printing – the area to be printed is raised above the non-printing surface. Letterpress is a process that uses this technique.*

Planographic *printing – uses a flat printing plate that has been treated so that certain areas reject or accept ink or water. An example of a process that uses this technique is lithography.*

Intaglio *printing – the printing areas are lower than the non-printing surface. The 'holes' in the printing plate are filled with ink, which is then transferred to the paper. Gravure uses this technique.*

Stencil *printing – parts of a mesh screen are left open or closed by a stencil, and the open parts allow ink to pass through onto the paper. An example of a process that uses this technique is screen printing.*

Digital printing

Traditional methods of mechanical printing such as off-set litho, flexography and gravure are still very much a part of the print industry, but digital printing, already commonplace in the home, school and office environment, is now becoming increasingly popular for commercial printing. This is because digital printers, such as inkjet and laser printers, are now capable of high-quality colour printing using **variable data**, and they are also cost effective for shorter print runs.

Digital technology has had a particularly large impact on the print industry which, until relatively recently, still relied on the more traditional mechanical methods of print production. New methods of production and distribution have led to a much greater emphasis on computer-based technology, and a need for a more highly skilled workforce.

What does it mean?

Variable data – *data that changes – in this context refers to the different information that can be sent to a printer when printing the same product.*

This feature of digital printing means that you can now quickly print letters from a standard template that are personalised and individually addressed. The use of variable data also means that you can produce personalised promotional material that has specific elements targeted at individual people.

Think it over

Think about the changes that digital technology has bought to both the **production** and the **distribution** of products such as newspapers, many of which are now also available as online versions on the Internet.

Think about the different ways in which you can now get information about what is going on in the world around you.

One of the biggest changes within the print industry has perhaps been on the pre-press side, with the introduction of ever more sophisticated computer-based programs to help with the design and layout of pages, replacing the traditional labour-intensive methods of cut and paste.

The increased use of computers and desktop-publishing (DTP) software means that a pre-press designer today needs to be familiar with a number of different software programs that are used within the industry to manipulate, control and combine text, image and graphic files.

Logos and graphics tend to be produced using programs such as *Adobe Illustrator*, *Macromedia Freehand* or *Corel Draw*, while the main program used within the print industry to edit and manipulate digital images is *Adobe Photoshop* (Figure 6.9).

The two main page layout programs used by pre-press designers are *Adobe InDesign* and *QuarkXpress*. Used to design and lay out the text and images in print products, they can handle a range of image and graphic files. They also allow type to be added directly into the page layout, or imported in from programs such as *Microsoft Word* or *Excel*.

■ **Figure 6.9** *A pre-press designer using Adobe Photoshop.*

 Remember

You will need to save your completed work as it will form part of the portfolio that your tutor will need to present to the moderator towards the end of the course.

Did you know?

Before the final proof is sent to print, a pre-press designer will often run the finished design through some additional software to check if there are any problems or conflicts with the various files.

Pre-flight *software, such as* FlightCheck *produced by Markzware, and* **post-flight** *software, such as* PitStop *produced by Enfocus, both analyse the digital files to ensure that they are fit and ready for their intended purpose, before they are sent to print. The software highlights potential problems, such as poor image resolution or problems with the colours, and suggest things that can be done to solve the problem. (The terms 'pre-flight' and 'post-flight' come from the checklist that pilots go through prior to take off.)*

Think it over

Why do you think pre- and post-flighting software has become so popular within the print industry?

Remember

Digital printing includes inkjet and laser printers that can produce high-quality prints very quickly.

Variable data (such as personalised details in marketing letters) can also be used in digital printing.

Pre-press processes are now largely computer-based, and pre-press designers work with a range of different software packages.

CTP (computer-to-plate) printing is now the main commercial process for printing media products such as newspapers, magazines and most books. CTP allows printing plates to be created directly from the computer.

Assessment task 1

- *Write a report on print techniques and technology. You will need to do some further research into the different techniques and technologies.*

- *Your report should have an appropriate structure using headings and sub-headings. You should also try to use appropriate language in the report and make sure you check your spelling and grammar.*

- *Include examples of some of the printed products that you have been looking at, either within the body of the report or in an appendices section. Annotate your examples to explain the processes and technologies that have been used.*

Assessment evidence

✅ Describe the print techniques and technologies that you have investigated.

✅✅ Ensure that the descriptions you provide are quite detailed and include well-annotated examples of print material to support the points you are making.

✅✅✅ You will need to explain, rather than just describe, the relevant techniques and technology, and provide an evaluation of them. You should also use technical and specialist language accurately and in an appropriate way.

6.2   Develop ideas for printed material

You should now be ready to start to develop some of your own ideas for printed material that you can then go on to produce later in the unit.

You will probably want to work with other students as part of a team so that you can share ideas and work together to produce a well-designed and professional-looking product. If you do work as part of a team it is important that you clearly show what your individual contribution has been to the group project.

For example, your group may decide to work together to produce a student magazine for your school or college. This is a good idea for this unit as it will allow each member of the group to take responsibility for the development, design and production of a specific section of the magazine, while you can all work together on the front cover.

Theory into practice

- Write down some ideas for print products that you and your team could develop and produce.

- Try to consider the main issues that will be involved in planning and producing each of these ideas.

- What strategies could you use to try to make sure that you and your group produce a successful product?

Brainstorming ideas is a good place to start, and at this point it is important to record the ideas in some way so that they do not get lost or forgotten. One method is to use a flip chart or whiteboard and write down key words from the discussion, or you might want to record the session as audio or video.

It is important that you try to capture all of the thoughts and ideas at this point, however strange some of them may seem, as you never know which ones are going to work.

When looking at the feasibility of each of the ideas, think about the cost of production and the budget that you would need to undertake it. You also need to think about the resources that are available to you and the timescale in which you have to complete the project.

Researching initial ideas

Once you have decided on some ideas that have potential, you and your team will need to undertake some further research so that you can make

Remember

Time spent planning, developing and researching your proposed production will be time well spent, and should improve the effectiveness and quality of the final product that you produce.

■ **Figure 6.10** *Use a flip chart or whiteboard to note down all the ideas you come up with in your brainstorming session.*

Remember

The production idea that you research and develop in this section will need to be carried through to the production stage in section 6.3 of this unit.

You will need to ensure that you and your team thoroughly evaluate your chosen idea. The project needs to be valid in terms of cost, time and resources.

Remember, too, that you will need to review your production work in section 6.4.

an informed decision as to which ideas have potential to develop and which are best left alone.

Building on the work that you completed for Unit 2, this research will probably involve both primary and secondary techniques, and you may get as far as conducting a short survey to find out the thoughts of your potential target audience about your ideas. It would be a good idea at this stage to look back at the key points that you learnt in Unit 2 about the different research methods and techniques that are available to you.

Case study

Researcing a college magazine project

Let's take a look at how some students tackled this part of the unit when they were developing their own ideas for a print product.

Casey and her team brainstormed a list of initial ideas that included a college magazine aimed at the students, a community newspaper targeting the unemployed and some promotional material for a company run by one of their parents.

They decided to research the viability of all three ideas and carried out some primary and secondary research. This included conducting a short questionnaire, interviewing some key people and looking at similar products that already existed.

After assessing each idea they decided that the team was best placed to further develop their print, design and journalistic skills by producing a college magazine that was aimed at 16–18-year-old students at the college.

Once this had been decided, they did further research into this idea, which included examining a range of printed products aimed at their target audience so they could get ideas for the style and content of their product. They also completed a more detailed survey of a sample of the target audience to see what they would like to see in the magazine, and to find out things like how often they would like it to come out, what size they would prefer and how much they were prepared to pay for it.

To extend their vocational knowledge they also decided to visit a local newspaper office to find out more about the actual process of putting together and printing a print product.

■ *Casey and her team visiting a local newspaper office.*

Theory into practice

- Decide on the initial ideas that you are going to research further.

- Assess each idea according to the following key questions:
  - What will be produced?
  - What is its purpose?
  - Who is the target audience?
  - How will it be produced?
  - Are there any ethical or legal issues, including copyright, to think about?
  - What other issues need to be considered?

- After assessing each idea, decide on the one you will take forward to the production stage and explain why you have chosen this particular idea.

Pre-production planning

Once you have chosen the idea that you are going to take through to the production stage and undertaken the necessary research, you can begin your detailed planning and preparation. This is called the **pre-production** stage and will involve you in producing rough drafts, designs and ideas of your proposed print product.

These might include **ideas sheets** on which you will produce a number of different sketches of your ideas, together with some brief notes. You can then develop these into **thumbnails**, which are small sketches that show details of the layout and composition (Figure 6.11). You can develop your thumbnails further into **concept drawings** and **rough drafts** of the finished product.

Getting feedback on your drafts and designs is important if you want your final product to be successful. If you have a client for your project then you should get feedback from them as you go through the pre-production stage to make sure that they are happy with what you are doing.

Remember

It is important that you keep all of your pre-production work and include it in your final portfolio. It will provide good evidence of the stages that you went through in developing your print product.

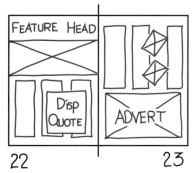

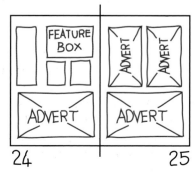

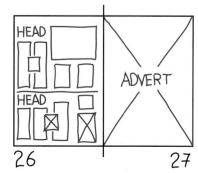

■ **Figure 6.11** *Example of a set of thumbnails used to draft page layouts for a magazine.*

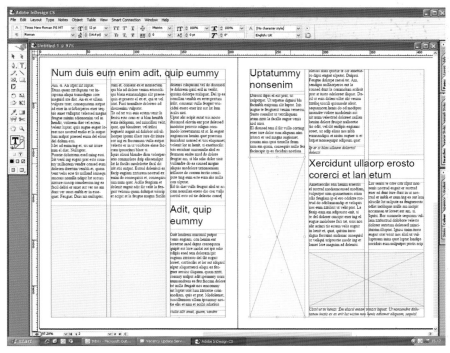

■ **Figure 6.12** *A rough draft of a newspaper layout with dummy text and placeholder boxes for images.*

During this stage you will need to think carefully about what the main purpose of the product is, what your target audience will expect to see in the product and, if you have a client, what he or she will require. You do not want to get to the end of the project and have your client tell you that it is not what they want, or your audience say that they do not like it.

Production issues

At this stage you also need to consider some of the production issues that you will have to face if you take your ideas through to the next stage.

You will need to consider very carefully the resources that you have available to you, the costs involved and the quantity of finished products you will need to print for your target market.

Whichever technology you use to print your final product, the principles are broadly the same and you need to make sure that the results are as good as you can make them within your set budget.

You will also need to consider any legal and ethical issues that there might be with your work. For example, copyright is an important factor to consider and you need to make sure that you do not copy or use anybody else's work without first asking their permission. You also need to make sure that anything that you write is true and that you do not make any claims or accusations that you cannot prove. If you do write things that are untrue and are negative about somebody, then you could be breaking the laws on libel. For much more on copyright, libel and other issues, look back at Unit 1.

Case study

McLibel

One of the most famous libel cases was brought by McDonald's against the publishers of a leaflet called 'What's wrong with McDonald's?'

The trial was one of the longest in British history and cost many millions of pounds in legal fees. The judge eventually found in favour of McDonald's because the publishers of the leaflet could not prove that all of the statements that they had made were true.

They were ordered to pay damages to McDonald's of £60,000.

 Assessment task 2

This assessment task is to bring together all of the work that you have carried out in developing, researching and planning your proposed print product.

- *Provide evidence that you have come up with several ideas and have explored each of these, including a consideration of the budget, resources and time required.*
- *You can present your work as a section of your portfolio. Include all of your notes and research material as well as the rough drafts and other pre-production paperwork that you and your team developed.*
- *Provide a commentary or narrative of some sort in which you describe and explain the processes that you went through.*
- *You can also present some of this information in the form of an oral presentation to the rest of your class, though you should remember to record details of it to include with your portfolio.*

Assessment evidence

✔ Describe your ideas for your print product. This means that you need to show that you have come up with some valid ideas for print products and have identified some of the relevant issues that might have an impact on the production of them.

✔✔ Describe your ideas in detail and ensure that the development of your ideas is competent. Show that you have put some thought into the relevant issues that you will need to consider throughout the production process.

✔✔✔ Explain and evaluate your ideas using appropriate and accurate technical language. Your ideas should show imagination and creativity and should begin to move beyond the conventional.

6.3 Produce print products

Most print products consist of a combination of both words and images, and once you have decided on your final idea and the planning stages have been completed, it is now time for the production of the text and images that will form the basis of the print product itself.

Copy

The original writing that is used in a print product is called **copy**, and the print industry employs journalists and copywriters to produce those all-important words that are used to communicate to the readers.

Producing original copy can be a demanding job, and it is often done to very tight deadlines, so when you are producing the copy for your product you will have to have a clear idea of when you need to have it finished by. You will have to research your topic thoroughly so that you can use a combination of your existing knowledge and the information that you have found out.

When writing copy you will need to think carefully about the audience that you are targeting, the context in which it will be placed and what the purpose of the writing is. Having a clear idea about who your target

■ **Figure 6.13** *Casey and her team working on their magazine project.*

audience are is probably the most important consideration when writing your copy, as it will have a big impact on the words and sentences that you produce.

The way that you write and the things that you write about would be very different for the following three items: a comic aimed at young children; an article on recycling for a local newspaper; a games review for a computer magazine. Similarly, the style of writing used in a news story in a national quality newspaper such as the *Independent* will be very different from the style used in a tabloid paper such as the *Sun*.

Theory into practice

- Collect a selection of newspapers from the same day. Look through each one and select examples of stories that appear in more than one paper.
- Try to identify the different styles and techniques of writing that are used in each paper. Look at the types of words that are used. Are they emotive words or has the writer chosen words that are more neutral? Are they negative or positive words? Are the sentences long or short?
- Explain why these different techniques have been used and what their impact on the reader might be.

You might find the information that is covered in Unit 11, Writing for the Media, useful when completing this activity.

You also need to think carefully about what the purpose of your print product is, as this will also have an impact on the style and form of the writing that you produce. Are you trying to persuade somebody to buy something, or are you trying to inform them about something more factual? Are you writing a piece to entertain, to shock, to make somebody laugh?

All of these decisions will influence the language that you use, the style of the writing, the length of the sentences and the structure of the text. It will also have an impact on the amount of words that you use. An advertising poster might have only one or two very carefully chosen words on it, a flyer or leaflet might have a few hundred, whereas a newspaper or magazine article might consist of many thousands of words.

Images

The pictures and images in a print product are often used as a way of attracting the right audience to notice the product and to pick it up and read it. You only have to look at the different images that newspapers and magazines put on their front covers to get some idea of the sort of audience that they are targeting.

■ **Figure 6.14** *With well-known brands, a minimum of words can have a powerful effect in advertisements.*

Think it over

- Why are images so important in media products?
- What information and messages do they give us about the world around us?
- People say that 'the camera never lies'. Is this true?

■ **Figure 6.15** *How might the images used on these magazine covers help attract readers from the target audience?*

Theory into practice

- Collect examples of print products that have used an image to attract people's attention.
- Describe what the images are and how they have been produced
- What messages are they trying to communicate to the audience?

You can produce images for your print product in a number of different ways. Depending on what sort of equipment you have, you can use traditional or digital methods to produce your own original photographic images, or you can use a scanner and picture editing software to copy and manipulate existing images. You can also use a scanner to convert copies of images that you have taken with a film-based camera to a digital format.

If you choose to use a digital camera from the start, then you need to make sure that the quality and resolution of the images is high enough to allow successful printing to take place. Once taken, it is a simple procedure to transfer the images from the camera to the computer.

Once they are in a digital form, you can control and manipulate images using software packages such as *Adobe Photoshop*, and then import them into design software such as *QuarkXpress* or *InDesign*.

Remember

When using a computer to design and put together a product such as a newspaper, magazine or poster, remember that what looks good on the computer screen can sometimes be disappointing once it is printed on the page. Checking for potential problems before you send a job for printing can save you time and money in the long run. Programs such as *FlightCheck* and *PitStop* will go through your software and highlight any problems for you.

Graphics

Photographic images are not the only images that are used in printed products. Cartoons, line drawings, logos, charts and diagrams can all be used to illustrate a piece of copy and attract the attention of potential readers.

You might have somebody in your team who is good at drawing and able to produce original illustrations, or you may want to use computer software to produce charts and diagrams from the data that you have collected.

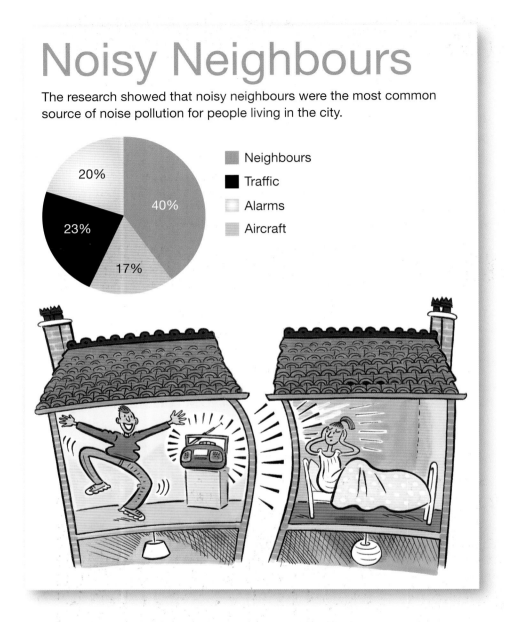

Noisy Neighbours

The research showed that noisy neighbours were the most common source of noise pollution for people living in the city.

- Neighbours
- Traffic
- Alarms
- Aircraft

40%
20%
23%
17%

■ **Figure 6.16** *The chart and cartoon in this article draw the attention of potential readers and add extra information about the topic being written about.*

Whatever type of images you include in your product, you need to make sure that they have a clear purpose, are of a high quality and are clearly captioned or labelled so that they communicate the right message to the readers. Pictures are capable of generating a wide range of meanings to different people, and a caption can help to narrow down this range of potential meanings and direct the audience to the meaning that you want.

Theory into practice

- What sort of graphics and images are you planning to have in your printed product?
- How are you going to produce them and ensure that they are of the highest quality possible?
- Think about what they will look like when they are printed. Remember, just because something looks good on a computer screen does not mean it will always look as good when printed on the page.

Theory into practice

- Look at the news picture in Figure 6.17 and write down the different meanings that this image could communicate.
- Try to think of a caption for each of the meanings you have come up with. Each caption should encourage people to accept that particular meaning
- Which types of news stories might each of the different picture/caption combinations appear in?

■ **Figure 6.17** *Write your own captions for this photograph.*

The editing process

Once you have produced your copy and images and combined them in your page layout, you will need to edit your product to make sure that it makes sense and has no mistakes in it.

Did you know?

The publishers of newspapers and magazines employ an editor to oversee the whole product and sub-editors to edit specific parts of the publication.

A sub-editor might be responsible for checking the copy for accuracy, adding or deleting words to make it fit the space available, adding headlines and strap-lines, and restructuring the material.

A sub-editor might also manipulate the images: scaling a graphic or image (increasing or decreasing the size) to make it fit the available space, cropping the image to get rid of unwanted parts of the picture, or adding a caption to make its meaning clearer.

If you are producing a group project like a magazine, then it would be a good idea for all members of the team to undertake the role of sub-editor for somebody else's work. This will allow all members of the team to carry out the role of journalist and sub-editor. You might want to do the same thing for the images in the magazine, with each person responsible for producing their own images and also sub-editing somebody else's.

Case study

Team roles

Remember Casey and her team? When they were producing their magazine they decided that all four of them would be members of the editorial board to oversee the production and decide what the front cover would look like. This board met regularly and they took turns to take minutes so that they always had a record of what was said.

In their first meeting they decided that each member of the team would be responsible for a different section of the magazine. Casey chose to produce a section on fashion. Raj chose to write an article on computer games. Florence decided to produce a section on music, while Ashton concentrated on a section with advice for young people. In addition they all contributed articles about life at their college.

They all produced their own images for their work and acted as a sub-editor for somebody else's work.

Their client was the head of the college Media department, and they also arranged regular meetings with her so that they could get feedback on their progress.

You might not want to appoint a single editor to oversee the whole project, and instead prefer to adopt a more collective approach with all members of the team as part of an editorial board that will manage the production process.

Design

Putting the copy, images and graphics together in a way that is pleasing to the eye and satisfies the demands of the brief is a skilled job. You will probably want to use one of the desktop-publishing or design software packages used in the industry such as *QuarkXpress* or *InDesign*.

You will need to experiment with the alignment of text and images, the use of columns and boxes to structure the page. Make sure you include headings, sub-headings and strap-lines to break up the text and guide the eye of the reader.

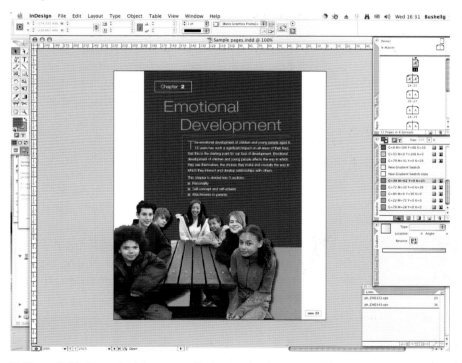

■ **Figure 6.18** *A page in the process of being put together using DTP software.*

Fonts

There are literally thousands of different **typefaces** or **fonts** available, each of which has its own distinctive style and is capable of generating its own set of meanings to the reader. Some are designed to look like handwriting, others to look funny or old-fashioned.

The two main types of font are **serif** and **sans serif**. Serif typefaces have a decorative flourish to the letters, while sans serif typefaces are plainer. As a general rule, serif typefaces tend to be used in the main body of a text and sans serif typefaces tend to be used for titles and headings.

Remember

Learning to use design software takes time, and you will need to learn about the basic techniques and functions before trying more complex tasks.

Remember to save examples of your experimental work to include in your final portfolio as evidence of your skill development.

Think it over

See how many different fonts you can find. What sort of meanings does each font communicate to you? What sort of publication might you expect to see each one in?

Times New Roman
ABCDEFGabcdefg

Palatino
ABCDEFGabcdefg

Baskerville
ABCDEFGabcdefg

Gill Sans
ABCDEFGabcdefg

Arial
ABCDEFGabcdefg

Trade Gothic
ABCDEFGabcdefg

■ **Figure 6.19** *Examples of serif and sans serif typefaces.*

The choice of font and text size, and the use of such features as italics, underlining and bold text, will all have an effect on the final look of your product, what the audience thinks of it and whether it communicates the intended messages to them. Whatever decisions you make, be sure to apply them consistently. For example, if you decide to put your sub-headings in italics, make sure you do so to all of them.

Take care not to introduce too many different styles and features into your product. A page, poster or flyer that uses too many different styles and is too cluttered will often put off the potential reader. Also, do not be afraid of white space. With page design less is often more, and you should aim to produce a well-designed page with clean lines and a consistent, coherent style throughout.

The printing process

Once you have finalised your design, put all the copy and images in place, edited your work and got the client to sign it off, you are finally ready to print your product.

In section 6.1 we looked at the range of printing technologies that are available to the print industry, with the choice dependent on the type of product being printed, the quality of reproduction that is needed, the amount of money available and the size of the print run.

Theory into practice

Unless you are working in a school or college that has its own print department, or have links with a printing company, it is unlikely that you will have access to anything more sophisticated than a domestic computer printer and a photocopier to print and reproduce your finished products.

However, whichever technology you use, the principles are broadly the same, and it is the way in which you have produced your product and the quality of the final work that are most important for this part of the unit.

■ **Figure 6.20** *A student printing his finished publication.*

The printing process needs to be carefully monitored and controlled so that the same high quality can be maintained throughout the whole of the print run. You do not want hours of careful planning, design and production to be ruined by a poorly printed final product.

Print finishing

Print finishing refers to the processes used to complete a product after it has been printed and before it can be distributed and used.

The finishing process usually includes cutting and trimming the product to the appropriate size using a guillotine. If the product is a book, leaflet, newspaper or magazine, then the pages will need to be collated together in the right order, folded and then bound using staples, glue or stitching.

 Remember

You will need to produce a number of test prints, and make any necessary adjustments, before beginning the print run proper. The test prints might be useful evidence to include in your portfolio.

 Think it over

Think about the ways in which your product will be 'finished'. If it consists of more than one page, how will you keep these pages together? Is a simple staple the best method for you to use?

If you are producing a newspaper or magazine, or leaflets and flyers, how are you planning to distribute your final product to your audience?

Assessment task 3

Produce the print product that you planned and researched in Assessment task 2.

- *If you are working as part of a group, you will need to decide who is doing what and agree an action plan which shows the deadlines you are working to and clearly defines the roles and responsibilities.*
- *Do not forget to include feedback from your client or audience into this plan, and time to make any additional changes.*
- *You will need to produce the copy and images for the product and make sure that somebody sub-edits your work. You will then need to combine all the elements together and get the product as a whole ready for press.*
- *Once printed, you will need to 'finish' your product in an appropriate way and get it out to the audience.*
- *Do not forget to keep examples of your work as you go through each of the production stages, and to keep a diary or commentary that explains what you are doing.*

Assessment evidence

✔ Your final print product should show some relation to the original idea and should demonstrate that you have used relevant techniques and technology to produce it.

✔✔ Your final print product should demonstrate competent use of the relevant techniques and technology, and show that you have clearly thought about how the final product should look.

✔✔✔ Your final print product should provide evidence of the use of high-level skills and a creative approach to print production. Your product will show that techniques and technology have been used to very good effect.

6.4   Review your print production work

You should now have finished your production work and be ready to reflect on how it went and review what you have completed. This is a very important part of the unit, as you need to understand what went well so that you can do these things again in your future projects. You also need to understand the things that went wrong or did not go as well as you planned. Learning from your mistakes is an important part of any process and will make you better at doing things next time.

You can present your review in any form that you choose. You might prefer to present it in the form of a written report or you might want to use an audio-visual format of some kind. You need to discuss this with your tutor so that you can decide what is the best format for you.

The three key areas that you need to look at when reviewing your print work are

- the finished product or products that you printed
- the production processes that you went through
- the sources of information that you used.

When reviewing your completed work you will need to compare the finished product with your original ideas and intentions. To what extent have you carried through your original ideas into the final version? What did you have to change and what were the reasons for these changes?

■ **Figure 6.21** *You might want to present your review in a audio-visual format.*

■ **Figure 6.22** *Reviewing your print work is an important final stage of the unit.*

You will also need to describe and account for the technical quality, such as the quality of the paper used, what the quality of the final print run is like, how bright and sharp the images are and how clear the copy is.

You must also examine how suitable your printed product is for the target audience and to what extent it meets the requirements and the needs of the client.

You also need to review the production processes that you used when designing, developing and printing your work. You will need to comment on the way that you and your team managed the design and production process, and describe and explain the technical and creative skills that you used throughout the process.

You will also need to review your own working methods and those that you used when working as a member of a team.

Finally, you will need to review the sources of information that you used, which will include your research material, your self-evaluation of your work as it developed, details from your production logs and the feedback that you received from your audience, your client, tutor and peers.

Think it over

Think about what went well during the production process and what you had some difficulties with. If you were to do this unit again, is there anything that you would do differently?

Assessment task 4

Review and evaluate your print product and the processes that you went through. In this review you should clearly identify your contribution to any group work and the roles that you undertook.

Assessment evidence

✔ Describe your own print work. As well as describing the finished product, you also need to describe the processes that you went through and comment on your own skill development and the role that you as an individual played in any group work.

✔✔ Ensure that the descriptions you provide are quite detailed and include some examples to support the statements you are making.

✔✔✔ Explain, rather than just describe, the product and the processes, methods and technology that you used. Justify and support your comments with specific and well-chosen examples. You should also use technical and specialist language accurately and in an appropriate way.

7 Advertising Production

Introduction

The media industry and advertising are inextricably linked by the need of the media industry to produce advertising material to support its other programmes and publications. It is therefore essential for the industry to understand the audience for advertisements.

In this unit you will be looking at advertising techniques and how advertisers produce material to attract particular audiences. You will be able to generate ideas for an advertisement in whatever media format you wish to use and then create the advertisement. This may be based on the work you have done in other units and you will want to choose the media format in which you feel you can achieve the highest marks. Finally, you will learn how to review your advertising production work.

Learning outcomes

On completion of this unit you should:

- understand advertising techniques
- be able to develop ideas for an advertisement
- be able to create an advertisement
- be able to review your own advertising production.

7.1 Advertising techniques

When you get on a bus or a train, read a newspaper, listen to the radio or watch the television you see or hear advertisements. You are also bombarded with pop-up advertisements and banners on websites.

Advertising has been around for a long time, at first just as word of mouth. The ancient Egyptians used papyrus to create sales messages. As printing techniques developed in the fifteenth and sixteenth centuries, advertising moved on to handbills or leaflets. It was not until the seventeenth century that newspapers appeared and, with them, newspaper advertisements.

Advertising has come a long way from those early days. Every daily or weekly newspaper contains a huge amount of advertising. Magazines are crammed full of colour advertisements that are designed to 'sell' to the magazine's target audience.

Next time you go to the cinema try to arrive early and watch the advertisements that appear before the feature film. When you arrive at the cinema look around and see how many advertisements you can see for the latest films. When you are watching the film try to notice if there are any products being promoted by the film – this type of advertising is called **product placement**. In the film *I, Robot*, Will Smith mentions his classic shoes by name and in *The Matrix Reloaded*, Cadillac cars are used extensively. Recent James Bond films feature Omega watches and BMW cars. Why would these companies want to place their products in a film? What benefit could this have for the sales of the products?

Think it over

Why do you think advertisers use the television as an advertising medium?

Why do you think advertisers use newspapers and magazines as an advertising medium?

Why do you think that many advertisers now use the Internet as an advertising medium?

Figures 7.1 and 7.2 show examples of advertisements that are designed to encourage you either to see a film or to enter a website where you can buy a DVD and merchandise. How effective are they? Would you go and see the film? Would you click on the box and enter the site? Ask yourself what it is about these advertisements that might attract you.

Did you know?

Some commonly used advertising techniques are:

Celebrity endorsement – *the product is linked to a celebrity who appears in the advertising – the idea is that people might think that buying this product will make them like the celebrity.*

Peer approval – *advertisers suggest that using this product will win you friends (and that not using it could lose you friends).*

Nurture – *these advertisements appeal to your paternal or maternal instincts – the use of animals and children are key features of advertisements of this type.*

Escape – *these advertisements appeal to people who want to get away from it all and fly away to far off places.*

Beauty appeal – *these advertisements draw people to beautiful people, places and things.*

Intelligence – *the advertisement associates the product with people who are smart and who cannot easily be fooled.*

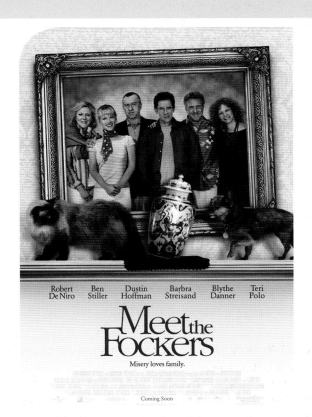

■ **Figure 7.1** *A billboard advertisement for the film* Meet the Fockers.

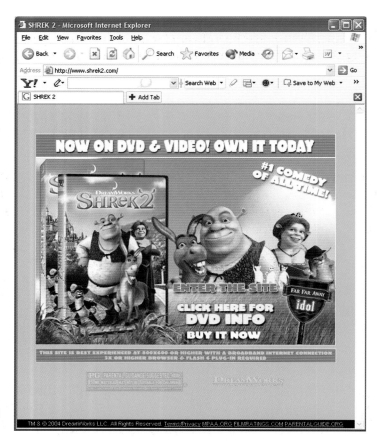

■ **Figure 7.2** *An advertisement for the website of the film* Shrek 2.

Think it over

Think about a product that you own, for example an MP3 player, mobile phone or a computer.

- What prompted you to buy this product?
- Did you see an advertisement for the product?
- Did you see someone else using it?
- Did you feel that without owning this product you were missing out or you were inferior in some way?

Target audience

Placing advertisements within products aimed at an appropriate target audience is crucial for advertisers. It would be no use advertising products such as nappies or baby oil in *Saga Magazine*, which is aimed at people of retirement age. Products advertised in this magazine are more likely to be health-related or for travel aimed at retired people. Equally, you would not advertise a holiday for retired people in *Mother & Baby* magazine.

Advertisers take great care to select the correct medium for their advertisements. Companies spend very large sums of money on advertising their products so they must ensure that this money is spent wisely.

Did you know?

The advertising budgets of some of the largest companies are enormous. In the 12 months to 31 August 2006, the biggest advertising spender in the UK was Unilever – which had spent £192.5 million, closely followed by Procter & Gamble at £182.9 million. And in third place? You may be surprised to learn that it was the UK Government, which spent £154 million on advertising.

The two biggest supermarket chains, Tesco and Sainsbury's were also both big spenders: £68.5 million and £54.4 million respectively.

Source: Daily Telegraph, 31/08/2006

Theory into practice

Get hold of a copy of a tabloid newspaper and a broadsheet or compact newspaper. Choose at least three advertisements from each one.

For each advertisement, identify the target audience, the type of language used and the type of images used.

Are there any differences between the types of advertisement that appear in these two newspapers? If so, why do you think this is?

Did you know?

Soap operas were first heard on the radio in the USA in the 1930s and expanded into television in the 1940s. The commercials aired during these programmes were largely aimed at housewives and were for laundry and cleaning products.

Internet advertising

More and more companies are now advertising on the Internet. In 2004, for the first time, the amount spent on Internet advertising in the UK was more than the amount spent on radio advertising.

Did you know?

In 2004, £16.9 billion pounds were spent on advertising in the UK. Internet advertising is on the increase, but it is still a long way behind some of the more popular advertising media: 41.5 per cent of the spend was on advertising in the press, 23.9 per cent on TV adverts, 14.6 per cent on direct mail, 3.9 per cent on the Internet and 3.8 per cent on radio advertising.

E-commerce

By setting up an electronic shop on its website, a company can advertise its products or services directly to any potential customers who visit the site. The number of sales will be enhanced by having an e-commerce facility, which allows customers to buy directly from the website. Most such websites now accept credit card payments, which makes buying easier.

Banner ads

As you have spent time surfing the Internet, you have probably seen more than your fair share of banner ads. Because of its graphic element, a banner advertisement is quite similar to a traditional advertisement that you would see in a printed publication such as a newspaper or magazine. These small rectangular advertisements appear on all sorts of web pages and vary considerably in appearance and subject matter, but they all share a basic function – if you click on them, your Internet browser will take you to the advertiser's website. It is almost like being taken instantaneously to the advertiser's shop – an extremely powerful marketing tool for the advertiser.

Pop-ups

Pop-up ads are a form of online advertising intended to increase web traffic or capture email addresses. They appear in a separate web browser window, usually of a fairly small size. Pop-ups are usually generated by JavaScript, but can be generated by other means as well. Many Internet users find pop-ups annoying and disruptive.

A variation on the pop-up is the pop-under advertisement. This opens a new browser window behind the active window. Pop-unders interrupt the user less, but are not seen until the main window is minimised or closed, making it more difficult for the user to determine which website opened them.

Viral advertising

Viral advertising is a marketing technique that relies on people sharing Internet content that interests them among their social and professional networks. It is called 'viral' because it is supposed to spread quickly as people pass on information about the website. It is an up-to-date version of word of mouth – which can be one of the most effective forms of advertising, as satisfied customers recommend a company, product or service to their friends and colleagues.

Viral adverts often take the form of funny video clips or interactive Flash games, images and even text – these will be sponsored by a company that wants to increase awareness of its product or service. The advantage of this type of advertising for advertisers is that it is relatively low cost.

Theory into practice

Try to identify some of the advertisers who use the Internet to advertise their products.

You may have to seek permission from your teacher or network administrator in order to allow some forms of advertising to appear on your school or college computer.

Theory into practice

We have looked in detail at advertising on the Internet. Investigate advertising in another medium of your own choice. How many different kinds of advertising can you identify in this medium? Which do you think are the most effective and why?

Assessment task 1

*Consider the following three advertising scenarios and then answer questions **a** to **d** below.*

1 *A company has developed a hand-held game console that can be linked to two or more other consoles. It has been designed for high-speed gaming and is to be sold at low cost.*

2 *A new low-cost airline wants to develop their market in fun holidays designed to appeal to the young adult market – one of the key features of the holidays is late-night partying in bars and night clubs.*

3 *A toy company wants its talking robot to become the top toy this Christmas. This toy is priced at more than £200.*

a *Describe the target audience for each of the three products.*
b *Discuss the most effective form of advertising for each of these products.*
c *Produce an initial outline of the advertising techniques you would use to advertise each of these products.*
d *Explain why you chose these techniques.*

Assessment evidence

✔ Describe the kinds of advertisements and advertising techniques that you would use.

✔✔ Discuss the kinds of advertisements and advertising techniques that you would use, using appropriate examples.

✔✔✔ Criticially discuss the kinds of advertisements and advertising techniques that you would use.

7.2 Developing ideas for an advertisement

Exploring ideas

In order to produce your own advertisement you will need to come up with some ideas. First you will need to choose a product to advertise. This might be a fictitious product such as a new chocolate bar, a new design of mobile telephone or a range of clothing. Alternatively, you may decide to produce an advertisement for something you have produced as part of this course. For example, if you produced a magazine or school newspaper for Unit 6 Print Production, you could develop an advertisement to sell the product to the teachers, students and parents. Or, if you produced an exhibition of photographs for Unit 9 Photography Techniques, you could develop an advertisement to encourage people to come and see the exhibition.

Whatever you choose to advertise, you must develop your ideas carefully in order that your advertisement will hit the mark and be successful. Figure 7.3 is a diagram that will help you understand all the processes involved in producing an advertisement and how they all fit together.

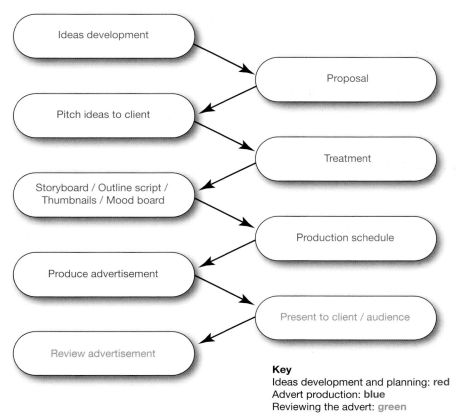

Key
Ideas development and planning: **red**
Advert production: **blue**
Reviewing the advert: **green**

■ **Figure 7.3** *The processes involved in advertisement production.*

Case study

Media productions

Media Productions is a media company with a number of different departments, one of which is an advertising department that creates advertisements in a number of different media, including print, interactive media, on DVD and for televison and radio.

An existing client, Yorkshire Pottery, wanted to promote their new range of kitchenware (a retro-look range called Yorkshire Blue) and asked Media Productions to develop some ideas for an advertising campaign. The team at Media Productions had previously worked with this company to produce a video about the range of pottery they produced. The advertising department produced a number of ideas for the client to consider:

- a point-of-sale video about the way in which the kitchenware was made
- a leaflet that would be available on the point-of-sale stand
- an opportunity to visit the factory and the factory shop
- a magazine advert
- a newspaper advert
- a commercial to be shown on national television
- a commercial to be aired on local and national radio.

Media Productions produced a presentation of their ideas for the client which included some initial mock-ups of how each of the ideas would look on paper or on screen. They used a PowerPoint presentation to do this, together with some mock-ups of the leaflets and a demonstration of what the television and radio commercials might look and sound like.

Theory into practice

Decide on the product or service that you will be advertising.

Discuss with your client or group how you will start to plan for production.

Producing a mind map is a good way of generating and recording your initial ideas for an advertisement.

The team at Media Productions researched all the ideas and then presented the best ones to the client. The Media Production team met as a group and spent some time going though each of the ideas and then dismissing any that would not produce the desired result or might be too expensive for the client.

■ **Figure 7.4** *A record of the mind mapping exercise undertaken by the team at Media Productions for their client Yorkshire Pottery.*

Media Productions also had to consider the time available, as the client wanted the advertisement to be ready for a planned launch at a London venue.

Theory into practice

Produce a mind map of your initial ideas for your advertisement.

Go through all the ideas with your group and dismiss any ideas that might be difficult or impossible to produce.

Think about the time you have to make the advertisement and the resources you have available.

Think about the restrictions you might have on the resources available to you. Considering the following questions is a good start.

■ Do I have the equipment for making the advertisement?

■ Will I have sufficient time to make it?

■ Will I have the materials available to make the advertisement?

■ Will there be sufficient time to review my advertisement and make changes if necessary?

You will need to include some contingency in your planning. This means allowing for things going wrong and equipment failure. You will be able to plan for contingency when you produce your treatment.

The proposal

Once you have chosen an idea to work with, the first stage of the planning process is to produce a proposal. This document will set out your ideas for your advertisement. The proposal will allow you to expand on some of your ideas and to try to sell them to a client. In this instance your client will probably be your teacher, but you may have the opportunity to work with a real client, perhaps a local company or charity that would like some advertising.

As you can see from the example proposal in Figure 7.5, the proposal is used as a document to 'sell' the ideas to the client, in this case a romantic approach to the advertising campaign. It also gives the client an idea about the alternatives available to them, such as involving a celebrity and the use of atmospheric music.

 Remember

Your proposal should be a based on an idea that is feasible and something you really feel you could make. Your advertisement can be in whatever media format you want to use. So if, for example, you decide you want to produce an advertisement for your school or college, you could:

- make a short video advertisement suitable for sending to a potential student or parent
- make a website advertisement that would be viewable by a student or parent
- produce an advertisement for your local newspaper
- produce a radio commercial
- produce a television commercial
- make an advertising poster or billboard.

You should base your proposal on the media format in which you think you have the best skills to produce the work. You must also consider your audience. When Media Productions were writing their proposal they had to consider who their target audience would be and where to place their advertisements in order to reach this audience. They had to consider the language to be used, as well as appropriate music and images for their audience.

It would be no good producing an advertisement aimed at kitchenware purchasers in a department store and then using drum and base music as the soundtrack. Equally, it would be inappropriate for this product to include bad language or images of violence.

Proposal
for
an advertising package

Yorkshire Blue

Prepared by
Sandra Ahmed

Media Productions

21st July 2006

for
Yorkshire Pottery

copyright © 2006

PROPOSAL

Prepared by Sandra Ahmed

Media Productions will produce a package of advertising materials to encourage consumers to purchase a new and exciting range of pottery. The package will be aimed at an audience of shoppers in kitchenware departments of high street shops and will be informative and educational. The programme will provide evidence of the romantic link between this range of pottery and the public's concept of 'the old days'.

The package will feature:

- Point-of-sale material including a video programme and a leaflet
- A commercial for local and national radio
- A series of print advertisements for specialist magazines
- A series of print advertisements for national newspapers
- A competition to win a trip to the factory and factory shop

The point-of-sale material will feature the production process of the range of pottery as it progresses through the factory right up to the sale.

The theme of the point-of-sale video and the commercials and print advertisements will be the romantic notion of having something that looks like the pottery your grandmother might have had on her dresser. This will encourage a whole new generation of buyers looking for that retro feel in their kitchen.

The final shot in the point-of-sale video and commercials will be in a department store with racks of the pottery looking clean and bright. There will be a range of atmospheric and romantic music used throughout the point-of-sale video and commercials. The images used in all the material will be of the wide range of kitchenware available and the handmade processes used in their production. A television personality, who collects kitchenware, could be approached to appear in all the advertising material.

The point-of-sale video and the television commercial will be produced on high-definition format cameras and edited using the latest high-definition digital editing technology at our Birmingham editing facility. The radio commercial will be produced using the latest digital technology. The photographic images used in the magazine and newspapers will be produced in our digital photography facility.

The budget is subject to discussion but will be approximately £75,000.

■ **Figure 7.5** *The proposal prepared by the team at Media Productions for their client Yorkshire Pottery.*

Legal and ethical issues

You will also need to consider legal and ethical issues when preparing your proposal. Legal considerations include copyright – you might need to obtain permission to use some of the material you would like to use in your advert. Ethical issues include representation – for example, your client might not want women to be stereotyped as working in the kitchen, or to include images that might alienate some parts of society.

Did you know?

In 2004 the clothing retail company French Connection used the logo FCUK in their advertising. The Advertising Standards Authority, which regulates advertising in the UK, issued a strong rebuke to the fashion retailer as they considered their advertising campaign to be in poor taste. The ASA said French Connection had 'brought the advertising industry into disrepute', with advertising that was 'offensive and irresponsible'. French Connection was banned from putting up any more adverts without prior approval from the regulator for a period of two years.

The Advertising Standards Authority (ASA) is an independent regulator for advertising in the UK. It publishes rules on advertising and investigates complaints about advertisements from members of the public. The ASA can have misleading or offensive advertising stopped. The basic rules are that all advertisements and marketing materials should be:

- legal
- decent
- honest
- truthful
- socially responsible
- respectful of the principles of fair competition generally accepted in business.

Figure 7.6 contains some material taken from the ASA website about the advertising codes. It will help you to understand the way in which advertising is regulated in the UK. You can find out more about the role of the ASA by visiting their website at www.asa.org.uk.

The advertising industry is self-regulating and this is overseen by the Committee of Advertising Practice (CAP). Figure 7.7 contains some information from the CAP website, explaining what they do.

The dos and don'ts of advertising

Every advertisement – whether it appears on the TV, radio, Internet, in a newspaper or on a poster, or if it drops on your doormat – is required to meet certain codes of conduct. Administered by the Advertising Standards Authority (ASA), these codes are there to prevent advertising that is either misleading or offensive.

Codes of conduct govern advertising in the UK. The advertising industry takes responsibility for the Codes, which apply to radio and television commercials, ads in non-broadcast media, sales promotion and direct marketing. Here are some of the key rules contained in the Codes:

Misleading advertising

Advertisements are not allowed to mislead consumers. This means that advertisers must hold evidence to prove the claims they make about their products or services before an ad appears.

Offensive advertising

Ads are not allowed to cause serious or widespread offence. Special care needs to be taken on the grounds of sex, race, religion, sexuality and disability. We consider many factors before deciding whether or not the ad is offensive – including where the ad appears, the audience, the product and what is generally acceptable conduct at the time. It's not simply about the number of complaints made.

Other rules

The Codes also contain specific rules about sales promotions and direct marketing, including how advertisers can use certain types of personal data and the non-receipt of mail order items. Other rules cover ads aimed at children and ads for alcohol, health products, beauty products, financial services, employment and business opportunities, and gambling. There are also rules governing the types of ads that can be shown around certain programmes.

■ **Figure 7.6** *Information about the UK advertising codes from the ASA.*   Source: *ASA website* 2006

CAP

The Committee of Advertising Practice (CAP) is the industry body responsible for the UK's advertising Codes. CAP's Non-broadcast Committee writes and enforces the British Code of Advertising, Sales Promotion and Direct Marketing (the Code). The Committee comprises representatives of advertisers, agencies, media owners and other industry groups, all of which are committed to upholding the highest standards in advertising.

What we cover

As well as regulating the content of advertisements in print, on posters, in new media and the cinema, we cover all sales promotions, the use of personal data for direct marketing and the delivery of mail order goods or refunds.

We also regulate the content of all TV and radio commercials on channels and stations licensed by Ofcom. We also regulate advertising on interactive television services, TV shopping channels and Teletext services.

We don't, however, cover programme sponsorship, the amount of permitted advertising, the use of commercial breaks (except for advertisement content) or judgments about whether advertising is "political" (and therefore prohibited); those are the responsibility of Ofcom.

The Codes

Two sets of rules apply to broadcast advertisements – a set for TV and another for radio. In broad terms, they state that all types of broadcast advertising shouldn't mislead, offend or cause harm.

You may download free copes of all the Codes from our website at www.cap.org.uk.

■ **Figure 7.7** *Extract from the CAP website, with information about the sorts of advertising that they cover.*

Source: CAP website 2006

What does it mean?

Pitch – *a presentation in which you attempt to sell your product or idea to a potential client – also known as a* **sales pitch**

Pitching

As we discussed earlier, the purpose of the proposal is to try to sell your ideas to your client. When an advertising agency or media production company has finished preparing their proposal, they will make a **pitch** to their client. (In your case, your client may well be your teacher.)

There are several ways of presenting your pitch. One way that will help make you look professional is to create a PowerPoint presentation with your ideas. The aim of your pitch should be to persuade the client that your ideas are feasible and exciting. In the real world, the client is likely to be investing a lot of money in their advertising campaign, so the pitch needs to be very convincing and persuasive. Make sure that your pitch persuades the client:

- that your advertisement will help them achieve their goals
- that it will increase their sales and make them money
- that it includes all the elements that they have asked for
- that your ideas are creative and exciting.

You may wish to enhance your pitch with an illustrated handout that the client can take away – it could contain a summary of your proposal with examples of what the finished advertisement might look like. Make sure that all your presentation material is produced to a professional standard – the more professional you look, the more convincing you will be. Make sure that you check your spelling in any PowerPoint slides and handouts.

You may find that the client likes you ideas but wants to make some suggestions about them. Record all of these carefully and try to find out why they want to make changes. After the meeting, go back to your proposal and make any changes necessary in order to include your client's suggestions. Make sure that you keep a record of the changes that you have made. You will need to use these records when you review your advertising work at the end of this unit.

The creative director at Media Productions pitched the proposal to the advertising manager and the managing director at Yorkshire Pottery in a meeting at the client's head office. They recorded the meeting carefully, particularly all the comments and suggestions raised by their clients, as shown in Figure 7.8.

Assessment task 2

1 *Using your initial idea for an advertisement, prepare a proposal that you can pitch to your client (this may be your teacher).*
2 *Include your ideas about the content and style of your advertisement. Be as descriptive as possible and really sell your idea to the client.*
3 *Include as much information as you can to convince your client that you have thought about legal and ethical considerations.*
4 *Prepare a pitch using appropriate techniques and pitch your ideas to the client.*
5 *Make a note of any suggestions that the client makes and follow their suggestions to amend your proposal if necessary.*

Assessment evidence

✔ Describe an idea for an advertisement.

✔✔ Demonstrate competent application of advertising techniques in your description of your idea.

✔✔✔ Demonstrate creative application of advertising techniques in your description of your idea.

Treatment

Once you have decided on your idea and produced your proposal, the next step is to develop a treatment. The treatment contains much more detail than the proposal and will provide a detailed snapshot of the advertisement – this will be useful information for both the client and for yourself when you come to actually produce your advertisement.

As a result of the meeting with their client, Media Productions produced a treatment, developing their ideas for a point-of-sale video advertisement. In their treatment, they made sure that they addressed the suggestions made by their client at the sales pitch meeting. The form that they used is shown in Figure 7.9.

A treatment should be produced using DTP software and must look professional. The first page is a cover sheet identifying the name of the advertisement, the client, your name and the date. The rest of the treatment is divided into sections, each of which describes and explains different aspects of the advertisement. The headings allow the writer to give more detail of the project. You should complete all the sections of the treatment – some sections will be quite short but others may take up one or more pages.

Remember

It is vital that you keep careful records of meetings. If you keep careful records and make sure you carry out any suggestions made, you may be able to meet the requirements for a merit or distinction grade.

CLIENT MEETING RECORD SHEET

Date: 26 July 2006	**Time:** 10.45 a.m.	**Place:** Yorkshire Pottery head office

Present: Sandra Ahmed (Media Productions)
Gill Somerton (Managing Director Yorkshire Pottery)
Barry Smith (Marketing Director Yorkshire Pottery)

Apologies for absence: None

Items discussed

1. SA introduced the concept for the Yorkshire Pottery advertising campaign.
2. SA presented the proposal using a PowerPoint presentation and talked about the ideas one by one.
3. SA asked for the client's comments.
4. GS liked the ideas proposed but wanted more detail about potential costs.
5. BS liked the range of ideas but felt that to implement all of them would be costly and he felt that he would prefer to have a more focused advertisement.
6. GS thought that the romantic idea was fine but wondered how this would translate into a point-of-sale programme and leaflet.
7. SA suggested that Media Productions could develop their idea for a point-of-sale video further.
8. GS and BS thought that this would be a sensible idea and agreed to Media Productions developing the idea further.
9. SA suggested that the team at Media Productions produce a treatment that explored the idea further and expanded on the content.
10. This was agreed and date for a further meeting was agreed.

Date of next meeting: 2 August 2006

■ **Figure 7.8** *Example of a client meeting record sheet, showing suggestions from the client and what was agreed.*

PRODUCTIONS

TREATMENT	
Advertisement:	Yorkshire Blue
Client:	Yorkshire Pottery
Writer:	Sandra Ahmed
Date:	1st August 2006

Introduction

Outline script

Storyboard/thumbnails/layout

Production schedule

Outline budget

Contingency plan

Talent

Production staff

Research

media
PRODUCTIONS

Treatment
for
Point-of-sale Video Advertisement

Yorkshire Blue

Prepared
by
Sandra Ahmed

Media Productions

1st August 2006

Client
Yorkshire Pottery

Copyright © 2006

■ **Figure 7.9** *The treatment form used by Media Productions for their Yorkshire Blue point-of-sale video.*

The treatment should include the following sections:

Introduction

A short opening section which summarises the original proposal and the approach that you will take in your advertisement. This is an opportunity to really sell your idea. The introduction should also include details of the size and content of the advertisement.

Outline script

Writing an outline script will help you to work out the resources that you will need for your advertisement. It allows you to bring your ideas together to show what the finished advert will contain and what it will look like. It should include the characters used and the dialogue or narration. In order to complete the outline script, you must have a clear picture of your advertising product.

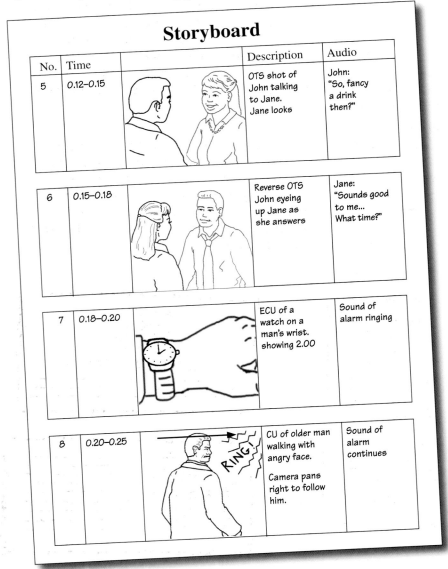

■ **Figure 7.10** *An example of a storyboard.*

Figure 7.12 *You will probably want to carry out more than one role yourself, but think about how much you can realistically achieve in the time available and who you can get to help you.*

Production schedule

This important document will include all your plans for production of your advertisement, together with the details of what is involved and when. A production schedule will help you to plan effectively for pre-production, production and post-production.

Building from the outline schedule you included in your treatment, the production schedule includes details of when the work for your advertising project started and when various activities are planned to take place. This information is vital for your records as it will form a major part of the evidence required for this unit. Your production schedule should contain:

- details of the start and finish dates for producing the proposal and the treatment and when these were circulated to the client
- agreed dates for activities such as location shooting, photography or sound recording, editing and review by the client
- details of the production equipment required and where you will obtain this from

- your transport requirements
- crewing requirements, with names of personnel
- the talent (actors) required, with names
- the properties required for the production and whose responsibility they are
- your post-production equipment requirements.

The production schedule helps to clarify all of the details of the production in one document. This document is a vital piece of evidence of your planning and production work, so you must store it carefully and have it available for the assessment of your work.

Monitor your production schedule regularly and record any changes as soon as they occur. Figure 7.13 shows the first part of the production schedule for Media Production's Yorkshire Blue advertising video. It includes all the key dates for this project and provides a clear picture of the way that the project is progressing.

For your own project, you might need to change some of the items included, depending on the type of product you are creating. For example, if you are producing a magazine advertisement, you will need to include dates for sample layouts and copywriting, instead of shooting script and storyboard.

Part 2 of the production schedule should include a complete list of all your requirements for the production, including equipment, personnel, talent, transport, props and post-production requirements such as sound effects, music, etc.

Think it over

The production schedule part 2 shown in Figure 7.14 was produced for a point-of-sale video advertisement.

What would you have to include if you were making each of the following advertisements?

- a radio commercial
- a television commercial
- a newspaper or magazine advertisement
- a poster or flyer
- a website

As well as the production schedule, if you are producing a radio or TV commercial, you will also find a **call sheet** useful. A call sheet is a detailed schedule produced for each day of production. It contains details of date, time and location, the crew and actors involved. It also contains details of transport arrangements, props needed, materials required for the day's work and location catering arrangements.

PRODUCTION SCHEDULE PART 1	
Programme Title:	Yorkshire Blue
Client:	Yorkshire Pottery
Writer:	Sandra Ahmed
Date:	21st August 2006

	Date		Date
Programme started:	01/06/06	Completed:	
Proposal started:	27/07/06	Completed:	21/07/06
Treatment started:	31/07/06	Completed:	01/08/06
Agreement from client:	05/08/06		
Shooting script started:	05/08/06	Completed:	09/08/06
Storyboard started:	13/08/06	Completed:	16/08/06
Production started:	12/09/06	Completed:	
Post-production started:	03/10/06	Completed:	
Rough-cut supplied to client:	14/10/06	Agreed with client:	
Final version to client:	21/10/06		

■ **Figure 7.13** *Part 1 of the production schedule gives all the key dates for the production of the advertisement.*

PRODUCTION SCHEDULE PART 2	
Programme Title:	Yorkshire Blue
Client:	Yorkshire Pottery
Writer:	Sandra Ahmed
Date:	25th August 2006

Production equipment required

cameras
lights
microphones
tripod

Crewing requirements

cameraperson
sound recordist
production assistant
lighting technician
props technician

Actors

1 male actor
1 female actor

Transport requirements

Transport to pottery required for approximately 10 people

Props/scenery

All kitchenware to be supplied by Yorkshire Pottery, from their Yorkshire Blue range

Post-production requirements (format, effects, music, voice-over)

Editing using Final Cut Pro
Graphics for titles and credits
Music throughout programme
Sound effects where necessary

■ **Figure 7.14** *Part 2 of the production schedule lists all the requirements for the production and post-production stages.*

When you do your planning, remember to keep everyone informed about the schedule. If you give everyone involved a call sheet (Figure 7.15), they are much more likely to be in the right place at the right time and with the right equipment.

PRODUCTION SCHEDULE CALL SHEET	
Programme Title:	Yorkshire Blue
Client:	Yorkshire Pottery
Writer:	Sandra Ahmed
Date:	16th September 2006

Crew	
Camera:	Robin Williams
Sound:	Rory Smith
Lighting:	Jill Sparks
Production Assistant:	Kate Azhami
Technicians:	John Brown/Bill Bailley
Transport:	Just Cars
Props:	Gary Musazawksi

ARRANGEMENTS	
Meeting at:	Yorkshire Pottery, 2 Chapel Steet, Grisdon Meet at front gates
Location Venue:	Interior of pottery
CALL DATE:	**20th September 2006**
CALL TIME:	**6.30 a.m.**
Transport:	Leaving from Media Productions offices at 6 a.m. prompt

INSTRUCTIONS:	No special instructions for this shoot

Actors:	Bill Foreman: Interviewer	Jane Smith: Pottery enthusiast
Wardrobe:	Bill: 7 a.m.	Jane: 7.30 a.m.
Make-up:	Bill: 7.30 a.m.	Jane: 8 a.m.

Location catering:	Breakfast for 10 people from 7 a.m. Lunch for 10 people from 12.30 p.m. Evening meal for 10 people from 6 p.m. Coffee/tea available at all times Chuck Wagon caterers on site at all times
Properties:	Pottery provided by Yorkshire Pottery

■ **Figure 7.15** *The call sheet used by Media Productions for the first day of their Yorkshire Blue video shoot.*

Remember

■ You will need to keep careful records of your planning and production.

■ Update your production schedule regularly to reflect any changes that occur.

■ Make sure that you record any changes in an appropriate way. Keep a copy of the original schedule so you can comment on why any changes were necessary.

Location reconnaissance

For a moving image production (such as a promotional video or TV commercial) and perhaps also for an audio production (such as a radio commercial), you will need to carry out a location reconnaissance (usually known as a **recce** for short).

This is where you can visit any locations or the studio that you are planning to use and check out the lighting, power supply and accessibility for your crew and cast. You may have to organise a contact person to let you in early to set up your equipment.

Your location recce will also allow you to identify potential hazards so that you can compile a risk assessment document – this is a vital document for any professional production company planning to do location work.

Use a **location visit sheet** to record all of the information that you gather during your recce – an example is provided in Figure 7.16.

When working on location, you also need to make sure that you obtain the permission of anyone who appears in your production. For more on this, see the section on location considerations on page 159–161 of Unit 4.

Health and safety issues

Look at the sections on health and safety issues in Unit 1 and Unit 4. Ask yourself – will there be any problems when producing my product? It is essential that you consider the possible risks to yourself, your crew and the general public when planning for your production and post-production work.

You may have to allocate some of your budget to ensure that there are no problems with health and safety. Media production companies might have to consider issues such as:

■ security on site when working with famous actors

■ finding out the hazards and safety precautions necessary for working in a particular location – e.g. a building site or factory using hazardous chemicals.

Remember

Always make sure that you gain permission to film on location and notify the police if you are planning to film in a public area.

PRODUCTION SCHEDULE LOCATION VISIT SHEET	
Programme Title:	Yorkshire Blue
Client:	Yorkshire Pottery
Writer:	Sandra Ahmed
Producer:	Amanda Phillips
Director:	Barry Norman
Date:	2nd September 2006

Rough sketch of location including electricity points:
Yorshire Pottery

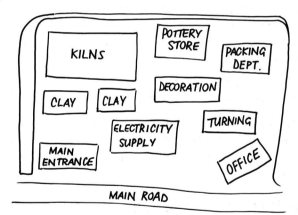

Access to location via:
Main road and through access gates via security

Name and number of location contact:
Declan Harris, Site Manager

Health and safety issues to note:
• Working machinery
• Some toxic substances stored on site
• Close to main road
• Possibility of causing an obstruction to factory employees
• Very hot kilns used for firing the pottery: up to 1100°C
• Location of emergency services
• Availability of first aid

Potential filming problems:
• Electricity not available in all areas of the factory
• Machinery working in location
• Noise when recording live interviews
• Avoid blocking pathways and corridors
• Tight space in working areas
• Poor lighting in some areas of the factory

Notes:

■ **Figure 7.16** *The location visit sheet for the day of filming planned by Media Productions at Yorkshire Pottery.*

You must follow safe working practices at all stages of work on your advertisement. You have to work with equipment, with other people and sometimes with the general public. No one wants to work in a dangerous situation if this can be avoided. Try to think about the health and safety issues that will affect your own production work.

You can use your location visit record to produce a **risk assessment** to help ensure the safety of everyone involved in your location work. You can find out more about risk assessments on page 151 of Unit 4. Figure 7.17 is the risk assessment done by Media Productions for their location filming at Yorkshire Pottery. You will notice that the risk assessment lists solutions for the hazards identified at the recce.

Theory into practice

Media production companies have to make sure that they have the correct insurance in place for their production work.

- Public liability insurance will cover any damages awarded to a member of the public as a result of damage or injury caused to them by the company.
- Employers' liability insurance covers any compensation claimed by employees due to accidents or illness at work.

Find out more about these two types of insurance and why they are needed.

Theory into practice

There is a wide range of regulation covering health and safety issues in the work place. See if you can find out a bit more about each of the following pieces of legislation. How might each one affect your own production work?

1 Health and Safety at Work Act 1974
2 The Management of Health and Safety at Work Regulations 1999
3 The Manual Handling Operations Regulations 1992
4 Display Screen Equipment Regulations 1992
5 Control of Substances Hazardous to Health Regulations (COSHH) 2002

RISK ASSESSMENT SHEET	
Programme Title:	Yorkshire Blue
Client:	Yorkshire Pottery
Writer:	Sandra Ahmed
Producer:	Amanda Phillips
Director:	Barry Norman
Date:	8th September 2006

FILMING AT YORKSHIRE POTTERY		
Possible hazards		
Risk	Level of risk	Safety measures to be taken
1. Working machinery	High	Arrange tour of premises by factory's health and safety officer for all crew, pointing out areas with working machinery. Instruct on the dangers involved.
2. Toxic substances stored on site	High	Do not film near the storage areas.
3. Kilns for firing the pottery: operate at up to 1100°C	High	Follow factory's safety procedures when filming in the vicinity of the kilns. Wear protective clothing as instructed.
4. Possibility of causing an obstruction to factory employees	Medium	Film only in areas we have permission to use. Provide ample warning of our presence to factory workers. Use clear signs to indicate when we are working in each area. Ensure no wires or leads are left trailing over pathways or corridors.
5. Site close to dual carriageway	Low	Film well away from the road.
Contacts		
• Site Safety Manager: Declan Harris 0320 719618		
Emergency Services		
• On-site first aid officer: Glynis Cole 0320 719543		
• Local police: 0320 765100		
• Local fire: 0320 765400		
• Local hospital: 0320 748333		

■ **Figure 7.17** *An example of a risk assessment. As well as identifying the risks and how to avoid them, contact numbers are included so that the appropriate people can be contacted if anything does go wrong.*

Remember

Here is a checklist to help you decide if you have finished all the pre-production work and are ready to more on to the production stage of your advertisement.

- Have I completed all of my pre-production paperwork?
- Do I have enough information to allow me to start producing my advertisement?
- Is there enough evidence in my folder to demonstrate that I have done my pre-production thoroughly?
- Have I considered all the health and safety issues (including a location recce and risk assessment)?
- Do all my crew understand what they need to do?
- Is my client happy with my planning?
- Do I have enough resources to undertake my production work?
- Do I have sufficient time to complete my work?

Production

Producing your material

In this section we will be looking at the techniques and technology you will use to produce material for your advertisement. You have now planned the production and you will have firm ideas about the content and look of your finished advertisement. The next step is to turn your ideas and planning into a reality.

Before you can start to create the content for your advertisement, you must ensure that you have the right equipment for the job. Choosing the right equipment depends on the nature of the media product you have chosen to produce.

- For **video** you will need: studio or location equipment – including a video camera, tripod, lights and microphones.
- For **audio** you will need: studio or location equipment – including a recorder or recording software on a computer or laptop, and microphones.
- For **print** you will need: a camera, a computer, a scanner, printers, DTP and picture-editing software.
- For **interactive media** you will need: a computer, a scanner, web design and picture-editing software.

You may need to consider how to record on location. For video, you will probably use one video camera and move it around to shoot from different angles – this will make it look as if you have used two or more cameras. If you try to use two cameras you will have many technical issues to deal with, such as balancing the colour of the two cameras.

Likewise, with sound recording you will use one recorder and one microphone to ensure that the quality of the sound recorded is consistent throughout.

For print and interactive media, the new generation of digital cameras can produce excellent images that equal the quality of film-based images. You will be able to upload your images directly on to a computer for editing.

If you are working on an interactive media advertisement, such as a website, you will be using a variety of media including text, graphics, photographs and perhaps video and audio. You will want to ensure that all the media you use is of excellent quality, so that both you and your client will be happy with the finished advertisement.

In order to successfully record material on location or in a studio, you must plan carefully to ensure that everything runs smoothly. You should make sure that:

- the crew and cast are aware of the time and location of the recording
- you have booked all the equipment that you need
- you have gathered together all the materials that you need – for example, cassettes, minidiscs, CD-ROMs, memory sticks, etc.
- all the batteries have been charged
- all the props you need are available.

Using the equipment effectively

You now need to make sure that you can produce the material accurately and that you create all the elements of your advertisement to a high quality. It is no good recording brilliant video footage if the sound is so poor that the audience will not be able to hear it. When taking photographs, you will need to make sure that the image is well lit and that the camera you are using will produce images of the quality required – this will depend on the format of your advertisement: the images used for a website will be more compressed than in a print product, and you will need images of a very high resolution for a full-page glossy magazine advertisement, for example. Sound recordings can easily be ruined by the sound of the equipment being handled or extraneous background sounds.

You must also have a clear understanding of all the elements that make up your production. Before you go out on location or use the studio, practise using the equipment to make sure you know what you are doing.

Keeping a record

Once you start to record your material, it is a very good idea to keep a careful record of everything you have recorded as you go along. In a media production company, this job is normally done by a production assistant, but for your advertisement you will probably do it yourself.

		SHOT MATERIAL LOG			
		YORKSHIRE BLUE LOCATION SHOOT			
Location:		Yorkshire Pottery factory			
Date:		13/09/2006			
Production assistant:		Sandra Ahmed			

SCENE NO.	TAKE NO.	TIME CODE IN	TIME CODE OUT	DESCRIPTION	COMMENTS
1	1	00.01	00.09	L/S exterior pottery	good
2	1	00.10	00.25	C/U pottery	out of focus
2	2	00.26	00.35	"	good
3	1	00.37	00.55	M/S workers in pottery	good
4	1	00.57	01.10	C/U workers	poor lighting
4	2	01.16	01.25	"	good
5	1	01.26	01.59	L/S factory interior	OK
6	1	02.00	02.45	M/S factory interior	good
7	1	02.46	03.04	C/U sign	good
8	1	03.05	06.50	interview manager	good sound
9	1	06.51	09.48	interview worker	poor sound
9	2	09.49	12.35	"	good

■ **Figure 7.18** *The records kept by the production assistant on the location shoot at Yorkshire Pottery. These notes will be invaluable when the editor goes into the edit suite.*

For video and audio, have a look at the section on keeping a record in Unit 4, page 159. Video producers will normally keep a 'shot material log' and audio producers will keep a 'recorded material log'. There is an example of a shot material log in Figure 7.18. If you are producing an audio advertisement, you will be able to adapt a log like this to include the details of your audio material.

When taking photographs for a print or interactive media advertisement, you may have the option to use a built-in log, which identifies each shot with a unique number. When writing the copy, you will probably revise your text several times before you are happy with it. Each time you revise your text, make sure you save the document with a different version number, so you can refer back to past versions if necessary. Also, keep a list of the names of all versions of the files, together with the date you saved them. Do the same when designing your layout – make sure you keep all the versions you produce, giving each file a different version number.

Theory into practice

Whichever media format you are using for your advertisement, you will need to keep records of all the materials produced. Consider the records you would need to keep if you were:

- producing a poster or flyer
- writing an advertisement feature for a newspaper or magazine
- recording a radio commercial
- developing pages for a promotional website
- producing an interactive advertisement, such as an information point
- recording a television commercial
- producing a press pack for the media.

Post-production

In this section we will consider the post-production process, including the various techniques used to manipulate and amend your original advertising material. Almost all advertising material needs to be edited before being released, whether it is video footage that needs to be joined together to create a fast-moving and exciting TV commercial or photographs that have to be cropped or colour corrected to make a promotional website or flyer look really inviting. The post-production process provides an opportunity to correct or improve the original material to make a finished advertisement.

You can, for example:

- correct errors in recording by omitting them from the finished advertisement

- choose to use alternative shots from the ones you originally thought would be appropriate
- shorten sequences that are uninteresting or repetitive
- control the overall length of the finished product by shortening or lengthening individual scenes or adding more information
- introduce special effects in moving image and audio adverts
- change the colour of images and manipulate them to alter their meaning
- reduce or enlarge file size to make an interactive media product run more effectively
- change text style or size
- cut or add text to fit the page better, or add or remove images.

Safe storage

It is very important to keep your advertising material safe. You will need to access this material throughout the editing process, so all tapes, memory cards and files need to be kept in a safe place. Make sure you follow these guidelines:

- Label the source material clearly with advertisement title, date recorded, location/studio, tape/disk/card number, etc.
- If you are storing your material on a computer hard drive or your school's network, you must have a clearly labelled folder structure in place. You must store your work in the correct folders and back up your work regularly.
- Use appropriate filenames for all your work, so you can find it easily and quickly. Stick to accepted file-naming conventions.
- Keep a copy of all previous versions of your work, using version numbers as you update the files.
- Keep the tapes, memory cards and files in a safe place.
- Make sure that no one can record over your source material by removing the recording tab or making files and disks 'read only'.

Losing your source material will result in you having to re-record all of your material. It may be impossible to recreate some of the original material and it will certainly put you behind your planned deadlines. Use clear labels for all of your tapes, cassettes, disks, etc. And attach clear descriptions to each of your computer folders and files. Your labels should include the information shown in Figure 7.19.

As well as labelling all your materials, it is a good idea to keep a material storage log with details of where all your materials are stored.

Editing

The editing process involves reviewing all the material you have created and putting together the pieces that you will be using in the finished

Video	Photographs
■ Name of advertisement	■ Name of advertisement
■ Cameraperson	■ Photographer
■ Location	■ Location
■ Date shot	■ Date shot
■ Filename/number or tape number	■ Image number/filename
Interactive media material	**Audio**
■ Name of advertisement	■ Name of advertisement
■ Date file created	■ Soundperson
■ Filename	■ Location
■ Folder name	■ Date recorded
	■ Filename/number or tape number

■ **Figure 7.19** *The information needed on labels for tapes, CD-ROMs and computer files that contain material for your advertisement.*

MATERIAL STORAGE LOG

Programme Title:	Yorkshire Blue
Client:	Yorkshire Pottery
Writer:	Sandra Ahmed
Producer:	Amanda Phillips
Director:	Barry Norman
Date:	4th October 2006

Tape number	Located
1	Tape storage locker – Edit Suite 1
2	Tape storage locker – Edit Suite 1
3	Tape storage locker – Edit Suite 1

Computer files	
Graphic designs for titles	Hard drive – folder: Yorkshire Blue / subfolder: Titles
Graphic designs for credits	Hard drive – folder: Yorkshire Blue / subfolder: Credits
Music tracks	Hard drive – folder: Yorkshire Blue / subfolder: Music
Voiceover	Hard drive – folder: Yorkshire Blue / subfolder: Voiceover
Backup files	CD-ROM labelled Yorkshire Blue backup, stored in filing cabinet Last backup made: 03/10/06

■ **Figure 7.20** *Some of the material for the Yorkshire Blue point-of-sale video is stored in lockers and some on computer. You can adapt this log for your own use.*

advertisement. Your shot material log (see Figure 7.18) will be invaluable in this process, as it will allow you to locate the relevant material quickly and easily and to identify the best version of each shot without having to trawl through hours of footage.

Video

There is a lot of information about editing video in Unit 4 (see pages 172–174). To summarise, the video editing process involves:

- Carrying out a **paper edit** based on the shot material log – an example of a paper edit is shown in Figure 7.21. This prepares you for carrying out the actual edit itself.
- Carrying out the **off-line edit** – editing together the sequences and making a version that can be viewed by colleagues and the client so they can suggest changes.
- Carrying out the **on-line edit** – this is the final edit and involves adding the final effects and finishing details.

Audio

There may be a number of reasons for editing audio material.

- Sometimes you will have recorded more than you need and so you will need to remove any excess audio.
- You may have recorded your material out of sequence. The editing process will allow you to rearrange the sequence.
- You may wish to delete recordings that are of poor quality.
- You may want to add sound effects or music to complete your advertisement.

Photographs

These are some of the reasons for editing photographic material.

- You may need to crop or stretch images in order to fit them into your layout.
- You may want to change the colour or contrast.
- You may wish to manipulate an image to create a special effect.

Text

When working with text, you will use the editing stage to do the following types of tasks.

- You may wish to change the font or type style.
- You might need to amend line lengths, columns or spacing on a page in order to fit in your material or for aesthetic reasons.
- You might add captions to your photographs and illustrations.
- You should also proof-read your text and carry out a spelling and grammar check.

PAPER EDIT	
Programme Title:	Yorkshire Blue
Client:	Yorkshire Pottery
Writer:	Sandra Ahmed
Producer:	Amanda Phillips
Director:	Barry Norman
Date:	8th October 2006

SCENE NO.	TIME CODE IN	TIME CODE OUT	DESCRIPTION	EFFECT	SOUND
1	00.01	00.09	L/S exterior pottery	fade in and cut to	atmos
2	00.26	00.35	C/U pottery	fade to	atmos
5	01.26	01.59	L/S factory interior	cut to	atmos
6	02.00	02.45	M/S factory interior	fade to	atmos
3	00.37	00.55	M/S workers in pottery	cut to	atmos
4	01.16	01.25	C/U workers	cut to	atmos
9	09.49	12.35	interview worker	cut to caption (name)	live interview
6	02.00	02.45	M/S factory interior	fade to	atmos & music
7	02.46	03.04	C/U sign	fade to	atmos & music
8	03.05	06.50	interview manager	cut to caption (name)	live interview

■ **Figure 7.21** *The paper edit is based on the records kept in the shot material log. The scenes are reordered as necessary and new instructions for effects and sound are added.*

Interactive media

An interactive media product will contain some or all of the elements listed above in this section. You can edit the text, images, video and sound separately, so part of the editing process will be combining them all in effective ways to create your finished advertisement. File size will be an important consideration as you make your editorial decisions.

■ You may need to change the format of a photograph or video or compress it further in order to improve download times.

■ You may need to shorten the length of video or sound extracts so that the file size is not too big.

Getting feedback

Once you have completed the initial edit of your advertisement, you will have a **rough cut** or **first draft** version. Show this to your client and try it out on a sample of your target audience. It is important that you understand that even at this stage you can still make changes to your advertisement if it does not meet the needs of your client or audience. You can incorporate any useful suggestions gained at this stage into your final edit.

It is very likely that you will have to make changes as a result of the feedback you receive. Do not be offended or discouraged by this. It is all part of the process of producing a successful advertisement that is fit for purpose, popular with its audience and that really sells the product or service it is advertising.

One way of getting feedback from your client and target audience is to hold a focus group in which you show your advertisement in order to get valuable feedback. Develop a questionnaire to use in the focus group that allows your participants to review your product in an appropriate way. You may want them to concentrate on certain aspects of the product more than others. A questionnaire is useful because it provides you with some written feedback that you can analyse afterwards and helps you to identify any changes you need to make.

Aspects of the product that you might like your focus group to consider include:

■ the length of the advertisement

■ the quality of the visual and sound elements

■ how well the advertisement conveys the product being advertised

■ consistency of style

■ the suitability of the advertisement for the target audience

■ how likely they are to buy the product after seeing the advertisement.

Remember

It will not help you if you choose people to review the advertisement who would not want to offend you. You must include a cross-section of people from your target audience.

Assessment task 4

Create an advertisement based on your proposed idea. Use all your planning documents to help you create it. Monitor your production and post-production work and keep careful records using the paperwork you have developed.

Assessment evidence

✔ Make sure that your advertisement follows the ideas you set out in your proposal and treatment.

✔✔ Demonstrate competent application of advertising techniques when producing and editing your advertisement.

✔✔✔ Demonstrate creative application of advertising techniques when producing and editing your advertisement.

7.4 Reviewing your advertising production

Keeping a log or diary

In order to produce a review of your production work, it is a good idea to keep a comprehensive diary or log of the work you have undertaken during the pre-production, production and post-production phases of your advertising work. This diary or log will help you to reflect on the work that you did and the help you had from colleagues. The following is a list of the points you could cover in your diary:

- how you thought of your idea
- how you developed the idea into a proposal
- how the proposal developed into a treatment
- a breakdown of the primary and secondary research methods you used
- notes of meetings with team members
- notes on the way that your team members worked
- notes on the work you undertook for others
- ongoing notes of the skills you are developing
- reflections on the quality of your work
- an analysis of your advertisement as compared to a professionally produced advertisement of a similar nature
- your understanding of the fitness for purpose of your own advertisement
- an analysis of how well your advertisement meets the client's brief and audience needs.

You might choose to keep a written diary or to use an appropriate format such as a PowerPoint presentation or a video or audio evaluation. Whichever method you use for your diary or log, you should use appropriate media language.

Figure 7.22 shows a page from the production diary kept by the producer from Media Productions.

Comments on your work

As part of your review of your work and how well you did, try to get a number of people to see and comment on your finished advertisement. Invite a selection of people from your target audience to review your work. Make sure that you also get feedback from your client (in this case it may be your teacher) and ask them to comment on the effectiveness of your advertisement.

PRODUCTION DIARY	
Name:	Amanda Phillips (Producer)
Production:	Yorkshire Blue advertisement (promotional leaflet for point of sale)

Date	Action Taken
1st August	Met with client to discuss the photographic images to be used in the leaflet. Client agreed that new photographs were needed of the new line of pottery.
3rd August	Met with photographer to discuss images that need to be shot in the studio.
7th August	Met with the creative director to discuss the style of photographs needed and the choice of model to be used. We agreed to use Sarah Cartwright as the model and to use a slightly retro style for the photographs.
15th August	Met with layout department to discuss the size and format of the photograhs needed.
16th August	Studio shoot day. Arrived on time at the studio. Creative director arrived 20 minutes late. The photographer was not ready to start on time and the model was 15 minutes late. However, we managed to shoot all the photographs we needed.
29th August	Meeting with client to look through initial copy. Client suggested several changes to the layout and text, which we will carry out by 5th September.

■ **Figure 7.22** *In your production diary it is important to keep a record of what you have done, any discussions that you have had and whether things went according to plan or not.*

If you want to get a wider range of feedback, consider making multiple copies of your advertisement and giving or sending it to people outside your school or college. This might include finding a group from your target audience from another school or college or from a local business or other group who could give you some good and impartial feedback.

If you send your advertisement in the post, make sure you include a stamped addressed envelope to encourage the recipient to return it to you. Alternatively, you may be able to upload your advertisement to your school or college website to make it available to a wider audience.

Include a questionnaire with your advertisement so that the audience can provide structured feedback to inform your review of your work. Put some thought into the design of your questionnaire. Providing options with tick boxes makes it much easier for people to respond than if you ask them to write answers to each question. However, you may want to include some questions that require short written answers in order to gain more detailed feedback. It is good practice to have a mixture of the two question types in the same questionnaire. For more information on writing questionnaires, see Unit 2.

Do not be disheartened by any negative views of your work. See them as a pointer to doing better next time. If there is still time, you could even use their comments to re-edit your advertisement or even re-record some of the material.

■ **Figure 7.23** *Showing your advertisement to a sample of the target audience is an important part of the review stage.*

■ **Figure 7.24** *The more focused the questions on your questionnaire, the more useful the information provided will be.*

It can also be useful to sit down with an audience after a viewing (or reading or listening) of your advertisement and ask for their immediate responses. You could record their views on video or audio and transcribe them (write or type them out) later. Some people will be more forthcoming in a face-to-face situation than in a written questionnaire.

The feedback you receive might indicate that the advertisement is too short or too long, the sound might be indistinct or the pictures might be blurred. Maybe the interactivity does not always work or some navigational buttons do not go anywhere. All of these things can be corrected if you know about them.

Evaluating your work

Once you have obtained sufficient feedback, you will need to analyse and record this information in a way that gives a representative view of what the audience thinks of your advertisement. This will form part of your review of your work.

In addition, try to answer the following questions when carrying out your review.

- What did I do?

- What did I learn and what skills did I develop?

Case study

Client review

Media Productions generally undertake a review of their work with a client.

The point-of-sale video they were making for Yorkshire Pottery was in the final stages of post-production. The client agreed to review the product with the director. The programme followed the making of a teapot from the initial cast to the finished product.

The client had a very firm idea that the programme should show the exact process involved in making a teapot and did not always agree with the 'poetic licence' used by the director in order to make the video more interesting. The client was particularly unhappy that the programme only showed one firing in the kiln when, in fact, the teapot had to be fired twice.

The director tried to persuade the client that in order to make the whole video flow there had to be some compromise in the sequences shot and how they were edited together. The client finally agreed and the programme was released.

Sometimes it can be hard to balance artisitic integrity with how things really are or what the client wants.

- What went wrong?
- What went right?
- What would I do if I could start again?

Refer back to all the records you have kept during the pre-production, production and post-production stages of your advertisement work. These will help you to identify when things went according to plan and when they did not. You will find your production diary particularly useful at this stage. You may find examples in your records of things you really want to emphasise in your review.

Remember

- Try to sell yourself in your evaluation. If you have done really good work, then say so. If you had problems, remember to say how you overcame them in order to achieve your aims.

- There is more than one way or recording your evaluation. You could use:
  - a video recording of your thoughts and comments
  - an audio recording
  - a PowerPoint presentation
  - a discussion with your teacher – make sure you record this conversation, perhaps in written or audio form.

- Whatever format you use, make sure you keep your review for assessment and store it safely.

Assessment task 5

*Produce a review of your work on your advertisement. Use the
following points and questions to help you.*

1 Check that the advertisement matches the intentions you set out
in your proposal and treatment.
2 Is the advertisement appropriate for the audience?
3 What about the technical qualities of your work?
4 How did you work with your team?
5 How well did you manage your time?
6 How was your work received by the client and audience?
7 Did you have to make any changes to your work?
8 Did feedback indicate that your advertisement will be successful in
selling the product or service that it is advertising?

Assessment evidence

✓ Describe clearly the work that you did, giving examples of what went wrong, what went
right and what you would do if you had the opportunity to work on this project again.

✓✓ Discuss your advertisement production work in detail, giving a range of relevant
examples of the factors involved in producing your advertisement.

✓✓✓ Explain clearly the work that you did, giving a range of relevant examples and
using correct technical language.

11 Writing for the Media

Introduction

Writing is a key activity that provides the content for the majority of the media products that we consume. The media industries employ journalists, script writers, authors and copywriters to produce the all-important words that are used to communicate the right message to the audience. Newspapers, magazines, leaflets and web pages are full of printed words, and many of the words we hear in films, television and radio programmes and computer games started off as printed words in a script of some kind.

Writing for the media is often done to very tight deadlines, and writers need to have a very clear understanding of the media product they are writing for, the purpose of the writing and who the target audience is. They must also be creative and able to use language with skill, accuracy and confidence.

In this unit you will be able to investigate the range of written material produced within the media industries and to learn about the different forms, methods and techniques involved. You will then be able to use this knowledge to generate your own ideas for written material, and develop some of these ideas into writing for your own selected media products. At the end of the unit you will have the opportunity to review and comment on your writing work.

Learning outcomes

On completion of this unit you should:

- know about different types of writing produced in the media industry
- be able to generate ideas for written material
- be able to produce written material
- be able to review your own writing work.

11.1 Types of writing produced in the media industry

The written word is an important element of most media products. Printed products such as newspapers and magazines are full of words, as are electronic media products, such as web pages and interactive CD-ROMs. Audio products, such as radio programmes, and moving image products, such as television programmes, also rely on written words throughout the development process as scripts are drafted and reworked.

Some media products, such as posters and flyers, might only have a few, well-chosen words on them, whereas a national newspaper, such as *The Times*, could have more than 100,000 words in each edition.

Scripts for films and television programmes include descriptions of what the location and scene looks like, and information about the camera shot, lighting and editing, as well as the words that will be spoken by the actors, presenters or narrators. Scripts for radio programmes will also include details of the music and sound effects that are included to create the right atmosphere.

There are two factors to consider when looking at the different types of written material produced by the media industries. The first of these is the **medium** that the written material has been produced for and the second is the **genre** of the media product.

■ **Figure 11.1** *Writing is a key component of most media products.*

EASTENDERS

EPISODE NINE HUNDRED AND EIGHTY SIX

By

JAMES PAYNE

SCENE 986/1. SQUARE. EXT. NIGHT. 00.48.

LOT

    [THE HOUSES OF ALBERT SQUARE ARE
STEEPED IN DARKNESS.

THE SQUARE GARDENS LOOK SIMILARLY
SLUMBERED. UNTIL...

THE LIGHT FROM A MOBILE PHONE
ILLUMINATES AN ANGELIC FACE: BEN'S.

HE SITS ON ARTHUR'S BENCH, LEGS
SWINGING BENEATH HIM, SCROLLING
THROUGH HIS LIST OF NAMES. THEY ALL
SAY 'PHIL'.

BEN LOOKS UP AT THE DARK WINDOWS OF
THE VIC, RUBS HIS FACE [THE SAME WAY
PHIL DOES], PUTS THE PHONE AWAY. WE
SEE IT'S NOT PROPERLY STOWED.

BEHIND HIM HE HEARS THE SOUND OF A
DOOR CLOSING. HE DUCKS DOWN BEHIND
SOME BUSHES AND SEES PHIL AND GRANT
EMERGING FROM THE MOONS' HOUSE]

GRANT: What a night, eh?

PHIL: Do you reckon he'll be alright?

GRANT: Good night's kip will do him the
power of good.

PHIL: [YAWNS] He ain't the only one.

    [GRANT LOBS THE CAR KEYS AT PHIL]

GRANT: Get the motor first. I'll stick
the kettle on.

    [PHIL TUTS, HEADS DOWN BRIDGE STREET
TO RETRIEVE THE RANGE ROVER. GRANT
HEADS INTO THE PUB SIDE GATE.

BEN EMERGES FROM HIS HIDING PLACE AND
WATCHES PHIL WALKING DOWN BRIDGE
STREET.

HE BITES HIS LIP, ANGRY, WANTING TO
SHOUT SOMETHING. NOTHING COMES.

INSTEAD HE TURNS AND MAKES FOR THE
OPPOSITE GARDENS EXIT.

HE DARTS FOR COVER AGAIN WHEN A DIM
LIGHT GOES ON AT THE BRANNINGS.]

■ **Figure 11.2** *Scripts for TV contain the words to be spoken and directions for the actors, as well as instructions about where the scene takes place, lighting, sound effects, etc.*

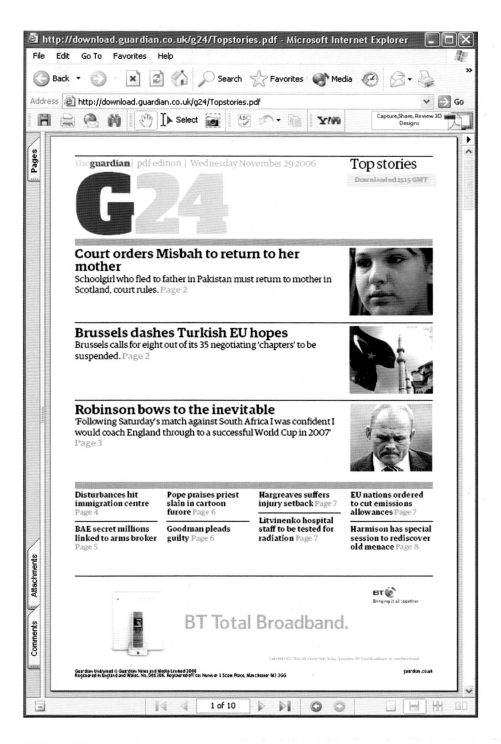

■ **Figure 11.3** *Many newspapers now have an online version.*

Medium

The medium that the written material is being produced for will have a big influence on the format that it will take and the way it is presented. A basic distinction to be made is between printed and audio–visual media.

Printed media include such products as newspapers, magazines, comics and promotional material such as leaflets, flyers and posters. For these products the written material is usually combined with still images to form the basis of the product itself. Many newspapers and magazines now also have online versions that are viewed using the Internet.

Most audio and moving image products start off as a written **treatment** which outlines the initial ideas for the film or programme. Once this has been accepted, a **script** is then developed which describes the product as it will look and sound when finished. It can be seen as a kind of map or plan that is then used by the production team as a guide when recording and editing the product.

The film, radio and television industries employ the services of scriptwriters and editors to produce and rework scripts. Many of these are self-employed **freelancers** who either work on fixed-term contracts or produce scripts of their own that they then try to sell to a production company.

The written words produced for a printed product such as a newspaper, magazine, leaflet or poster are normally called **copy** and the industry employs journalists and copywriters to produce the copy for a specific product. Writers who work for magazines and newspapers tend to be called **journalists** and those who work within the advertising industry are often called **copywriters**.

Some organisations still employ full- and part-time journalists and copywriters on permanent contracts, but there are now many people working as freelancers within the media industry. They will be contracted to write a particular article, column or review, or to work on a specific advertising campaign.

 Did you know

There is a growing demand for professional writers within the games industry to develop the plots, storylines and dialogue that many of today's computer games now have.

■ **Figure 11.4** *Many computer games now have quite complex plots, storylines and dialogues.*

What does it mean?

Copy – *the original writing that is used in a print product*

Journalist – *someone who writes stories and articles for newspapers, magazines and television and radio news programmes*

Copywriter – *someone who produces the words for advertising and promotional material*

Freelancer – *a person who is self-employed and who will hire out their services to a company for a fixed period of time or to complete a specific project*

Treatment – *a written summary of the final proposal that includes details of the product's theme, content and format as well as information about target audience, budget and timescale*

Script – *a detailed account of what is to be spoken in a particular audio or moving image product. A script will include a description of the location and what the characters or presenters have to do and, for moving image scripts, what camera shots are needed. Details of any music or sound effects that are to be used are also included.*

Case study

Martin Rockley: Copywriter

Martin graduated with a degree in Communication Studies in 1984 and immediately began looking for a job as an advertising copywriter. He says, 'It's notoriously difficult to break into, but the industry always appreciates an innovative approach.'

Martin started by creating a portfolio of ads written from imaginary briefs and ads he had seen in the papers. Then, instead of writing to advertising agencies and asking if he could come in to show them his work, Martin wrote and stated he would be coming in unless they had an outstanding reason for not seeing him. 'This negative option paid off, and I got my first job inside a month.'

As a junior copywriter, Martin began by writing the body copy to the more experienced writers' headlines, before being given more free rein on his own briefs. 'At first, I was simply filling in the gaps and had little influence on the creative direction of the campaigns. But once I had proven myself, I was allowed to develop my own approaches.'

In 1992, Martin became Creative Director, responsible for the entire creative output of the advertising agency. 'By now, I was involved with clients and influencing the strategic direction of major campaigns as well as developing the creative work which was the expression of those strategies.'

'Being a copywriter is always interesting and often exciting. It's always a thrill to see your words and ideas in print, and working on different briefs for a wide variety of products means it's never boring.'

Theory into practice

- Do some research into the different types of written material produced within the media industries.
- Find examples of written material and collect them together in a folder.
- Do some further research to find out more information about them, such as:
  - who wrote the material
  - what the purpose of the writing was
  - who the target audience was
  - what media product it was written for.

Theory into practice

Try to find examples of scripts that have been produced for audio and moving image products such as films and television and radio programmes. Of course, many of these scripts will be quite long and you will only need to include an extract of the scripts that you have studied.

A careful Internet search should provide you with some examples of scripts that you can study.

- The script archive section of the BBC website is a good place to start for examples of television and radio scripts. Go to www.bbc.co.uk/writersroom.
- The British Film Institute has links to film scripts. Go to www.bfi.org.uk and search for 'scripts'.

Genre

Another way of describing different media products is by their genre. As you will have found out in Unit 3, the word **genre** is the French word for 'type' and is used in media studies to group together all the media products of one type. A media product can be said to belong to a particular genre if it shares most of the codes and conventions of other products in that genre.

■ **Figure 11.5** *A TV news presenter reading the news from the main studio.*

Think it over

Have you noticed that news presenters and reporters look directly at the camera, but any guests that are interviewed do not. Can you think why this has become a convention of news programmes?

Images and recorded sound accompanying images	Script
Medium shot of Channel 4 News presenter.	"Celebrity musicians and actors have gathered across the USA in an effort to raise money for the victims of Katrina – this is what it looked like…"
Low angle tracking shot around the edge of a stage upon which Bono and Mary J Blige are performing.	Voice over: "Another cause, another concert – but this time U2 sang with Mary J Blige to raise money for the Red Cross and the Salvation Army."
Medium shot of actor Morgan Freeman explaining his links to the Mississippi Delta, having been born and grown up there just inland from New Orleans.	
Shot of unidentified performer playing a guitar on stage.	Voice over: "In an echo of the post 9/11 Telethon, stars of stage and screen linked up Los Angeles and New York across six television networks for an hour."
Medium shot of actress Julia Roberts celebrating the spirit of generosity that she claims is flooding America: "Americans are opening their doors to people they have never met…"	
Long shot of lecture-hall style arrangement of seats and telephones – at each one sits a glamorous star taking calls.	Voice over: "Stars manned the phones …
Medium shot of actor Jack Nicholson singing down the phone to one prospective donor: "I'll never stop saying Maria…"	… offering the occasional unexpected serenade."
Tracking shot, circling the singer Paul Simon singing "In the city of my dreams…"	Voice over – over the top of the song: "No censorship or time delay, but although nobody bashed the President, there was some implicit criticism…"
Medium shot of actor and comedian Chris Rock: "We realise that not everyone can leap into an SUV or check into a nice hotel."	
Tracking medium shot of singer at piano performing a song – we hear the line: "Walking in New Orleans…"	Voice over: "They ended with the wishful thinking of one of New Orleans' favourite sons Dr John… "… The 9/11 Telethon raised $50 million – if they can do that this time they'll be happy."
Medium shot of bulletin presenter: "Till tomorrow at 6pm – that's Channel 4 News."	

■ **Figure 11.6** *Extract from a news script of a Channel 4 News story, broadcast on Saturday 10th September 2005. It concerns a celebrity telethon – involving music and movie stars handling calls from the public and trying to get them to pledge money to help the victims of Hurricane Katrina.*

OPENING TITLES
10:00:00
MUSIC IN: 10:00:00

ASTON: WRITTEN AND
PERFORMED BY

10:00:14
ASTON: MATT LUCAS
10:00:17
ASTON: DAVID WALLIAMS
10:00:25
ASTON: LITTLE BRITAIN

MUSIC OUT: 10:00:29

10:00:29
MUSIC IN: 10:00:30

MUSIC OUT: 10:00:39

V.O.
Britain, Britain, Britain, land of
technological achievement. We've had
running water for over 10 years, an
underground tunnel that links us to Peru
and we invented the cat.

But none of these inventions would have
been possible if it had not been for the
people of Britain and it's those people
we look at today.

Let's do it.

SEQ. 1: EXT./INT. INNER CITY
COMPREHENSIVE SCHOOL

V.O.
It's half past Rene at this comprehensive
school in Darkley Noone, lessons are
coming to an end.

INT. COMPREHENSIVE SCHOOL THE CLASSROOM
IS FULL OF FIFTEEN YEAR OLDS. MR.
COLLIER, THE TEACHER, IS AT THE
BLACKBOARD SCRIBBLING AWAY. THE BELL
RINGS AND THE CLASS IMMEDIATELY PACK
THEIR BAGS AND BEGIN TO EXIT.

MR. COLLIER
Projects in by first thing next week.
Vicky Pollard, stay behind please.

WE REVEAL VICKY IN SCHOOL UNIFORM BUT
WITH MAKE UP. SHE'S SMOKING. SHE TUTS AND
PUTS OUT HER CIGARETTE ON THE FLOOR.
VICKY'S FRIEND KELLY LURKS BY THE DOOR.

KELLY
Good luck Vicky.

MR. COLLIER
Yes, thank you Kelly.

THE DOOR SHUTS. EVERYONE ELSE HAS LEFT.

MR. COLLIER
Right, come here please Vicky.

VICKY SLOUCHES OVER, KICKING HER BAG IN
FRONT OF HER AS SHE DOES SO. SHE SITS
DOWN IN A CHAIR OPPOSITE THE TEACHER.

■ **Figure 11.7** *Extract from* Little Britain *script.*

MR. COLLIER
Vicky, it's been two weeks now and I still haven't received your essay on Lord Kitchener.

VICKY
No but because what happened was was I was going round Karl's but then this whole fing happened right because Shelley Todd who's a bitch anyway has been completely going around saying that Destiny stole some money out of Rochelle's purse but I ain't never not even some to Rochelle 'cause she spat in Michaela's hair.

MR. COLLIER
Vicky, I'm not interested in that. I'm more interested in your coursework.

VICKY
Yeah because but what happened was was this whole fing happened what I don't even know anyfin about because Ashley Cramer has been going around saying that Samantha's brother smells of mud but I ain't so shab never even not even stole no car so shab.

MR. COLLIER
Vicky, have you even started this essay?

VICKY
No but yeah but yeah but yeah no but yeah no but yeah but no because I'm not even going on the pill because Nadine reckons they stop you from getting pregnant.

For example, most television news programmes tend to have a brief opening sequence that includes a title, dramatic music and some headlines of the major news items. The news is usually read by one or two smartly dressed people, often sitting behind a desk in a studio and delivered in a serious manner (Figure 11.5). Each news item will have some kind of visuals to illustrate the story, and the studio presenter will often talk to a reporter out on location who gives an update on what has happened and maybe interviews somebody connected to the news event.

The genre of a media product will have a big impact on the tone, style and form of the writing produced. For example, the language used in a television news programme will be very different from that used in the script for a comedy show such as *Little Britain*.

Look at the two examples of scripts shown in Figures 11.6 and 11.7. Both of the scripts include some detail of the location, the camera shots and the visuals used. They also detail the words that are spoken by the news presenter in Figure 11.6, and by the actors in Figure 11.7. The news script uses much more formal language and care is taken to describe the events in a balanced way without the use of too much emotion. The comedy script uses much more informal language and some of the language is exaggerated for comic effect.

Theory into practice

Try to find examples of other comedy scripts and identify some of the ways in which the writers have used language to create humour.

The opening sequence of *Borat: Cultural Learnings of America for Make Benefit Glorious Nation of Kazakhstan*, purportedly showing Borat's home town in Kazakhstan, is shot in Glod. Glod, incidentally, means "mud".

"We thought they came here to help us, not mock us," said one resident while she swept a manure-stained street lined with shabby homes of crumbling brick and corrugated iron sheeting. "We haven't got anything here. We haven't got running water. We can't even bathe," she said. "We are poor people, but we are still people."

Roma community leader Nicolae Staicu said he and other officials would meet with a public ombudsman today to map out a legal strategy against Borat creator Sacha Baron Cohen and distributor 20th Century Fox.

Staicu accused the producers of paying locals just $3.30 to $5.50, misleading the village into thinking the movie would be a documentary, refusing to sign proper filming contracts and enticing easily exploited peasants into performing crass acts.

■ **Figure 11.8** *Example of an article from* The Guardian *newspaper.*

It is presented as a typical Kazakhstan town.

Just four of the 1,000 residents have a job, so they welcomed the £3 fee for appearing in the film.

Grandfather Nicu has got together with some of the other villagers to pool funds in order to sue the film-makers. They believe they have been exploited and humiliated,

Nicu lost an arm in an accident and in the film had a rubber sex toy attached instead. He claims he had no idea what it was and now feels ashamed and deeply disturbed by the incident.

He said: "Our region is very poor, and everyone is trying hard to get out of this misery. It is outrageous to exploit people's misfortune like this — to laugh at them. We will try to hire a lawyer to take legal action for being cheated and exploited."

Spirea Ciorobea was dubbed "village mechanic and abortionist." He is furious with his portrayal.

He said: "What I saw looks disgusting. Even if we are uneducated and poor, it is not fair that someone does this to us." But vice-mayor Petre Buzea said: "They got paid so I'm sure they're happy."

■ **Figure 11.9** *Example of an article from the* Sun *newspaper.*

Different types of newspapers also have different styles. We can look at the different ways in which language is used in a newspaper such as *The Guardian* (sometimes referred to as one of the 'quality' newspapers) and the *Sun* (sometimes referred to as one of the 'popular' newspapers).

Consider the two articles in Figures 11.8 and 11.9 which cover the same news story. Look carefully at the way that language has been used in the two articles. Which words have been used to describe the event? Can you identify examples of any emotive language in the two articles? How long are the sentences that have been used? How has each journalist broken up the text? What message does each article give to the readers?

Think it over

News, comedy and horror are common genres that can be used to describe different media products. How many more genres can you identify? What are the main codes and conventions that define these genres? You may find it useful to look back at some of the work that you did on genre in Unit 3.

Theory into practice

- Do some research of your own and find examples of a story that appears in different newspapers.
- Try to identify the different codes and conventions and writing techniques that have been used in each article.
- Explain what different meanings are communicated by each of the articles. How successful do you think each one has been?

Having looked at the different types of writing produced by the media industries, you should now be ready to start the assessment task that will be marked for this part of the unit. To complete the task you will have to do some further research into different media products and include examples of some of the written material that you have been looking at.

Your completed work will form part of the final portfolio that your tutor will need to present to the moderator towards the end of the course.

Assessment task 1

Write a report on the written material that you have learnt about and researched.

- *Give your report an appropriate structure and use appropriate headings and sub-headings.*
- *You should also try to use appropriate language in the report and make sure you check your spelling and grammar.*
- *Include examples of some of the written material that you have been looking at, either within the body of your report or in an appendices section.*

Assessment evidence

✔ Describe the different types of writing produced within the media industries. Include some comments on why each type of writing can be identified as belonging to a particular genre.

✔✔ Make sure that the descriptions you provide are quite detailed and include appropriate examples of written material. Describe the codes and conventions used in these examples that show they belong to a particular genre.

✔✔✔ Explain, rather than just describe, the different types of writing produced in the media industries, and provide a comparative evaluation of them. You should also use technical and specialist language accurately and in an appropriate way.

11.2 Generate ideas for written material

You should now be ready to start to develop some of your own ideas for written material that you can then go on to produce in the next part of the unit.

To pass this part of the unit you need to develop ideas in two distinct ways:

- develop ideas for written material in response to a brief from a potential client
- develop ideas that you have thought up yourself.

It is very important that you show evidence that you have worked in these two different ways in the final portfolio that you present to the moderator towards the end of the course.

Working to a brief

The processes that you will go through when working to a brief are slightly different from those involved in generating your own ideas. When you are working to a brief you will need to consider very carefully what the client is asking you to do and what their expectations are.

It is also important that you communicate on a regular basis with your client and listen carefully to the feedback that they give you. Remember, they are the boss and you will not see your written material developed into a finished media product if the client does not like it, no matter how good you think it is.

■ **Figure 11.10** *Make sure that you get regular feedback on your work from your client to check that you are heading in the right direction.*

PAA

Creative Director
Pazim Advertising Agency
New Gate
Nottingham
NG1 6EY

Dear Sir/Madam

Pazim Advertising Agency has been asked by the government to help communicate a healthy living message to young people. As part of this message, we are planning to run a media campaign warning young people about the dangers of alcohol abuse.

The campaign will be targeted at young people between the ages of 14 and 17 and will include the production of an information leaflet that will be distributed to all schools and colleges.

We are keen to involve media students in the writing process and are inviting you to send in your ideas for an information leaflet that will get the message across successfully to this age group.

I look forward to hearing from you.

Yours,

Peter King
Creative Director

■ **Figure 11.11** *This brief is a letter to your school/college inviting students to write an information leaflet.*

If you or your school or college has good links with industry, then you might be lucky enough to be able to work on a real brief from a real client. If not, do not worry, as your tutor or somebody else at your school or college can play the role of the client and give you a brief to work from. Figures 11.11 and 11.12 contain two examples of briefs that ask you to produce written material.

Video and Multimedia Festival for Young People

This summer the local council is organising a Video and Multimedia Festival for young people. It is due to run from the 7th to the 10th of August and involves the screening of films and videos aimed at young people, together with short video and multimedia pieces made by young people in the area.

We are looking to produce a newsletter to help promote the festival and to get people talking about video and multimedia production.

We would like your school or college to help us write this newsletter and we are asking you to send us your ideas.

The newsletter should cover 4 sides of A4 paper and will need to engage and stimulate the target age group, who are 15–18 year olds.

I look forwarding to hearing from you and hope that you can play a role in promoting this festival.

Please send your ideas to Nadia Green at the Department of Leisure. which is located in the Council House in the High Street.

■ **Figure 11.12** *This brief has been received by your school/college – it is asking students to write a newsletter about a video and multimedia festival.*

Case study

Working in a team

In Unit 6 we looked at the way in which a group of students researched and developed a college magazine that was aimed at 16–18-year-old students at their college.

All of these students also chose to do Unit 11, as they wanted to develop their writing skills and make sure that their magazine was as professional as it could be and really did engage and interest the audience.

The team brainstormed what the content of the magazine could be and designed a research study to look at other written material targeted at the 16–18 age group. They also wanted to find out in more detail what their target audience looked for in a college magazine, and in particular what style of writing they expected to see.

They made sure that all of their team meetings were recorded by taking minutes and that the agreed actions were tracked and monitored. This evidence was included in their final portfolio for the unit. Their tutor also observed some of the team meetings and her observational records were included as evidence in each of the student's portfolios.

■ *The group of students holding a team meeting with their tutor observing.*

Remember

Because there will be no client to get feedback from, it is even more important for this type of writing that you get some feedback from a sample of your target audience.

Generating your own ideas

As well as developing ideas for written material from a given brief, you also need to show that you can develop ideas using your own initiative. These might be based on a personal interest or hobby that you have, or a particular genre that you have always been interested in.

Maybe you have always wanted to write a comedy sketch or the opening for a new science fiction film or a review of your favourite computer game. Well, now is your chance.

When developing ideas of your own it is still important that you have a clear idea of the medium and genre that you are working in, and that you consider very carefully the audience and market that you are writing for.

Working as part of a team

You may want to work with other students as part of a team for at least part of this stage so that you can generate a greater range of ideas and discuss them with each other. If you do work as part of a team, then as with your work in the other units, it is important that you document the decisions that are made and clearly show what your individual contribution has been to the group activity.

You can of course link the work you do in this unit with that of another production unit. If, for example, you are also taking Unit 6 and have decided to produce a student magazine for your school or college, then it would make sense to use the written material that you develop in this unit as the copy for the product that you will design and print in Unit 6. Similarly, you could develop a video script for your work in Unit 7.

Theory into practice

- Write down your initial ideas for written material that you could develop and produce.
- Try to consider the main issues that are involved when planning and producing each of these ideas.
- What strategies could you use to try to make sure that you are able to develop a successful piece of writing?

Brainstorming ideas is a good place to start, and at this point it is important to record the ideas in some way so that they do not get lost or forgotten. If you are working together as a group, then a good method is to use a flip chart or whiteboard to write down key words from the discussion, or you might want to record the session as audio or video.

It is important that you try to capture all of your thoughts and ideas at this point, however strange some of them may seem, as you never know which ones are going to work.

When looking at the feasibility of each of the ideas you should think about the amount of work involved and the timescale in which you have to complete your writing. You might have a great idea for a feature film, but it is unlikely that you will have the time to develop a full script for the film. It would be better at this stage to work on a number of smaller ideas so that you can develop your skills in a number of different written forms and genres.

You might want to try writing one or more of the following:

- a script for the opening sequence of a film or the first few scenes of a television soap or radio play

- some short articles for different types of newspaper or magazine that have different target audiences and a different purpose

- some persuasive copy for a poster or leaflet that is trying to sell a particular product.

Researching initial ideas

Once you have decided on the ideas that have potential, you will need to undertake some further research so that you can make an informed decision as to which ideasare worth developing further and which are best left alone.

 Remember

You will need to take at least one of the ideas that you develop in this part of the unit through to a finished piece of writing in the next stage.

You will need to make sure that you have the necessary skills and knowledge to be able to develop one of the pieces into a finished piece of writing and that you have the time to complete it.

Building on the work that you completed in Unit 2, this research will probably involve both primary and secondary techniques, as you will need to look at existing examples of scripts, articles, reviews and promotional copy, as well as getting direct feedback about your ideas from the target audience and the client who gave you the brief.

You will need to undertake research for two distinct purposes:

The market
The first area of research is to look into the market. For this you will need to look at existing examples of the type of work that you are planning to produce to see what the current practices are, who the audience for these products are and what the production guidelines are.

The content
The second area of research is to gather material for the actual content of your written work. You may already have some information about the topic that you are going to write about, but you will need to get more

■ **Figure 11.13** *Carrying out research for the content of your writing is an important activity at this stage.*

information to make sure that you cover all of the topic areas and that your information is as up to date and accurate as it can be.

For example, if you are writing an article on pollution for a local newspaper, you might want to do some primary research and interview an expert on the subject and then do a survey of what local people feel about the pollution issue. You might then do some secondary research to get some facts and figures about the levels of recorded pollution in the atmosphere and how they have changed over the years. You might also read some articles and some textbooks to find out what the key points are and what can be done to reduce levels of pollution.

It might be worthwhile for you to look back at the key points that you learnt in Unit 2 about the different research methods and techniques that are available to you, so that you can make your research as successful as possible.

Remember

Time spent planning, developing and researching your written material will be time well spent, and should improve the effectiveness and quality of the final pieces that you produce.

Preparation

When you are developing your written material and preparing your chosen ideas for the production stage, you will need to think very carefully about the style and structure of your writing and the type of language you are going to use.

Tone

The tone of a piece of writing refers to the way in which language is used to communicate in a certain way. A basic distinction to be made is between a formal and an informal tone.

Think it over

Think about the sort of language you would use when texting or emailing your friends, and then compare it to the language you would use when writing to a company for a part-time job or to arrange some work experience.

Remember

You have already learnt about things like mode of address, style and narrative structure in Unit 3, and it will be worth looking back at this material to help you with your preparation and the development of your chosen ideas.

There are many more ways in which you can alter the language that you use in order to communicate things in a different way. For example, you might want to make the person who is reading your work laugh, and so adopt a humorous tone, or you might be very unhappy about something and adopt a critical tone.

A good way to explore the ways in which you can use language to change the tone of the piece of work is to write about something in a different tone from the one you would normally expect. For example, you could write a recipe in a very sarcastic tone, a review of a pop concert in a very formal, factual tone and an article about a serious news item in a humorous tone. Remember, you will only be doing these experimental pieces of writing to help you understand how to use language to change the tone. You will have to think more carefully about the tone that you choose for your final pieces of writing.

Theory into practice

- Decide on the initial ideas that you are going to research further.
- Assess each idea according to the following key questions:
  - What form will the writing take?
  - What media product will it be used for?
  - What is its purpose?
  - Who is the target audience?
  - What codes and conventions will I have to be aware of?
  - What skills and knowledge will I need to produce this writing?
  - What other issues do I need to consider?
- After assessing each idea decide on the ones you will consider taking forward to the final writing stage and explain why you have chosen these particular ideas. You will need to include a more detailed description of these chosen ideas that includes information about the style in which they will be written, any narrative structure that you are using and what the tone of the language is going to be.

Remember

It is important that you keep all of your notes, drafts and research materials and include them in your final portfolio. It will provide good evidence of the stages that you went through in developing your written material.

Think it over

Think about your own communication skills. Are you confident when speaking to other people? What can you do to improve the way in which you get your ideas across?

Presenting to others

To complete this part of the unit you also need to present your ideas to others. There are two main ways in which you can do this. The first is in the form of a pitch to a client, or somebody playing the role of a client. The second is in the form of an oral presentation of your ideas to the rest of your class.

Presenting your ideas in the form of a pitch is more realistic because if you were working within the media industry, you would usually make a pitch to the person or group of people who have the final say as to whether your ideas will be accepted or not.

Whether you decide to pitch your ideas to a client or to present your ideas to the rest of the class, you will need to make sure that your presentation skills are as good as they can be.

■ **Figure 11.14** *The pitch is an important part of the development of your ideas.*

11.3 Produce written material

When producing your final pieces of written material it is important that you are aware of the conventions of style and layout of each of the forms that you are working in.

Scripts

If you are writing a script for a moving image product it is important that you set it out in a structured way so that it is clear which characters or presenters say which words, and what they are doing at the time.

You also need to give some indication about the location in which the film or programme will be filmed, and what kind of shots the camera will be taking. Script writers will often use the industry-standard abbreviations to describe the different shots that are used.

What does it mean?

Some of the commonly used camera shots are:

Wide shot (WS) *or* **Long shot (LS)** *– the subject is shot from a distance so that all of the subject can be seen and so can the location they are in*

Mid-shot (MS) *– only about half of the subject is seen and you can see less of the surroundings*

Close-up (CU) *– with this type of shot, a part of the subject, such as the head, fills the whole frame and very little, if any, of the surroundings can be seen*

Extreme close-up (ECU) *– a very close shot of the subject, or some part of them, that is often used for dramatic effect*

Two-shot *– a shot of two people framed like a mid-shot*

Over-the-shoulder shot (OSS) *– a shot of the subject taken from just behind a person who is looking at that subject – this shot helps to establish the positions of each person*

Point-of-view shot (POV) *– a shot that shows the view of somebody as if you are looking through their eyes*

See Figure 4.20 in Unit 4 for examples of these camera shots.

In your script you should also include details of any music or sound effects that are to be included and any additional visual information such as captions or graphics that are to be used.

The *EastEnders* script shown in Figure 11.2 opens with a description of the scene that the viewers will see. The script writer has given some factual information (the scene is set outside in Albert Square, it is dark and the time is 48 minutes past midnight), and also describes the situation that the character Ben finds himself in and they way that he looks and feels.

The dialogue that is actually spoken by the characters is clearly marked out, and their actions are also identified, as the extract in Figure 11.15 from the same script shows. The dialogue is written in upper and lower case to differentiate it from the instructions, which are all in upper case.

```
GRANT:   Good night's kip will do him the
         power of good.

PHIL:    [YAWNS] He ain't the only one.

         [GRANT LOBS THE CAR KEYS AT PHIL]

GRANT:   Get the motor first. I'll stick
         the kettle on.

         [PHIL TUTS, HEADS DOWN BRIDGE STREET
         TO RETRIEVE THE RANGE ROVER. GRANT
         HEADS INTO THE PUB SIDE GATE.
```

■ **Figure 11.15** *Extract from EastEnders script.*

Far from home
A radio drama by
Michael Butt

SCENE 1 HOME
EVENING. JANE, TERRY AND BETH ARE EATING. PAUSE.

BETH: Anyway so I…so I…so I've got to choose: Science or Arts.

        PAUSE

TERRY: Do both.

BETH: Crr.

TERRY: What?

        PAUSE

BETH: You got to choose. You can't do both.

TERRY: Why's that?

        PAUSE

BETH: Mum…

JANE: So they don't have enough teachers, or something. She has to choose. They all have to choose. Then she goes on, and goes to college.

BETH: Well…

JANE: Your music.

■ **Figure 11.16** *Opening of the radio drama* Far From Home *by Michael Butt.*

Also note that the dialogue written for the characters is realistic and includes informal language and non-standard forms. For example, the writer has used the word 'kip' instead of 'sleep' for Grant and 'ain't' instead of 'is not' for Phil, as this is how the characters the actors play actually speak.

Scripts for radio plays follow a similar style and structure, though of course will not include any visual information. Look at the extract from a radio play broadcast on BBC Radio 3 shown in Figure 11.16.

Printed products

There are also certain codes and conventions used in the writing of copy for printed products such as newspapers or magazines, and these are often dependent on the specific publication in which the copy will appear.

Most newspapers and magazines organise the words into columns as it is easier to read the relatively small type if it is organised in this way. Headings and sub-headings can also be used to break up the text, and of course images and graphics are also used to accompany and support the written words.

When producing articles for newspapers and magazines, it is a good idea to lay out the final version in a way that is appropriate to the type of writing. For example, if it is a magazine article, lay it out in columns and with sub-headings and text boxes. If it is a radio script, set it out with the instructions in upper case and the speakers' names in a column on the left. Laying out your work in an appropriate way will show that you understand the specific codes and conventions of each type of writing you have produced.

■ **Figure 11.17** *Columns, sub-headings and text boxes are found in many magazines.*

Remember

Remember to consider the layout of your written work. Check the font size and the use of columns to make sure that the words can be easily read. Also check the use of spacing between paragraphs and the alignment of any graphics or images. If you are producing a long text, you will also need to number the pages.

■ **Figure 11.18** *Examples of creative uses of typefaces and patterns.*

You might also want to experiment with the codes and conventions and come up with some more imaginative pieces of work. For example, you could experiment with different typefaces to communicate extra meaning, or the shape in which you present the words. Some examples are shown in Figure 11.18.

Writing skills

The unit specification requires you to demonstrate good technical writing skills as well as some degree of imagination and creativity. Spelling, punctuation and grammar are all very important – your final script, article or review might be very interesting and entertaining, but it will not pass if it is full of spelling and punctuation errors and simple grammatical mistakes.

Simply running your work through the spellchecker on your computer is not enough, as it will not pick up all of the errors, so you will need to proof-read your work carefully. It is also a good idea to let somebody else check your work. In the publishing industry, a journalist or author will pass their finished work on to an editor or sub-editor who checks their work and makes any necessary amendments.

Theory into practice

Can you spot the two deliberate errors in each of the sentences below? A spellchecker might pick up some of the mistakes, but not all of them. Check the correct answers at the end of the unit on page 353.

1 The group took there work and put it over their.

2 I asked the man were he had being on his holidays.

3 If we go over hear we will be able to here the band more clearly.

4 The greengrocers carrot's are very cheap.

5 What time does the concert start she asked. I think about eight, I replied.

Assessment task 3

You should now be ready to produce the final piece or pieces of written material that you will present in your portfolio of evidence.

■ *You will have been working on a number of different pieces of written material when completing section 3.2 of this unit, and you now need to decide which of these you will take forward.*

■ *The unit specification states that one long finished piece of written material is acceptable for this element, as are several shorter pieces. You will need to discuss with your tutor which is the best option for you.*

■ *You might want to develop and complete a script for a short film or television programme that you have been working on to link in with your work on Unit 4. Or you might want to complete two or three articles for a magazine or newspaper that you and a group of other students have been working on for Unit 6.*

■ *If you are working as part of a group on a college magazine, for example, then you will need to make sure that you clearly identify which is your own work.*

■ *Do not forget to keep examples of your work as you go through the writing stages, and to keep a diary or commentary that explains what you are doing.*

Assessment evidence

✔ Your written material will have a recognisable genre and the expression will be reasonably clear throughout. The work will show evidence of basic technical writing skills.

✔✔ Your work is competent, has been produced with care and shows good results. The genre(s) of the finished writing will be clearly recognisable and will show the use of the correct codes and conventions. Expression and register will be appropriate and technical writing skills will show only occasional mistakes.

✔✔✔ You demonstrate the use of high-level skills and a creative approach to the production of the written material. Your writing will demonstrate a level of confidence. Register and expression will be consistently accurate and clear. Good technical writing skills will also be in evidence with only one or two errors in spelling, punctuation or grammar.

11.4 Review your own writing work

Once you have finished your written work you will be ready to reflect on how it went and review what you have completed. This is a very important part of the unit as you need to understand what went well so that you can do these things again in your future projects.

However, you also need to understand anything that went wrong or did not go as well as you expected. Learning from your mistakes is an important part of any process and will help you to be better at doing things next time.

The three key areas that you need to look at when reviewing your written work are:

- the finished piece or pieces of writing that you produced
- the processes that you went through
- the sources of information that you used.

When reviewing your work you will need to compare each finished piece of writing with the original ideas that you had for it. How has it changed? What were the reasons for these changes?

You also need to consider to what extent it is appropriate for the target audience and, for work that you produced in response to a set brief, to what extent it meets the requirements of this brief and the needs of the client.

You also need to review the skills and techniques that you used when writing each piece of work. You will need to comment on its form, structure and style, the register and tone of the language used, and the accuracy of your spelling, punctuation and grammar.

When reviewing the process of producing your written material you need to reflect on your research skills, your time management, the process of drafting and redrafting that you went through to arrive at the finished work, and the different forms of communication that you used throughout the process. You will also need to review your own working methods and those that you used when working as a member of a team.

Finally, your review of your sources of information will include the original notes and ideas that you generated and the initial drafts. You should also comment on your research material and the feedback that you received from your audience, your client (if you had one), tutor and peers.

You can present your review in any form that you choose. You might prefer to present it in the form of a written report, or you might want to use an audio–visual format of some kind. You need to discuss this with your tutor so that you can decide what is the best format for you.

Think it over

Think about what went well during the writing process and what you had some difficulties with. If you were to do this unit again is there anything that you would do differently?

Assessment task 4

Your final task in this unit is to review and evaluate your writing work and the processes that you went through. In this review you should clearly identify your contribution to any group work and the roles that you undertook.

Assessment evidence

✔ Describe your own writing work. As well as describing your finished products, you also need to describe the processes that you went through, and comment on your skill development and the role that you as an individual played in any group work that was undertaken.

✔✔ Make sure that the descriptions you provide are quite detailed and include some examples to support the statements you are making.

✔✔✔ Explain, rather than just describe, the processes, methods and techniques that you used. Justify and support your comments with specific and well-chosen examples. You should also use technical and specialist language accurately and in an appropriate way.

Theory into practice

Answers

1 *The group took there work and put it over their.* ✗

The words *'there'* and *'their'* have been used wrongly in this sentence. It should read:

*The group took **their** work and put it over **there**.* ✓

2 *I asked the man were he had being on his holidays.* ✗

The word *'were'* is incorrect in this sentence and should be replaced with *'where'*. Also the word *'being'* needs to be replaced with *'been'*.

*I asked the man **where** he had **been** on his holidays.* ✓

3 *If we go over hear we will be able to here the band more clearly.* ✗

The words *'hear'* and *'here'* have been used wrongly in this sentence. It should read:

*If we go over **here** we will be able to **hear** the band more clearly.* ✓

4 *The greengrocers carrot's are very cheap.* ✗

The apostrophe is used to indicate possession, and so it should be used in *'greengrocer's'* to indicate that the carrots belong to the greengrocer. It should not be used in *'carrots'* as this is simply the plural of carrot.

*The **greengrocer's carrots** are very cheap* ✓

5 *What time does the concert start she asked. I think about eight, I replied.* ✗

Inverted commas to mark off the actual words spoken have been missed out. The question mark has also been missed out. The correct version should read:

*'What time does the concert start**?'** she asked. '**I** think about eight,**'** I replied.* ✓

How well did you do?

17 Media Production Project

Introduction

In the media industry, the majority of products are produced by a team who are working to a brief for the product. The person who comes up with the idea for a product is not usually involved in managing the project itself. However, in this unit, you will be developing your own ideas in order to create an actual media product – in this way you will learn all the stages involved in the process. You will be able to work on your own or in a small group to plan and complete your product.

You will learn about the importance of the proposal and how to prepare one. Then you will develop the ideas you set out in your proposal to plan and create your media product. At the end of the unit, you will have the opportunity to review your production work and evaluate what went well, what you could improve on next time and the skills that you have learnt.

Learning outcomes

On completion of this unit you should:

■ be able to prepare a proposal for a media product

■ be able to develop a proposal for a media product

■ be able to create a media product following a proposal

■ be able to review your own production work.

17.1 Preparing a proposal for a media product

A **proposal** is a document that sets out your ideas for a media product and is a key document in the planning stages of the project. It is designed to help sell your idea to your client so that they will want to invest in your product and give it the go ahead. The diagram shown in Figure 17.1 will help you understand the processes involved in producing a media product. The tasks you need to perform at each stage will vary depending on the medium you are using, but the sequence of processes will be the same whatever your product. You can see from the diagram that the proposal comes right at the beginning of the process.

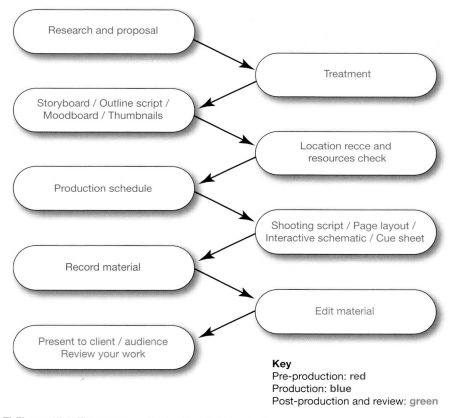

Research and proposal

Treatment

Storyboard / Outline script / Moodboard / Thumbnails

Location recce and resources check

Production schedule

Shooting script / Page layout / Interactive schematic / Cue sheet

Record material

Edit material

Present to client / audience Review your work

Key
Pre-production: **red**
Production: **blue**
Post-production and review: **green**

■ **Figure 17.1** *The processes involved in media production.*

Which medium?

Before you can start preparing your proposal you will need to decide on the product you want to work on. The first step is to decide on the medium you would like to work in. You may have already developed skills in one medium that you would like to develop further or you might want to try something new. Think carefully about where your strengths lie – perhaps you have a strong artistic and visual sense or maybe you enjoy speaking and listening or have excellent writing skills that you would like to use. Think about the medium that you would enjoy working in most and that would be drawing on your strengths. You might decide to make:

- a short video or DVD
- a website
- a newspaper, magazine or leaflet
- a radio programme or commercial
- an interactive CD-ROM or DVD
- a computer game
- an animation.

Researching ideas

Once you have decided on the medium you will be working in, you need to come up with some ideas for a product. There might be something you have always wanted to make or alternatively you might have to come up with a new idea from scratch. Think about the subjects that really interest you and that would inspire you when making a programme – for example, you might be really interested in global warming and want to inform others about it too, or you might have a favourite sport or hobby that you think would make an interesting subject for a media product.

Carrying out some initial research will help you to come up with some ideas and to decide which of those ideas will work best for your purpose. Here we will look at some of the areas that you need to research.

Client

Generally, media products are made for a client – the person who pays for the work. The client could be, for example, a local charity that wants a media product in order to publicise its work or your headteacher who wants to provide information to parents about your school or college – you could use this opportunity to produce a short video or website about the school. Or you might hear about a competition that you would like to enter that will provide ideas for your product.

If you are working for a client, their needs and requirements will clearly influence the type of product you will produce. Any guidelines that they give you will help you to come up with some initial ideas.

Target audience

You will need to think about your target audience and the kinds of products that they like – appealing to your target audience is crucial to the success of a media product. (For much more on the audiences of media products, refer to Unit 3.)

Theory into practice

Look at a range of products in your chosen medium and identify the target audience for each product.

OR

Decide on the target audience you would like to make a product for and identify some products in your medium that are aimed at this target audience.

What is it about each of these products that shows who the target audience is? How successful is each product in appealing to its intended audience?

Your target audience will have a huge impact on the content and style of the product you will be making, so it is important to define it quite clearly. You will need to make sure that all aspects of your product will be appropriate for your audience – including language, content, style and choice of actors or presenters. For example, you would not use a fluffy animal cartoon character to present a programme for 11–14 year olds, but you might choose a character who was similar to, say, Bart Simpson.

Theory into practice

Look at a range of products in your chosen medium that focus on environmental issues. For example:

- interactive media: websites of environmental groups; educational CD-ROMS about the environment; news sites with articles on the environment
- print: leaflets from environmental groups, local councils, etc.; books; newspaper articles; specialist magazines
- TV and video: documentaries; news items; dramas with an environmental theme
- radio: documentaries; news reports; dramas with an environmental theme; debates.

Make a list of all the products that you find and identify the target audience for each one. Which do you think have been made to appeal to young people of your own age?

Remember, too, any restrictions on content for certain age groups, especially in products for young children. This might affect your product, depending on your target age group.

Genre

You will also need to decide on the **genre** of product you would like to make. Carrying out some research into the different genres and sub-genres available in your chosen medium will help you to come up with some ideas. You can find out more about the genres within each medium in Unit 3, particularly pages 113–114.

Case study

Media Productions

Throughout this unit, we will be following a real media project as it is developed by a company called Media Productions.

As its name suggests, Media Productions is a production company that creates media products in a number of different media, including print, interactive media, on DVD and for televison and radio.

They have been commissioned by a local pottery manufacturer, Yorkshire Pottery, to produce a promotional point-of-sale video for their new range of kitchenware called Yorkshire Blue. This range of pottery has a 1940s style and is very distinctive, with white and blue banding. The point-of-sale video will be played in retail outlets as shoppers are walking by.

The client wanted Media Productions to come up with a variety of ideas for the video and then pitch their proposal to the managing director. After an initial meeting with the client, Media Productions started by sending a researcher to the Yorkshire Pottery factory and then to a local retail outlet to get some ideas for the content of the video.

The researcher then did a brainstorming exercise and used a mind map to record all her ideas. You can see this in Figure 17.2.

■ **Figure 17.2** *A record of the mind mapping exercise undertaken by the researcher at Media Productions for their client Yorkshire Pottery.*

Mind maps
One way of exploring ideas for a new product is to start with a mind map exercise. The idea is to brainstorm all your ideas, either on your own or in a group, and record them all in a diagram. Include all your ideas at this stage, not just the ones that seem the most sensible.

 Case study

Settling on an idea

The researcher then presented all her ideas to the production team at Media Productions. They discussed each idea so they could choose the best idea to develop into a proposal.

They discounted some ideas which they felt would not be appropriate. For example, filming in the USA would be too expensive so they dismissed that idea. They thought that a simple slide show might not be interesting or eye-catching enough so they dismissed that idea too.

In the end, they settled on the idea of a poetic video about the making of a teapot. They thought that this would fit the client's requirements well and that the poetic style would complement the retro look of the pottery range.

They then carried out some further research in order to be able to prepare their proposal for the video.

 Theory into practice

Brainstorm a number of ideas for your media product.

Produce a mind map showing all your ideas.

Go through all the ideas one by one and dismiss any ideas that might be difficult or impossible to produce.

Then decide on the idea that will work best for your product: it must be both achievable and something that you really want to make.

The proposal

Once you have chosen an idea to work with, the next stage of the planning process is to produce your proposal. This document will set out your ideas for your media product. The proposal will allow you to expand on your idea and try to sell it to a client. In this instance your client will probably be your teacher, but you may have the opportunity to work with a real client, perhaps a local company or charity that would like some advertising materials.

Remember

Here is a checklist of items to include in your proposal:

- the medium you will be working in
- the working title of your product
- the genre (and maybe the sub-genre)
- what the content will be
- the style
- the audience
- the length.

Content and style

The content refers to what is actually in your product. The content of the Media Productions video will be the making of a teapot and how it fits into the products in the Yorkshire Blue kitchenware range.

Style

The big factors involved in determining the style of your product are the subject matter and the target audience. Media Productions' video is about the making of a teapot and will be viewed by shoppers in the kitchenware department. Media Productions will have to make sure that they choose language, music and images that will be appropriate for presenting their subject to the audience. It is very unlikely that violence and swearing will be appropriate! Similarly, they will probably want some quite gentle, possibly retro-style, music in their programme, rather than the latest drum and base track.

Theory into practice

Does your school or college have a prospectus or promotional website or video? If so, read it carefully and think about the message that the prospectus is trying to get across:

- What kind of language is used in the text? Is it generally positive or negative?
- What do the photographs show? Do the images show people who are happy or sad? Does the school or college look clean or dirty?

Think about your answers to these questions and how what you have discovered can help you with the style of your own product.

Legal and ethical constraints

When preparing your proposal, you will also need to consider any legal and ethical constraints on your production, for example:

- Will you be in danger of libelling anybody?
- Have you considered issues of representation?
- Will you need to obtain permission to use any copyright material?
- Are you aware of the codes of practice for your sector of the media industry?
- Is the product likely to offend anyone?
- If you are creating an advertisement, does it represent the product accurately?
- If you are creating a TV programme, is it suitable for airing before the 9 p.m. watershed?
- If you are creating a film, will it need a classification certificate?

For more on the legal and ethical constraints that you will need to consider, have a look at Unit 1, pages 29–45. If there are any issues that will affect your production, make sure you mention them in your proposal and how you intend to deal with them.

 Case study

Issues of representation

The Media Productions point-of-sale video will be shown in department stores across the UK. Here are some of the issues that Media Productions had to consider:

- They could not use a voiceover actor with a really broad local accent that might not be understood in other regions.

- They wanted to show a wide range of people using the Yorkshire Blue pottery, so that it would appeal to both the younger and older generations.
- They wanted to be representative of different ethnic and social groups so that the range would have a wide appeal all over the country.

As you can see from the example proposal in Figure 17.3, the proposal is a document designed to sell the idea to the client, in the hope that the client will ask for a further development of the product idea. It also gives the client an idea about the alternatives available to them, such as involving a celebrity and the use of atmospheric music.

media
PRODUCTIONS

Proposal
for
a point-of-sale video

Yorkshire Blue

Prepared by
Sandra Ahmed

Media Productions

21st July 2006

for
Yorkshire Pottery

copyright © 2006

PROPOSAL

Prepared by Sandra Ahmed

Media Productions will produce a ten-minute point-of-sale video programme to encourage consumers to purchase the new and exciting range of pottery Yorkshire Blue. The programme will be aimed at an audience of shoppers in kitchenware departments of high street shops and will be informative and educational. The video will aim to create a romantic link between the range of pottery and the public's concept of the 'old days'.

The video will feature material shot on location at the pottery and at a large department store. It will focus on the production process of a teapot from the range as it progresses through the factory, on to the shelf in the department store and is sold.

The theme will be the romantic notion of having something that looks like the pottery your grandmother might have had on her dresser. This will encourage a whole new generation of buyers looking for that retro feel in their kitchen.

The programme will start with a shot of the factory and then follow the pottery on its long journey through moulding and firing. The final shot will be in a department store with racks of the pottery looking clean and bright.

There will be a range of atmospheric and romantic music used throughout the point-of-sale video. There is no intention to use interviews or voiceover in this programme. We have approached a television personality who collects kitchenware to appear in the programme. They could appear to talk us through the production process and/or at the end of the programme to endorse the product.

The video will feature atmospheric sounds in the factory and department store scenes.

The video will be produced on high-definition format cameras and edited using the latest high-definition digital editing technology at our Birmingham editing facility.

The budget is subject to discussion but will be approximately £20,000.

■ **Figure 17.3** *The proposal prepared by the team at Media Productions for their client Yorkshire Pottery.*

Theory into practice

Look at the proposal shown in Figure 17.3. Identify the parts of the proposal that include the following information:

- *the medium*
- *the working title of the product*
- *the genre (and maybe the sub-genre)*
- *what the content will be*
- *the style*
- *the audience*
- *the length.*

In your own proposal, you may prefer to use subheadings to divide up the information into different sections.

Remember

Your proposal should be based on an idea that is feasible and something you really want to make. It can be in whichever media format you want to use.

Assessment task 1

1 *Using your initial idea for a media product, prepare a proposal that you can pitch to your client (this may be your teacher).*
2 *Include in your proposal: the medium, the working title, the genre, the content, the style, the audience and the length of your product.*
3 *Show that you have thought about legal and ethical considerations that might affect your product.*

Assessment evidence

✓ Present a written proposal for a media product.

✓✓ Prepare a detailed written proposal for a media product.

✓✓✓ Prepare a detailed written proposal that shows you have used high-level skills and creativity.

Pitching your proposal

As we discussed earlier, the purpose of the proposal is to try to sell your ideas to your client. When a media production company has finished preparing their proposal, they will make a **pitch** to their client. (In your case, your client may well be your teacher.) For ideas on how to present a pitch, have a look at page 284 in Unit 7.

■ **Figure 17.4** *Dressing smartly for your proposal pitch will help to give the right impression to your client.*

Client comments

Whether you deliver your proposal in an oral pitch or give your client a copy of the written document to read, your client might well have some suggestions about your ideas. Record all of these carefully and try to find out why they want to make these changes. Then go back to your proposal and make any changes necessary in order to include your client's suggestions. Make sure that you keep a record of the changes that you have made. You will need to use these records when you review your production work at the end of this unit.

Case study

Meeting records

The creative director at Media Production pitched the video proposal to the marketing manager and the managing director of Yorkshire Pottery in a meeting at the client's head office. They recorded the meeting carefully, particularly all the comments and suggestions made by their clients, as shown in Figure 17.5. A copy of this meeting record was distributed to the Media Productions team and to the team at Yorkshire Pottery.

CLIENT MEETING RECORD SHEET

Date: 26 July 2006 | **Time:** 10.45 a.m. | **Place:** Yorkshire Pottery head office

Present: Sandra Ahmed (Media Productions)
Gill Somerton (Managing Director Yorkshire Pottery)
Barry Smith (Marketing Director Yorkshire Pottery)

Apologies for absence: None

Items discussed

1. SA introduced the concept for the Yorkshire Pottery point-of-sale video.
2. SA presented the proposal using a PowerPoint presentation and talked about the ideas one by one.
3. SA asked for the client's comments.
4. GS liked the ideas but was a little concerned about the logistics of filming in the factory.
5. BS suggested that he could make arrangements to avoid any disruption to the workers in the factory. He also offered to arrange a department store location.
6. GS thought that the romantic idea was fine but wanted more details about what the final programme would look like.
7. SA suggested that Media Productions could develop their idea for a point-of-sale video further by producing a treatment that expanded on the content.
8. GS and BS thought that this would be a sensible idea and agreed to Media Productions developing the idea further in a treatment.
9. This was agreed and date for a further meeting was agreed.

Date of next meeting: 2 August 2006

■ **Figure 17.5** *Example of a client meeting record sheet, showing suggestions from the client and what was agreed.*

Remember

It is vital that you keep careful records of meetings. If you keep careful records and make sure you carry out any suggestions made, you may be able to meet the requirements for a merit or distinction grade.

Assessment task 2

Deliver a pitch of your proposal to your client. Make a note of any suggestions that the client makes using a meeting record sheet – include as much detail as possible so that you have an accurate record of the meeting. If necessary, follow your client's suggestions to amend your proposal.

Assessment evidence

✔ Pitch your written proposal for a media product to your client.

✔✔ Present a detailed written proposal for a media product in a pitch to your client.

✔✔✔ Present a detailed written proposal in a pitch that shows you have used high-level skills and creativity.

Remember

Make sure that someone records your pitch and that you keep all PowerPoint slides and any handouts that you produce. These will all provide essential evidence for your assessment.

17.2 Developing a proposal for a media product

Developing your proposal means building on the ideas contained in it to create a more detailed picture of the product you intend to create. You need to develop your content ideas further and plan and prepare for all the tasks that need to be completed during production and post-production.

Treatment

Once you have decided on your idea and presented your proposal, the next step is to produce a treatment. The treatment contains much more information than the proposal and will provide a detailed snapshot of the media product – this will be useful for both the client and yourself when you come to actually produce your media product.

Case study

The treatment

As a result of the meeting with their client, Media Productions produced a treatment, developing their ideas for the point-of-sale video product. In their treatment, they made sure that they addressed the suggestions made by their client at the sales pitch meeting. They spent two weeks developing their treatment, which gives an indication of the amount of work that needs to go into it.

A treatment should be produced using DTP software and must look professional. The first page is a cover sheet identifying the name of the media product, the client, your name and the date. The rest of the document is divided into sections, each of which describes and explains different aspects of the media product. The headings allow the writer to give more detail of the project. You should complete all the sections of the treatment – some sections will be quite short but others may take up one or more pages.

The treatment should include the following sections:

Introduction
A short opening section which summarises the original proposal and the approach that you will take in your media product. This is an opportunity to really sell your idea. The introduction should also include details of the size and content of the media product.

TREATMENT	
Programme Title:	Yorkshire Blue
Client:	Yorkshire Pottery
Writer:	Sandra Ahmed
Date:	1st August 2006

Introduction

Outline script

Storyboard

Production schedule

Outline budget

Contingency plan

Talent

Production staff

Research

media
PRODUCTIONS

Treatment
for
Point-of-Sale Video
Yorkshire Blue

Prepared
by
Sandra Ahmed

Media Productions
1st August 2006

Client
Yorkshire Pottery

Copyright © 2006

■ **Figure 17.6** *The treatment form used by Media Productions for their Yorkshire Blue point-of-sale video.*

Outline script

Writing an outline script will help you to work out the resources that you will need for your media product. It allows you to bring your ideas together to show what the finished product will contain and what it will look like. It should include the characters used and the dialogue or narration. In order to complete the outline script, you must have a clear picture of your media product.

Storyboard/structure diagram/mood board/thumbnails

What you include here will depend on the format of the media product you have decided to produce.

■ A **storyboard** is a paper visualisation of a moving-image product. It will help you to form ideas about what scenes will look like, the positions of characters, the way that the visual and sound aspects of your product will work together, etc. Television media products will have a detailed storyboard developed before a single frame is shot. This is done to ensure that all of the scenes are feasible before expensive equipment is hired and staff employed. You can see an example of a storyboard in Unit 7, Figure 7.10.

■ The equivalent of the storyboard for an interactive media product is a **structure diagram**, which shows the hierarchy of the pages and all the links between them. It may also have examples of the text, pictures and sound to be used. Figure 17.7 shows an example of a structure diagram for a college website.

■ **Figure 17.7** *A structure diagram is a clear way of planning a website or other interactive product.*

- For a print product, you may need to produce a **mood board** that gives the feel of the product you are hoping to create. It will include examples of the colours and text styles that you will use, as well as the types of photos, illustrations and other graphic items that you want to include.

- **Thumbnails** are a useful way of planning layouts for print products or pages of an interactive media product. They are rough sketches in pencil or pen, used to explore layout options. The idea is just to put in the main elements of a page – shaded rectangles for images and lines for text. These rough sketches will help you come up with the best design and will give your client an idea of the layout you are thinking of. You will need to do thumbnail layouts for all the different pages in your print publication. You can see an example of some thumbnail sketches in Unit 7, Figure 7.11.

Production schedule

Include the key dates for your production work here. Make sure you allow enough time for the following tasks: planning, creating content (e.g. designing a leaflet, magazine or website, shooting a video, recording a radio show, etc.), editing your content and for the client to review. Include the date for delivery of your finished media product. Make sure that you will be able to fit in all the tasks before your deadline.

Outline budget

Understanding the cost requirements of your planned media product is very important. You will have to produce a realistic budget for your production, including real costs for equipment hire, actor fees, fees for use of locations, etc. For the treatment approximate costs are fine, but later you will also need to prepare a complete budget with details of all the costs you will incur.

Contingency plan

It is not always possible to plan a production down to the last detail – things often change as the production progresses. Reasons for this could be:

- the client changes their mind about the content after production has started

- the price of materials or equipment changes

- an actor is ill or unavailable for another reason

- equipment breaks down during production

- severe weather means you have to postpone your location work or hire a studio instead.

So it is always a good idea to plan for contingency – give an idea of what could go wrong and what you would do about it if it did. It is a good idea to allow extra time in the schedule for things going wrong, and some extra money in the budget for unforeseen expenses.

Personnel

Include the names and roles of all the staff who will be working on the production.

Talent

Include ideas for appropriate actors, presenters and/or voiceover artists. This will give the client a real feel for who could appear in their media product. A famous name could help sell their product, though of course it will add to the costs.

Research

It is a good idea to include details of the research you have carried out for the production, into the target audience, for example.

Make sure you spend enough time researching and developing your treatment. It might take you two weeks or more to gather all the information you need and to prepare scripts, storyboards, layouts, etc., but this time will be extremely well spent. Not only will it impress your client and convince them to go with your solution, it will also save you time later as you will already have done a large amount of the planning you need for your production. You will be able to develop the production paperwork you need using the information in the different sections of your treatment.

Remember

When planning and producing the treatment for your own media product, make sure that you research:

- the time you have available for planning and production

- the resources you have available for pre-production, production and post-production.

Do not put anything into your treatment that you will not have the resources or time to achieve.

Assessment task 3

Produce a treatment for your media product. Include all the details necessary for the client to see that you have made sufficient plans for the product to be produced. Make sure that you complete all the sections using the headings listed in this section. Once you have completed your treatment, give a copy to your client or teacher for them to review.

Assessment evidence

✔ Develop your proposal for a media product into a treatment.

✔✔ Competently develop your proposal for a media product into a treatment.

✔✔✔ Develop your proposal for a media product into a treatment that demonstrates application of high-level skills and creativity.

Personnel requirements

Part of the planning for your product involves thinking about who you will need to help you produce it in time and to the required quality. It is unlikely that you will be able to do everything yourself. Think about your media product in terms of the different roles that are needed in order to carry out all the production and post-production tasks. For example, to produce a website, you might need:

- A **producer** – responsible for managing the whole project and making sure it is completed on time.
- An **information architect** – plans the structure of the website: how pages are linked, navigation, etc.
- A **web designer** – designs the layout of the web pages, including the fonts, images, colours and branding.
- A **content developer** – writes the copy (the text) that appears on the website, and makes suggestions for images to illustrate the text.
- A **programmer** – creates the functionality of the website, including any dynamic aspects involving databases.
- A **photographer/picture researcher** – provides the images for the website.
- A **tester** – carries out thorough testing of the website to make sure it works properly on a variety of platforms and reports any bugs that need fixing.

You will probably want to carry out more than one role yourself, but think about how much you can realistically achieve in the time available and who you can get to help you.

Once you have arranged who will be on your production team, you should hold regular team meetings to ensure that everything is on track and that all members of the team know what is expected of them. Keeping a chain of communication in place and having regular updates will keep you aware of any problems that are arising or any delays in the project being completed.

Keep a record of what is said in your production team meetings – you might like to use a version of the meeting record sheet shown in Figure 17.5. List each item that is discussed as a numbered point.

■ **Figure 17.8** *Holding regular team meetings will keep everyone up to date with developments and allow people to contribute their creative ideas.*

Production schedule

This important document will include all your plans for production of your media product, together with the details of what is involved and when it will take place. A production schedule will help you to plan effectively for pre-production, production and post-production.

Building from the outline schedule you included in your treatment, the production schedule includes details of when the work for your media project started and when various activities are planned to take place. This information is vital for your records as it will form a major part of the evidence required for this unit. Your production schedule should contain:

- details of the start and finish dates for producing the proposal and the treatment and when these were circulated to the client
- agreed dates for activities such as location shooting, photography or sound recording, editing and review by the client
- details of the production equipment required and where you will obtain this from
- your transport requirements
- crewing requirements – with names of personnel
- the talent (actors) required, with names
- the properties required for the production and whose responsibility they are
- your post-production equipment requirements.

The production schedule helps to clarify all of the details of the production in one document. This document is a vital piece of evidence of your planning and production work, so you must store it carefully and have it available for the assessment of your work.

PRODUCTION SCHEDULE PART 1	
Programme Title:	Yorkshire Blue
Client:	Yorkshire Pottery
Writer:	Sandra Ahmed
Date:	21st August 2006

	Date		Date
Programme started:	01/06/06	Completed:	
Proposal started:	20/07/06	Completed:	21/07/06
Treatment started:	31/07/06	Completed:	01/08/06
Agreement from client:	05/08/06		
Shooting script started:	05/08/06	Completed:	09/08/06
Storyboard started:	13/08/06	Completed:	16/08/06
Production started:	12/09/06	Completed:	
Post-production started:	03/10/06	Completed:	
Rough cut supplied to client:	14/10/06	Agreed with client:	
Final version to client:	21/10/06		

■ **Figure 17.9** *Part 1 of the production schedule gives all the key dates for the production of the media product.*

Monitor your production schedule regularly and record any changes as soon as they occur. Figure 17.9 shows the first part of the production schedule for the Media Productions Yorkshire Blue point-of-sale video. It includes all the key dates for this project and provides a clear picture of the way that the project is progressing.

For your own project, you might need to change some of the items included, depending on the type of product your are creating. For example, if you are producing a magazine, you will need to include dates for sample layouts and copywriting, instead of shooting script and storyboard.

Part 2 of the production schedule should include a complete list of all your requirements for the production, including equipment, personnel, talent, transport, props and post-production requirements such as sound effects and music.

Think it over

The production schedule part 2 shown in Figure 17.10 was produced for the point-of-sale video media product.

What would you have to include if you were making each of the following media products?

- a radio play
- a television commercial
- a newspaper or magazine
- an animation
- a website

As well as the production schedule, if you are planning any location or studio work, you will also find a **call sheet** useful. A call sheet is a detailed schedule produced for each day of production. It contains details of date, time and location, the crew and actors involved. It also contains details of transport arrangements, props needed, materials required for the day's work and location catering arrangements.

When you do your planning, remember to keep everyone informed about the schedule. If you give everyone involved a call sheet, they are much more likely to be in the right place at the right time and with the right equipment.

Remember

- You will need to keep careful records of your planning and production.

- Update your production schedule regularly to reflect any changes that occur.

- Make sure that you record any changes in an appropriate way. Keep a copy of the original schedule so you can comment on why any changes were necessary.

PRODUCTION SCHEDULE PART 2

Programme Title:	Yorkshire Blue
Client:	Yorkshire Pottery
Writer:	Sandra Ahmed
Date:	25th August 2006

Production equipment required

cameras
lights
microphones
tripod

Crewing requirements

cameraperson
sound recordist
production assistant
lighting technician
props technician

Actors

1 male actor
1 female actor

Transport requirements

Transport to pottery required for approximately 10 people

Props/scenery

All kitchenware to be supplied by Yorkshire Pottery, from their Yorkshire Blue range

Post-production requirements (format, effects, music, voice-over)

Editing using Final Cut Pro
Graphics for titles and credits
Music throughout programme
Sound effects where necessary

■ **Figure 17.10** *Part 2 of the production schedule lists all the requirements for the production and post-production stages.*

PRODUCTION SCHEDULE CALL SHEET	
Programme Title:	Yorkshire Blue
Client:	Yorkshire Pottery
Writer:	Sandra Ahmed
Date:	16th September 2006

Crew	
Camera:	Robin Williams
Sound:	Rory Smith
Lighting:	Jill Sparks
Production Assistant:	Kate Azhami
Technicians:	John Brown/Bill Bailley
Transport:	Just Cars
Props:	Gary Musazawksi

ARRANGEMENTS	
Meeting at:	Yorkshire Pottery, 2 Chapel Steet, Grisdon Meet at front gates
Location Venue:	Interior of pottery
CALL DATE:	**20th September 2006**
CALL TIME:	**6.30 a.m.**
Transport:	Leaving from Media Productions offices at 6 a.m. prompt

INSTRUCTIONS:	No special instructions for this shoot

Actors:	Bill Foreman: Interviewer	Jane Smith: Pottery enthusiast
Wardrobe:	Bill: 7 a.m.	Jane: 7.30 a.m.
Make-up:	Bill: 7.30 a.m.	Jane: 8 a.m.

Location catering:	Breakfast required for 10 people from 7 a.m. Lunch required for 10 people from 12.30 p.m. Evening meal for 10 people from 6 p.m. Coffee/tea available at all times Chuck Wagon caterers on site at all times
Properties:	Pottery provided by Yorkshire Pottery

■ **Figure 17.11** *The call sheet used by Media Productions for the first day of their Yorkshire Blue video shoot.*

Always make sure that you gain permission to film on location and notify the police if you are planning to film in a public area.

Location reconnaissance

For a moving image production (such as a film or TV programme) and perhaps also for an audio production (such as a radio programme), you will need to carry out a location reconnaissance (usually known as a **recce** for short).

This involves visiting any locations or the studio that you are planning to use and checking out the lighting, power supply and accessibility for your crew and cast. You may have to organise a contact person to let you in early to set up your equipment.

Your location recce will also allow you to identify potential hazards so that you can compile a risk assessment document – this is a vital document for any professional production company planning to do location work.

Use a **location visit sheet** to record all of the information that you gather during your recce – an example is provided in Figure 17.12.

When working on location, you also need to make sure that you obtain the permission of anyone who appears in your production. For more on this, see the section on Location considerations on pages 159–161 of Unit 4.

Health and safety issues

Look at the sections on health and safety issues in Unit 1 and Unit 4. Ask yourself – will there be any problems when producing my product? It is essential that you consider the possible risks to yourself, your crew and the general public when planning for your production and post-production.

You may have to allocate some of your budget to ensure that there are no problems with health and safety. Media production companies might have to consider issues such as:

- security on site when working with famous actors
- finding out the hazards and safety precautions necessary for working in a particular location – e.g. a building site or factory using hazardous chemicals.

You must follow safe working practices at all stages of work on your media product. You have to work with equipment, with other people and sometimes with the general public. No one wants to work in a dangerous situation if this can be avoided. Try to think about the health and safety issues that will affect your own production work.

PRODUCTION SCHEDULE LOCATION VISIT SHEET	
Programme Title:	Yorkshire Blue
Client:	Yorkshire Pottery
Writer:	Sandra Ahmed
Producer:	Amanda Phillips
Director:	Barry Norman
Date:	2nd September 2006

Rough sketch of location including electricity points:
Yorshire Pottery

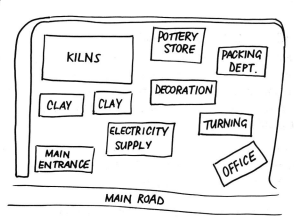

Access to location via:
Main road and through access gates via security

Name and number of location contact:
Declan Harris, Site Manager

Health and safety issues to note:
• Working machinery
• Some toxic substances stored on site
• Close to main road
• Possibility of causing an obstruction to factory employees
• Very hot kilns used for firing the pottery: up to 1100°C
• Location of emergency services
• Availability of first aid

Potential filming problems:
• Electricity not available in all areas of the factory
• Machinery working in location
• Noise when recording live interviews
• Avoid blocking pathways and corridors
• Tight space in working areas
• Poor lighting in some areas of the factory

Notes:

■ **Figure 17.12** *The location visit sheet for the day of filming planned by Media Productions at Yorkshire Pottery.*

■ **Figure 17.13** *Carrying out a recce will help you to identify any potential hazards for when you do your location work.*

Theory into practice

Media production companies have to make sure that they have the correct insurance in place for their production work.

■ Public liability insurance will cover any damages awarded to a member of the public as a result of damage or injury caused to them by the company.

■ Employers' liability insurance covers any compensation claimed by employees due to accidents or illness at work.

Find out more about these two types of insurance and why they are needed.

You can use your location visit record to produce a **risk assessment** to help ensure the safety of everyone involved in your location work. You can find out more about risk assessments on page 151 of Unit 4. Figure 17.14 is the risk assessment done by Media Productions for their location filming at Yorkshire Pottery. You will notice that the risk assessment lists solutions for the hazards identified at the recce.

RISK ASSESSMENT SHEET	
Programme Title:	Yorkshire Blue
Client:	Yorkshire Pottery
Writer:	Sandra Ahmed
Producer:	Amanda Phillips
Director:	Barry Norman
Date:	8th September 2006

FILMING AT YORKSHIRE POTTERY		
Possible hazards		
Risk	**Level of risk**	**Safety measures to be taken**
1. Working machinery	High	Arrange tour of premises by factory's health and safety officer for all crew, pointing out areas with working machinery. Instruct on the dangers involved.
2. Toxic substances stored on site	High	Do not film near the storage areas.
3. Kilns for firing the pottery: operate at up to 1100°C	High	Follow factory's safety procedures when filming in the vicinity of the kilns. Wear protective clothing as instructed.
4. Possibility of causing an obstruction to factory employees	Medium	Film only in areas we have permission to use. Provide ample warning of our presence to factory workers. Use clear signs to indicate when we are working in each area. Ensure no wires or leads are left trailing over pathways or corridors.
5. Site close to dual carriageway	Low	Film well away from the road.
Contacts		
• Site Safety Manager: Declan Harris 0320 719618		
Emergency Services		
• On-site first aid officer: Glynis Cole 0320 719543		
• Local police: 0320 765100		
• Local fire: 0320 765400		
• Local hospital: 0320 748333		

■ **Figure 17.14** *An example of a risk assessment. As well as identifying the risks and how to avoid them, contact numbers are included so that the appropriate people can be contacted if anything does go wrong.*

Theory into practice

There is a wide range of regulation covering health and safety issues in the work place. See if you can find out a bit more about each of the following pieces of legislation. How might each one affect your own production work?

1 Health and Safety at Work Act 1974
2 The Management of Health and Safety at Work Regulations 1999
3 The Manual Handling Operations Regulations 1992
4 Display Screen Equipment Regulations 1992
5 Control of Substances Hazardous to Health Regulations (COSHH) 2002

Assessment task 4

Produce all the paperwork that you need to help you plan your production. As well as the treatment that you have already produced, you should create:

- *a list of the roles involved in your product and who will do them*
- *records of all team meetings, with details of decisions made*
- *a production schedule, including all the key dates and a list of the resources you will need*
- *call sheet(s) for location work*
- *a location recce visit sheet*
- *a risk assessment.*

You should also finalise your plans for the content of your product, including finishing off scripts and agreeing on layouts and designs.

Assessment evidence

✔ Do the planning and produce all the pre-production paperwork needed for your production.

✔✔ Show competence in your planning and pre-production paperwork.

✔✔✔ Show high levels of technical skills and creativity in your planning and pre-production paperwork.

Remember

Your work at this stage should show that you have completed the pre-production stage and are now ready to more on to the production stage. Use the following questions to check that you are ready.

- Have I completed all of my pre-production paperwork?

- Do I have enough information to allow me to start producing my media product?

- Is there enough evidence in my folder to demonstrate that I have done my pre-production thoroughly?

- Have I considered all the health and safety issues (including a location recce and risk assessment)?

- Do all my crew understand what I am doing?

- Is my client happy with my planning?

- Do I have enough resources to undertake my production work?

- Do I have sufficient time to complete my work?

17.3 Creating a media product following a proposal

In this section, you will be creating your media product following your original proposal and using all the planning paperwork that you created in the last section. You will need to undertake a variety of production and post-production tasks in order for your project to be successful. It is important that you stick closely to your plans and that you keep careful notes of the processes you use – these will provide the evidence you need for assessment.

Production

Producing your material

You have now planned the production and you will have firm ideas about the content and look of your finished media product. The next step is to turn your ideas and planning into a reality. In this section we will be looking at the techniques and technology you will use to produce material for your media product. You will find more information on the techniques you will need for your chosen medium in the appropriate unit of this book: Unit 4 for video, Unit 5 for audio, Unit 6 for print.

Before you can start to create the content for your media product, you must make sure that you have the right equipment for the job. Choosing the right equipment depends on the nature of the media product you have chosen to produce.

- For **video** you will need: studio or location equipment – including a video camera, tripod, lights and microphones.
- For **audio** you will need: studio or location equipment – including a recorder or recording software on a computer or laptop, and microphones.
- For **print** you will need: a camera, a computer, a scanner, printers, DTP and picture-editing software.
- For **interactive media** you will need: a computer, a scanner, web-design and picture-editing software.

You may need to consider how to record on location. For video, you will probably use one video camera and move it around to shoot from different angles – this will make it look as if you have used two or more cameras. If you try to use two cameras you will have many technical issues to deal with, such as balancing the colour of the two cameras.

Likewise, with sound recording you will use one recorder and one microphone to ensure that the quality of the sound recorded is consistent throughout.

For print and interactive media, the new generation of digital cameras can produce excellent images that equal the quality of film-based images. You will be able to upload your images directly on to a computer for editing.

If you are working on an interactive media product, such as a website, you will be using a variety of media including text, graphics, photographs and perhaps video and audio. You will want to ensure that all the media you use is of excellent quality, so that both you and your client will be happy with the finished media product.

In order to successfully record material on location or in a studio, you must plan carefully to ensure that everything runs smoothly. You should make sure that:

- the crew and cast are aware of the time and location of the recording
- you have booked all the equipment that you need
- you have gathered together all the materials that you need – for example, cassettes, minidiscs, CD-ROMs, memory sticks, etc.
- all the batteries have been charged
- all the props you need are available.

Using the equipment effectively

You now need to make sure that you can produce the material accurately and that you create all the elements of your media product to a high quality. It is no good recording brilliant video footage if the

■ **Figure 17.15** *Practising with the equipment will help ensure that you record high-quality material when you come to use it for real.*

SHOT MATERIAL LOG					
YORKSHIRE BLUE LOCATION SHOOT					
Location:	Yorkshire Pottery factory				
Date:	13/09/2006				
Production assistant:	Sandra Ahmed				

SCENE NO.	TAKE NO.	TIME CODE IN	TIME CODE OUT	DESCRIPTION	COMMENTS
1	1	00.01	00.09	L/S exterior pottery	good
2	1	00.10	00.25	C/U pottery	out of focus
2	2	00.26	00.35	"	good
3	1	00.37	00.55	M/S workers in pottery	good
4	1	00.57	01.10	C/U workers	poor lighting
4	2	01.16	01.25	"	good
5	1	01.26	01.59	L/S factory interior	OK
6	1	02.00	02.45	M/S factory interior	good
7	1	02.46	03.04	C/U sign	good
8	1	03.05	06.50	interview manager	good sound
9	1	06.51	09.48	interview worker	poor sound
9	2	09.49	12.35	"	good

■ **Figure 17.16** *The records kept by the production assistant on the location shoot at Yorkshire Pottery. These notes will be invaluable when the editor goes into the edit suite.*

sound is so poor that the audience will not be able to hear it. When taking photographs, you will need to make sure that the image is well lit and that the camera you are using will produce images of the quality required – this will depend on the format of your media product: the images used for a website will be more compressed than in a print product, and you will need images of a very high resolution for a full-page glossy magazine media product, for example. Sound recordings can easily be ruined by the sound of the equipment being handled or extraneous background sounds.

You must also have a clear understanding of all the elements that make up your production. Before you go out on location or use the studio, practise using the equipment to make sure you know what you are doing.

Keeping a record

Once you start to record your material, it is a very good idea to keep a careful record of everything you have recorded as you go along. In a media production company, this job is normally done by a production assistant, but for your media product you will probably do it yourself.

For video and audio, have a look at the section on keeping a record in Unit 4, page 159. Video producers will normally keep a 'shot material log' and audio producers will keep a 'recorded material log'. There is an example of a shot material log in Figure 17.16. If you are producing an audio media product, you will be able to adapt a log like this to include the details of your audio material.

When taking photographs for a print or interactive media product, you may have the option to use a built-in log, which identifies each shot with a unique number. When writing the copy, you will probably revise

Theory into practice

Whichever media format you are using for your media product, you will need to keep records of all the materials produced. Consider the records you would need to keep if you were:

- producing a poster or flyer
- writing an article for a newspaper or magazine
- recording a radio commercial
- developing pages for a website
- producing an interactive media product, such as a game or an information point
- recording a short television drama
- producing a press pack for the media.

your text several times before you are happy with it. Each time you revise your text, make sure you save the document with a different version number, so you can refer back to past versions if necessary. And keep a list of the names of all versions of the files, together with the date you saved them. Do the same when designing your layout – make sure you keep all the versions you produce, giving each file a different version number.

Post-production

In this section we will consider the post-production process, which is when you will manipulate and amend your original material in order to produce a complete product. Almost all media material needs to be edited before being released, whether it is video footage that needs to be joined together to create a fast-moving and exciting TV drama or photographs that have to be cropped or colour-corrected to make a website or magazine look really inviting. The post-production process provides an opportunity to correct or improve the original material to make a finished media product.

You can, for example:

- correct errors in recording by omitting them from the finished media product
- choose to use alternative shots from the ones you originally thought would be appropriate
- shorten sequences that are uninteresting or repetitive
- control the overall length of the finished product by shortening or lengthening individual scenes or adding more information
- introduce special effects in video and audio products
- change the colour of images and manipulate them to alter their meaning
- reduce or enlarge file size to make an interactive media product run more effectively
- change text style or size
- cut or add text to fit the page better, and add or remove images.

Safe storage

It is very important to keep your recorded material safe. You will need to access this material throughout the editing process, so all tapes, memory cards and files need to be kept in a safe place. Make sure you follow these guidelines:

- Label the source material clearly with product title, date recorded, location/studio, tape/disk/card number, etc.
- If you are storing your material on a computer hard drive or your school's network, you must have a clearly labelled folder structure in

Video	Photographs
■ Name of advertisement	■ Name of advertisement
■ Cameraperson	■ Photographer
■ Location	■ Location
■ Date shot	■ Date shot
■ Filename/number or tape number	■ Image number/Filename
Interactive media material	**Audio**
■ Name of advertisement	■ Name of advertisement
■ Date file created	■ Soundperson
■ Filename	■ Location
■ Folder name	■ Date recorded
	■ Filename/number or tape number

■ **Figure 17.17** *The information needed on labels for tapes, CD-ROMs and computer files that contain material for your media product.*

place. You must store your work in the correct folders and back up your work regularly.

■ Use appropriate filenames for all your work, so you can find it easily and quickly. Stick to accepted file-naming conventions.

■ Keep a copy of all previous versions of your work, using version numbers as you update the files.

■ Keep the tapes, memory cards and files in a safe place.

■ Make sure that no one can record over your source material by removing the recording tab or making files and disks 'read only'.

Losing your source material will result in you having to re-record all of your material. It may be impossible to recreate some of the original material and it will certainly put you behind your planned deadlines. Use clear labels for all of your tapes, cassettes, disks, etc. Remember to attach clear descriptions to each of your computer folders and files. Your labels should include the information shown in Figure 17.17.

As well as labelling all your materials, it is a good idea to keep a material storage log with details of where all your materials are stored.

Editing

The editing process involves reviewing all the material you have created and putting together the pieces that you will be using in the finished media product. Your shot material log (see Figure 17.16) will be invaluable in this process, as it will allow you to locate the relevant material quickly and easily and to identify the best version of each shot without having to trawl through hours of footage.

MATERIAL STORAGE LOG	
Programme Title:	Yorkshire Blue
Client:	Yorkshire Pottery
Writer:	Sandra Ahmed
Producer:	Amanda Phillips
Director:	Barry Norman
Date:	4th October 2006

Tape number	Located
1	Tape storage locker – Edit Suite 1
2	Tape storage locker – Edit Suite 1
3	Tape storage locker – Edit Suite 1
Computer files	
Graphic designs for titles	Hard drive – folder: Yorkshire Blue / subfolder: Titles
Graphic designs for credits	Hard drive – folder: Yorkshire Blue / subfolder: Credits
Music tracks	Hard drive – folder: Yorkshire Blue / subfolder: Music
Voiceover	Hard drive – folder: Yorkshire Blue / subfolder: Voiceover
Backup files	CD-ROM labelled Yorkshire Blue backup, stored in filing cabinet Last backup made: 03/10/06

■ **Figure 17.18** *Some of the material for the Yorkshire Blue point-of-sale video is stored in lockers and some on computer. You can adapt this log for your own use.*

Video

There is a lot of information about editing video in Unit 4 (see pages 172–174). To summarise, the video-editing process involves:

- A **paper edit** based on the shot material log – an example of a paper edit is shown in Figure 17.19. This prepares you for carrying out the actual edit itself.

- The **off-line edit** – editing together the sequences and making a version that can be viewed by colleagues and the client so they can suggest changes.

- The **on-line edit** – this is the final edit and involves adding the final effects and finishing details.

Audio

There may be a number of reasons for editing audio material.

- Sometimes you will have recorded more than you need and so you will need to remove any excess audio.

PAPER EDIT	
Programme Title:	Yorkshire Blue
Client:	Yorkshire Pottery
Writer:	Sandra Ahmed
Producer:	Amanda Phillips
Director:	Barry Norman
Date:	8th October 2006

SCENE NO.	TIME CODE IN	TIME CODE OUT	DESCRIPTION	EFFECT	SOUND
1	00.01	00.09	L/S exterior pottery	fade in and cut to	atmos
2	00.26	00.35	C/U pottery	fade to	atmos
5	01.26	01.59	L/S factory interior	cut to	atmos
6	02.00	02.45	M/S factory interior	fade to	atmos
3	00.37	00.55	M/S workers in pottery	cut to	atmos
4	01.16	01.25	C/U workers	cut to	atmos
9	09.49	12.35	interview worker	cut to caption (name)	live interview
6	02.00	02.45	M/S factory interior	fade to	atmos & music
7	02.46	03.04	C/U sign	fade to	atmos & music
8	03.05	06.50	interview manager	cut to caption (name)	live interview

■ **Figure 17.19** *The paper edit is based on the records kept in the shot material log. The scenes are reordered as necessary and new instructions for effects and sound are added.*

- You may have recorded your material out of sequence. The editing process will allow you to rearrange the sequence.

- You may wish to delete recordings that are of poor quality.

- You may want to add sound effects or music to complete your media product.

Photographs

These are some of the ways in which you might edit your photographic material.

- You may need to crop or stretch images in order to fit them into your layout.

- You may want to change the colour or contrast.

- You may wish to manipulate an image to create a special effect.

Text

When working with text, you will use the editing stage to do the following types of tasks.

- You may wish to change the font or type style.

- You might need to make amendments to line lengths, columns or spacing on a page in order to fit in your material or for aesthetic reasons.

- You might add captions to your photographs and illustrations.

- You should also proof-read your text and carry out a spelling and grammar check.

Interactive media

An interactive media product will contain some or all of the elements listed above in this section. You can edit the text, images, video and sound separately, so part of the editing process will be combining them all in effective ways to create your finished media product. File size will be an important consideration as you make your editorial decisions.

- You may need to change the format of a photograph or video or compress it further in order to improve download times.

- You may need to shorten the length of video or sound extracts so that the file size is not too big.

Getting feedback

Once you have completed the initial edit of your media product, you will have a **rough cut** or **first draft** version. Show this to your client and try it out on a sample of your target audience. It is important that you understand that even at this stage you can still make changes to your product if it does not meet the needs of your client or audience. You can incorporate any useful suggestions gained at this stage into your final edit.

It is very likely that you will have to make changes as a result of the feedback you receive. Do not be offended or discouraged by this. It is all part of the process of producing a successful media product that is fit for purpose, popular with its audience and will therefore sell well.

One way of getting feedback from your client and target audience is to hold a focus group in which you show your media product in order to get valuable feedback. Develop a questionnaire to use in the focus group that allows your participants to review your product in an appropriate way. You may want them to concentrate on certain aspects of the product more than others. A questionnaire is useful because it provides you with some written feedback that you can analyse afterwards and helps you to identify any changes you need to make.

Aspects of the product that you might like your focus group to consider include:

- the length of the media product
- the quality of the visual and sound elements
- consistency of style
- the suitability of the product for the target audience
- how likely they are to buy the product.

Remember

It will not help you if you choose people to review the product who would not want to offend you. You must include a cross-section of people from your target audience.

Assessment task 5

Create a media product based on your proposed idea. Use all your planning documents to help you create it. Monitor your production and post-production work and keep careful records using the paperwork you have developed.

Assessment evidence

✓ Make sure that your media product follows the ideas you set out in your proposal and treatment.

✓✓ As well as following the proposal and treatment, your media product will demonstrate competent technical and aesthetic qualities.

✓✓✓ You achieve the intentions set out in your proposal and treatment by the application of high-level technical skills and creativity.

17.4 Reviewing your production work

Keeping a log or diary

In order to produce a review of your production work, it is a good idea to keep a comprehensive diary or log of the work you have undertaken during the pre-production, production and post-production phases of your media project work. This diary or log will help you to reflect on the work that you did and the help you had from colleagues. The following is a list of the points you could cover in your diary:

- how you thought of your idea
- how you developed the idea into a proposal
- how the proposal developed into a treatment
- a breakdown of the primary and secondary research methods you used
- notes of meetings with team members
- notes on the way that your team members worked
- notes on the work you undertook for others
- ongoing notes of the skills you are developing
- reflections on the quality of your work
- an analysis of your media product as compared to a professionally produced product of a similar nature
- your understanding of the fitness for purpose of your own media product
- an analysis of how well your media product meets the client's brief and audience needs.

■ **Figure 17.20** *Keeping a production diary will help you to keep track of your project and to review how well your own skills are progressing.*

You might choose to keep a written diary or to use an appropriate format such as a PowerPoint presentation or a video or audio evaluation. Whichever method you use for your diary or log, you should use appropriate media language.

Figure 17.21 shows a page from the production diary kept by the producer from Media Productions.

PRODUCTION DIARY

Name:	Amanda Phillips (Producer)
Production:	Yorkshire Blue advertisement (promotional leaflet for point of sale)

Date	Action Taken
1st August	Met with client to discuss the photographic images to be used in the leaflet. Client agreed that new photographs were needed of the new line of pottery.
3rd August	Met with photographer to discuss images that need to be shot in the studio.
7th August	Met with the creative director to discuss the style of photographs needed and the choice of model to be used. We agreed to use Sarah Cartwright as the model and to use a slightly retro style for the photographs.
15th August	Met with layout department to discuss the size and format of the photograhs needed.
16th August	Studio shoot day. Arrived on time at the studio. Creative director arrived 20 minutes late. The photographer was not ready to start on time and the model was 15 minutes late. However, we managed to shoot all the photographs we needed.
29th August	Meeting with client to look through initial copy. Client suggested several changes to the layout and text, which we will carry out by 5th September.

■ **Figure 17.21** *In your production diary it is important to keep a record of what you have done, any discussions that you have had and whether things went according to plan or not.*

Comments on your work

As part of your review of your work and how well you did, try to get a number of people to see and comment on your finished media product. Invite a selection of people from your target audience to review your work. Make sure that you also get feedback from your client (in this case it may be your teacher) and ask them to comment on the effectiveness of your media product.

If you want to get a wider range of feedback, consider making multiple copies of your media product and giving or sending it to people outside your school or college. This might include finding a group from your target audience from another school or college or from a local business or other group who could give you some good and impartial feedback.

If you send your media product in the post, make sure you include a stamped addressed envelope to encourage the recipient to return it to you. Alternatively, you may be able to upload your media product to your school or college website to make it available to a wider audience.

Include a questionnaire with your product so that the audience can provide structured feedback to inform your review of your work. Put some thought into the design of your questionnaire. Providing options with tick boxes makes it much easier for people to respond than if you ask them to write answers to each question. However, you may want to include some questions that require short written answers in order to gain more detailed feedback. It is good practice to have a mixture of the two question types in the same questionnaire. For more information on writing questionnaires, see Unit 2.

Do not be disheartened by any negative views of your work. See them as a pointer to doing better next time. If there is still time, you could even use their comments to re-edit your media product or even re-record some of the material.

It can also be useful to sit down with an audience after a viewing (or reading or listening) of your product and ask for their immediate responses. You could record their views on video or audio and transcribe them (write or type them out) later. Some people will be more forthcoming in a face-to-face situation than in a written questionnaire.

The feedback you receive might indicate that the product is too short or too long, the sound might be indistinct or the pictures might be blurred. Maybe the interactivity does not always work or some navigational buttons do not go anywhere. All of these things can be corrected if you know about them.

Evaluating your work

Once you have obtained sufficient feedback, you will need to analyse and record this information in a way that gives a representative view of what the audience thinks of your media product. This will form part of your review of your work.

In addition, try to answer the following questions when carrying out your review:

■ What did I do?

■ What did I learn and what skills did I develop?

■ What went wrong?

■ What went right?

■ What would I do if I could start again?

Refer back to all the records you have kept during the pre-production, production and post-production stages of your media production work. These will help you to identify when things went according to plan and when they did not. You will find your production diary particularly useful at this stage. You may find examples in your records of things you really want to emphasise in your review.

Remember

■ Try to sell yourself in your evaluation. If you have done really good work, then say so. If you had problems, remember to say how you overcame them in order to achieve your aims.

■ There is more than one way or recording your evaluation. You could use:
   – a video recording of your thoughts and comments
   – an audio recording
   – a PowerPoint presentation
   – a discussion with your teacher – make sure you record this conversation, perhaps in written or audio form.

■ Whatever format you use, make sure you keep your review for assessment and store it safely.

Assessment task 6

Produce a review of your work on your media product. Use the following points and questions to help you.

1 *Check that the media product matches the intentions you set out in your proposal and treatment.*
2 *Is the media product appropriate for the audience?*
3 *What about the technical qualities of your work?*
4 *How did you work with your team?*
5 *How well did you manage your time?*
6 *How was your work received by the client and audience?*
7 *Did you have to make any changes to your work?*
8 *Did feedback indicate that your media product will be successful with its target audience?*

Assessment evidence

✔ Describe clearly the work that you did, giving examples of what went wrong, what went right and what you would do if you had the opportunity to work on this project again.

✔✔ Discuss your media product production work in detail, giving a range of relevant examples of the factors involved in producing your media product.

✔✔✔ Explain clearly the work that you did, giving a range of relevant examples and using correct technical language.

Glossary

Acoustics – the audio characteristics of a particular place. If you record in a washroom, for example, a voice will seem very different from when it is recorded outside.

Aesthetic – refers to something that is beautiful – so contributing to the aesthetic aspects of a video product means helping to make it look good.

Alternative reading – a meaning that is different in some significant way from the producer's preferred reading.

Anchorage – a means of 'tying down' the meaning of some part of a media text.

Artwork – all the text, photographs and illustrations that are intended to be printed.

Audience – a group of people targeted by the media industry because they share broadly similar characteristics and interests.

Average hours – How long the station or channel is consumed over a fixed period – this figure indicates how long audiences are listening or viewing.

Bibliography – a list of books that you have used in a particular research project.
You should reference the books in the following way:
Hart, J: *Storyboarding for Film, TV and Animation* (Focal Press, 1999)
Start with the author's surname followed by his or her initial, then the title of the book, which is often written in italics or in bold. Put the name of the publisher and the year of publication in brackets.
You should also include a list of other sources you have used, such as newspapers, magazines and websites.

Billboards – a feature in a radio programme of over a minute.

Close-up (CU) – a type of camera shot – a part of the subject such as the head fills the whole frame and very little, if any, of the surroundings can be seen.

Code – a way of conveying meaning to audiences without having to use words to explain what is happening.

Colour temperature is measured in degrees Kelvin. It refers to the colour of the light source and is indicated by the following scale:

Lighting	Approximate temperature in degrees Kelvin (K)
Candle	1,800 K
Indoor tungsten	3,000 K
Indoor fluorescent	4,000 K
Outdoor sunlight	5,500 K
Outdoor shade	7,500 K

The lower the Kelvin rating, the 'warmer' or more yellow the light. The higher the rating, the 'cooler' or more blue the light.

Convention – a feature of a particular type of media product – it will be used in most or all of that type of product.

Copy – the original writing that is used in a print product.

Copywriter – someone who produces the words for advertising and promotional material.

Cross-media – describes an organisation which operates in a number of different media, such as the BBC.

Cue – copy that is used to introduce audio, a **voicer** or a **wrap**.

Defamation – unfairly damaging somebody's reputation.

Demographics – ways of describing groups of people, based on characteristics such as where they live, age, how much they earn and what they spend their money on.

Digital print processes – include photocopying, laser printing, inkjet printing and the use of desktop-publishing (DTP) software.

Extreme close-up (ECU) – a very close camera shot of the subject, or some part of them, that is often used for dramatic effect.

Freelancer – a person who is self-employed and who will hire out their services to a company for a fixed period of time or to complete a specific project.

Hand-operated processes – in print, these include the use of etching, linocut, woodcut and screen print.

Horizontal integration – describes the structure of an organisation: different parts of an organisation do not supply or depend on each other, and may even operate in different media. For example, one of the BBC's local radio stations is a part of the same organisation as the BBC1 television channel, but they each lead a very separate existence, with the only similarities in content being in the national and international news they broadcast.

Human resources department – the part of an organisation that deals with staffing issues, such as recruitment, employment contracts, pension contributions and pay.

Intaglio printing – the printing areas are lower than the non-printing surface. The 'holes' in the printing plate are filled with ink, which is then transferred to the paper. Gravure uses this technique.

Intertextuality – where content crosses from one product to another.

Journalist – someone who writes stories and articles for newspapers, magazines and television and radio news programmes.

Libel – **defamation** that is broadcast, published, distributed to a large number of people on a leaflet or posted on the Internet.

Likert scale – a type of scale used in questionnaires: the people completing the questionnaire are asked how strongly they agree or disagree with a series of statements.

Market – the group of customers a media product can target.

Mechanical processes – in print, these involve the use of some form of machinery and include offset-litho, flexography and gravure.

Media company – an organisation which is mainly concerned with communication through one or more of the mass media.

Media industry – the industry in which the main activity is focused on communication through mass media.

Mid-shot (MS) – a camera shot in which only about half of the subject is seen and you can see less of the surroundings.

Niche – a specialised, and sometimes very narrowly defined, segment of the market – the smaller the niche, the more difficult it may be to make money from it.

Non-verbal communication (NVC) – all of the body language that occurs during interpersonal communication, including the clothes that you wear, your posture, facial expression and hand and arm movements.

Over-the-shoulder shot (OSS) – a camera shot of the subject taken from just behind a person who is looking at that subject – this shot helps to establish the positions of each person.

Package – in radio, the term used in the BBC for a **wrap**.

Paralanguage – the way that you speak, including pitch, tone, pace and volume, as well as all of the fillers and hesitations that we use in everyday language (e.g. 'er', 'well', 'OK', 'um').

Pitch – a verbal presentation of your ideas, including visual aids, that is delivered to the people who you are hoping will fund or purchase your proposed product.

Planographic printing – uses a flat printing plate that has been treated so that certain areas reject or accept ink or water. An example of a process that uses this technique is lithography.

Point-of-view shot (POV) – a shot that shows the view of somebody as if you are looking through their eyes.

Post-press or **print finishing** – the processes such as cutting, trimming, folding and binding that take place on the printed material before a product such as a newspaper or magazine can be distributed.

Preferred reading – the meaning the producer intended the audience to make from the text.

Pre-press – all of the design and preparatory work that takes place to get a product ready for print.

Press – the actual printing process.

Private ownership – an organisation is owned, bought or sold by other companies and individuals. In many cases shares in the organisation are traded on the stock exchange.

Foreign companies have invested heavily in buying media companies in the United Kingdom.

Psychographics – the science of measuring people's like and dislikes. This can be done by asking people questions about their lifestyles, what they do in their spare time, what they are most interested in and what they would like to do if they had the chance.

Public ownership – an organisation is owned for the public by the state.

Rank order scale – a type of scale used in questionnaires: people are asked to indicate their order of preference from a list of given answers, usually by putting a number next to each answer.

Ratings – how well different products do in the audience research – for example, the number one television show is rated higher than all the rest.

Reach – how many people the product 'reaches' – this could refer to a single issue or a single programme or to a whole radio station or television channel over a fixed period, such as a week or a month.

Reading – making meaning from a media text. For example, forming an understanding of what is happening in a radio play, or making sense of events in a news report.

Regulatory body – an organisation set up by law to control an industry – its powers are given to it by law, and it has to abide by that law.

Relief printing – the area to be printed is raised above the non-printing surface. Letterpress is a process that uses this technique.

Respondent – someone who provides responses in a survey.

Script – a detailed account of what is to be spoken in an audio or moving-image product. A script will include a description of the location and what the characters or presenters have to do and, for moving-image scripts, what camera shots are needed. Details of any music or sound effects that are to be used are also included.

Self-regulatory body – an organisation set up within an industry to set standards for that industry – the intention is to keep the industry's reputation clean by being responsible and showing it is capable of running itself without outside intervention.

Semantic differential scale – a type of scale used in questionnaires: uses a sliding scale between two opposing words and asks people to indicate where on the scale their opinion comes.

Share – how large a slice of the **market** a product has – the bigger the share, the better.

Slander – **defamation** on a small scale, for example through word of mouth. Because slanderous remarks can be repeated from one person to another, they can still be very damaging. Slander can occur in any area of human activity, including the workplace, school, college, clubs and societies – not just the media.

Spoken language – this includes not only what you say but also the way that you say it – known as **paralanguage.**

Stencil printing – parts of a mesh screen are left open or closed by a stencil, and the open parts allow ink to pass through on to the paper. An example of this technique is screen printing.

Stringers – freelance journalists who usually work for news organisations, often covering interesting court cases for newspapers or radio stations which cannot spare staff to sit in court for a whole day. They provide coverage of other types of news story, too – sometimes providing a tip-off to a news editor.

Sub judice – a Latin term which literally means 'under justice'. It is used to refer to a judicial process that is taking place. In order that justice takes its natural course, special restrictions apply to all reporting of a criminal court case.

Substrate – the material on to which printing ink is applied – usually paper or card, but can be textiles, plastics, etc.

Symbolic codes – these suggest meaning through the choice of content. For example, using the colour red might suggest danger in a vampire movie, because it is the colour of blood. Facial expressions on actors in a drama are also symbolic codes as they suggest the emotions that the people are feeling. Voice can portray emotion, too, and this is particularly important on radio, where faces cannot be seen and have to be imagined.

Technical – relating to the use of equipment and the specialist practical skills involved in an activity.

Technical codes are ones that use structural elements in a media product to make meaning. They include the way a picture is cropped, the way a television shot is framed, or boxes are drawn around certain parts of a text – as in this textbook, for example.

Text – any media product that is **read** (or consumed) by an audience. The text may include written words or it may consist entirely of sounds and/or images.

Trade union – an organisation formed to protect the interests of staff when dealing with their employers. Members pay monthly fees in order to benefit from a range of services, including help in any dispute with their employer. Some employers choose not to recognise trade unions or they may have a preferred union that they deal with on an exclusive basis.

Treatment – a written summary of the final proposal that includes details of the product's theme, content and format as well as information about target audience, budget and timescale.

Two-shot – a camera shot of two people, framed like a **mid-shot**.

Variable data – data that changes – in the context of printing, refers to the different information that can be sent to a printer when printing the same product. This feature of digital printing means that you can now quickly print letters from a standard template that are personalised and individually addressed.

Vertical integration – describes the structure of an organisation: different parts of an organisation come under others involved in the same process. For example, a Hollywood studio could produce films, own a distribution company that gets them to cinemas on time, and even own some of the cinemas which show the films.

Visual aids – props, objects and examples that you include in an oral presentation. Also slides, images and posters that can help to structure what you say.

Voicer or **voice piece** – in radio, a report from a reporter covering a story.

Wide shot (WS) or **long shot (LS)** – a type of camera shot in which the subject is shot from a distance so that all of the subject can be seen and so can the location that they are in.

Wrap – a mini-feature item in a radio programme of perhaps 20 seconds or so.

Index